Overleaf: Crabapples, page 168.

Hybrid rhododendron and shore juniper, pages 147 and 53.

Weeping Higan cherry, page 180.

Flowering quince and crepe myrtle, pages 146 and 172.

Southern Living Gardening
Trees & Shrubs
Ground Covers · Vines

by the Garden and Landscape Staff
Southern Living® Magazine

John Alex Floyd, Jr.	Senior Horticulturist
Glenn Morris	Landscape Editor
Norman K. Johnson	Garden Design Editor
Lois Trigg	Associate Garden Editor
Beth Maynor	Photographer
Van Chaplin	Photographer

Copyright © 1980 by Oxmoor House, Inc.
Book Division of The Progressive Farmer Company
Publisher of *Southern Living*®, *Progressive Farmer*®, and *Decorating & Craft Ideas*® magazines.
P.O. Box 2463, Birmingham, Alabama 35201

Eugene Butler	Chairman of the Board
Emory Cunningham	President and Publisher
Vernon Owens, Jr.	Senior Executive Vice President

Conceived, edited and published by Oxmoor House, Inc. under the direction of:

Don Logan	Vice President and General Manager
Gary McCalla	Editor, *Southern Living*
John Logue	Editor-in-Chief
Jerry Higdon	Production Manager

Southern Living*® *Gardening* • *Trees & Shrubs

Editor: Karen Phillips Irons
Book Design: Robert G. Herr, Charles Crone Associates, Inc.
Design Adaptation: James R. Weldon
Editorial Assistants: Cecilia Robinson, Annette Thompson
Illustrator: Ralph A. Mark

Library of Congress Catalog Number: 79-92605
ISBN: 0-8487-0512-2
Manufactured in the United States of America
First Printing

The Garden and Landscape Staff would like to thank coauthor Glenn Morris for coordinating the book.

Contents

Preface

A true appreciation of plants usually comes about through an early interest which was sparked by an influential individual's enthusiasm for plants, or perhaps by a good book on the subject. Each author of *Trees & Shrubs* had a special person who inspired their urge to learn everything about plants and to do research for new species.

For me, two people opened my eyes and gave me my great appreciation for the world of landscape plants. Henry Orr, a great horticulturist and professor of horticulture at Auburn University, introduced me to plants and showed me how they could be used in the Southern landscape. Then, while at Clemson University, Fred Thode, an avid horticulturist and landscape architect of the Horticulture Department, expanded my concepts and ideas about plant identification and their design uses.

Glenn Morris, a coauthor, became interested in landscape architecture and gained a respect for the careful use and placement of plants from Gilbert Thurlow while working on his master's degree in landscape architecture at North Carolina State University. He describes Mr. Thurlow as an "exacting plantsman."

Norman Johnson, another coauthor, was inspired by Robert Reich, Head of the Department of Landscape Architecture at Louisiana State University, who guided his development and appreciation for plants and practical planting design.

Lois Trigg expanded our knowledge of insects with her enthusiasm and fascination with the subject, for which she credits the late Milledge Murphey, her first professor of entomology at the University of Florida. As a result of her background in entomology and in her second major, horticulture, she has developed a great understanding of plants and their responses to various climatic ranges.

Also, acknowledgments must be made to numerous individuals who have contributed to the preparation of this book. Fred Bonnie, formerly of the Garden and Landscape Department at *Southern Living*, rendered invaluable assistance with parts of the manuscript, including the indexing of the book. Cathy Boozer, Assistant Copy Chief at *Southern Living*, helped with the style development, and DeAnn Wilson, Garden and Landscape Editorial Assistant, typed the rough draft and organized the photography. Special thanks should also go to Dr. Bill Barrick, Assistant Professor of Horticulture at the University of Florida; Buddy Hubbock, Director of Berheim Forest in Clermont, Kentucky; Fred Thode, Associate Professor Emeritus of Horticulture at Clemson University in South Carolina, who reviewed parts of the manuscript; and Dr. T.R. Dudley, of the National Arboretum, who reviewed the horticultural nomenclature. In addition, we are indebted to the reviewers of the insect and disease section—Dr. A. J. Lewis III, Assistant Professor of Horticulture at Virginia Polytechnical Institute and State University; Dr. Ronald Shumack, Ornamental Horticulturist with the Alabama Cooperative Extension Service at Auburn University; and Joan Green, Urban Horticulturist with the Dade County Cooperative Extension Service in Florida.

Finally, we hope that this book will help each of you, the readers, to share our enthusiasm for using, identifying, and growing trees, shrubs, ground covers, and vines in the South.

John Alex Floyd, Jr.
January 1980

Plant Hardiness Map

Compiled by
The Arnold Arboretum
Harvard University
Jamaica Plain, Mass.

Minimum Temperature Range
for Each Zone
Upper South $\frac{1}{M}$ -5° to 5°F.
Middle South $\frac{1}{M}$ 5° to 10°F.
Lower South $\frac{1}{M}$ 10° to 20°F.

Note: Piedmont is an area of the
Middle South
Gulf South is an area of the
Lower South

9

Introduction

Trees, shrubs, ground covers, and vines are the backbone of the Southern landscape and can have a major effect upon your garden. In addition to seasonal changes, your plants will undergo climatic changes which are created basically by regional temperature variations. While designed principally for the South, the information in *Trees & Shrubs* is also adaptable to other regions of the United States. Since the lowest average temperature in the South generally ranges from -5 degrees F. in the upper regions to above freezing year-round in parts of Florida (*see* Plant Hardiness Map), the plants discussed in *Trees & Shrubs* are by no means limited to the South. If you live outside the South and wish to evaluate whether one of these plants will grow in your yard, check with your local nurseryman or county agent as to its adaptability to your area.

Trees & Shrubs is divided into eight sections for easy use and is intended to serve as a quick guide as well as a comprehensive reference.

"Designing with Plants" gives the reader an overview of how to combine plants in various landscapes and how to apply the basic principles of planting design to improve your home landscape.

"Planting and Transplanting Ornamentals" describes how to handle bare-root, balled-and-burlapped, and container-grown ornamentals. It also advises you on how to protect new plants from the sun and cold weather and fertilize them after planting.

"Ground Covers" explains the use of these plants in the landscape. Since ground covers are usually less than 2 feet in height, they are one of the unifying elements in the landscape. Following this introduction, the individual plants' cultural and landscape uses are discussed.

"Vines" are often called the tracings of the landscape—the introductory material

Ground Cover (cast-iron plant)

Vine (trumpet creeper)

Shrub (Japanese pittosporum)

explains their means of attachment, an important factor when considering them for use on a structure. Following the introduction, the cultural and design uses of a few vines are presented.

"Shrubs" comprise the largest and most comprehensive section of the book. Classified as plants from 2 to 18 feet in height, the design introduction is followed by an extensive selection of individual genera.

"Small Trees" are the link between the shrubs and the large trees in the garden. Generally classified from 12 to 25 feet in height, small trees are one of the important design elements in the landscape. An explanation of how to use small trees is followed by a description of individual species.

"Large Trees" provide a canopy and have a major effect on the climate of the garden. The introduction to large trees gives a synopsis of how to use and evaluate them.

"Insects, Diseases, and Problems" introduces you to the common pests and diseases and how to control them. This is followed by an extensive chart of each plant discussed in *Trees & Shrubs* with its typical problems (pests and diseases) and controls for each.

The authors have attempted to present each plant discussed in this book with an acceptable common name and an accurate botanical name. They used *Hortus Third* as the basis of the plant identification system with help from the United States National Arboretum and Southern botanical gardens as well as colleges and universities which are active in horticulture throughout the South. Botanical names are important when evaluating plants because of their diverse shapes and growth rates. Also, to eliminate confusion, only the term selection or type is used to denote variation within a species. *Trees & Shrubs* is completely indexed and cross-referenced for easy use.

Small Tree (myrobalan plum)

Large Tree (tulip tree)

Designing with Plants

When designing with plants, you should remember that certain principles govern any type of design. Proportion, balance, rhythm, continuity, and emphasis are as much a part of choosing plants as of selecting a wardrobe or furnishing a room. The ultimate objective is always to create a practical, appealing combination from your selections.

However, one basic difference sets designing with plants apart from other types of design. The difference is that plants are not static but change with time through both the cycle of the seasons and the long-term maturation of a plant. This constant change is both a challenge and a delight; however, working with it requires great patience, skill, and planning.

Planting design is essentially a matter of problem-solving. The problems may be functional, such as the need for shade, privacy, or erosion control. Or, they may be a matter of aesthetics. Nevertheless, they are problems that can be solved with plants. When you select a plant to solve a functional problem, you should consider aesthetics; it is this relationship of practicality and beauty that gives planting design its true vitality and merit.

As the ambitious gardener knows, it takes years to master the complexities of blending textures, forms, and colors, and of coordinating seasonal effects. Not surprisingly, some of the most outstanding works of landscape design in the South—Dumbarton Oaks, in Washington, D.C.; Biltmore House, in Asheville, North Carolina; Oatlands, in Leesburg, Virginia; Middleton Place, in Charleston, South Carolina; Rosedown Plantation, in Baton Rouge, Louisiana; Longue Vue Gardens, in New Orleans, Louisiana; and Duke Gardens, in Durham, North Carolina—are the products of mature designers. For example, Frederick Law Olmsted was nearly 70 when he developed the landscape plan for Biltmore House; Beatrix Farrand continued to refine the gardens at Dumbarton Oaks for almost 20 years.

Aside from patience, time, and practice, planting design requires continual experimentation, constant garden work, the "discovery" of new plants, and the development of new plant combinations. In this respect, designing with plants is not unlike developing a new

A bank of rhododendrons lines this drive, creating a sweeping effect that is handsome year-round.

recipe. The basic ingredients remain essentially unchanged, but it is the way they are combined that is important.

One of the simplest approaches to planting design is to list the functions that plants must fulfill. These functions may be as varied as providing shade, screening an undesirable view, hedging or enclosing a space for privacy, stabilizing the soil on an eroding bank, or covering the ground with a low-maintenance cover. After making this list, you should consider which plant will best meet your objective.

Now you should list your garden's aesthetic needs. Some common aesthetic problems, particularly for newly constructed homes, are the removal of the natural landscape, the lack of unity in the planting of the lot, or the lack of a suitable environment to complement the architecture of the house. These are major problems and usually require a comprehensive landscaping plan. With older houses, landscape problems usually involve overgrown or inappropriate plantings. In these instances, it may be desirable to remove the existing shrubbery and to restructure the garden. No two homeowners will formulate the same list of plants and their functions, and it is also unlikely that any two designers, observing the same house or garden, would offer the same recommendations.

Mondo grass is a favorite Southern ground cover. In this garden, it is a lush underplanting for a bird-of-paradise.

Compiling this second list helps you to establish the atmosphere or personality of a garden—formal or naturalistic; multiseasonal or homogeneous throughout the year; evergreen or deciduous. Regardless of what you wish to achieve in your garden, there are certain criteria that you should follow when selecting your plants. Although the exact horticultural requirements vary in each region, the basic approach to plant selection remains essentially the same.

Selecting Plants for Their Form

One of the most important considerations (perhaps the most important) in choosing a plant for a particular location is the form of the plant. A plant retains its form throughout the year. Certainly this is true with evergreen plants; and even deciduous plants, which

Shore juniper, massed in an underplanting, ties the three palm trees together in a unified island of soft, wavy textures.

undergo noticeable seasonal changes, retain their form for almost 8 months of the year. Since the form of a plant is consistent, it should be afforded more importance than its seasonal characteristics.

A plant's form is easily described and usually remains constant. Each plant may change its form somewhat as it matures; quite frequently this change is characteristic of the species and may be considered a design feature. Red maple is such a plant. Young red maples are irregularly branched with upright, rounded crowns, but the weeping characteristics of the older trees give them a grace unforeseen in the younger plants. Similarly, mountain laurel will frequently be dense and bushy when young; but after many years, the plant develops wandering, twisting trunks and limbs that make it uncommonly elegant. The plant's form may also change with the horticultural conditions. For example, a dogwood planted in full sun will grow hunched and sheltered, trying to protect itself from the damage of the sun. Grown in the understory, however, dogwoods will have the open-layered appearance which is this tree's hallmark.

Categorizing plants according to their form is useful and should be automatic as you learn new plants. Some commonly used terms and examples of each are: spreading or

The handsome presentation of this residence is created by three elements: the small wooden gates, a magnificent river birch, and an earth berm. The visitor views only the best of the residence on the approach.

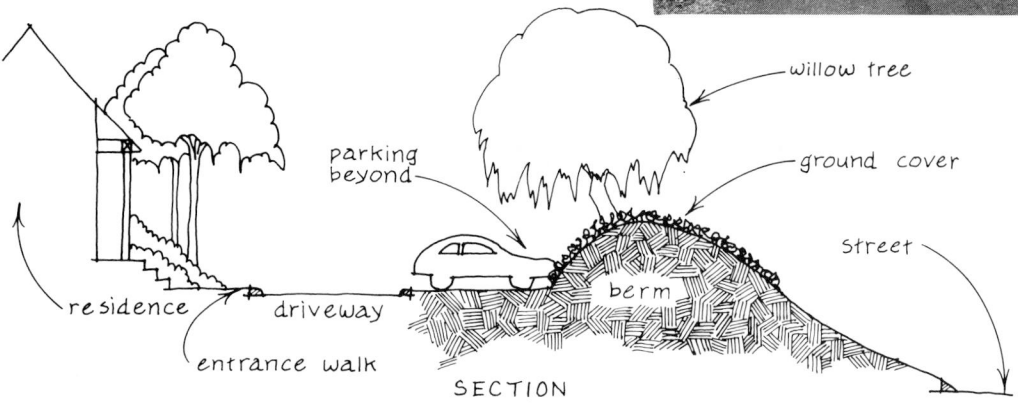

horizontal—junipers, shore juniper; prostrate or flat—blue rug creeping juniper, Sargent Chinese juniper, cotoneaster; mounding—Heller holly, dwarf yaupon; arching or cascading—forsythia, jasmines; upright—photinia, Bradford pear; oval or rounded—osmanthus, boxwoods; vase shaped—burning bush, chaste tree; pyramidal—American holly, the spruces; pendulous or weeping—willow, grafted species of ornamental cherry. If you do not know the exact plant that you need, you can describe the way you wish the plant to grow and the horticultural conditions at the site to a local nurseryman. From that description, a nurseryman should be able to recommend a plant.

Since you may begin your landscape planting dealing with pure forms rather than specific plant names, it is useful to know that some forms have certain strengths as landscape elements. The introductions to the chapters elaborate on these points, but some other suggestions are as follows.

—Cascading–as a soft cascading cover on steeply inclined grades; useful to gently tie strong vertical elements to ground plants

—Mounding–as a dense ground cover or underpinning of larger plants; foundation plantings

—Oval or rounded–the largest and most varied group, comprising the bulk of most plantings; best used to create form in the landscape or to define space

—Pyramidal–visually powerful plants; best used as accents or massed as a backdrop planting

—Spreading or prostrate–as ground covers or on gently inclined grades for erosion control

This curving walkway is framed by multitrunked dogwoods and edged with a sweeping mass of dwarf pfitzer juniper. Installed 20 years ago, the massed planting gently lines the curve and helps settle the house onto the site.

Designing with Plants

—Upright–as a substitute for architecture or as strong vertical accents; living fences

—Vase shaped–a difficult shape to use: in trees, the ideal shade tree; in shrubs, a good choice for specimens or accents

—Weeping–accent plants

If these were rules, numerous exceptions can be found in gardens throughout the South. The above generalizations are merely guidelines; ultimately, the total effect desired in the garden will determine the placement of the plants. Picking the form of the plant is only a beginning. By selecting the form and categorizing the plants according to their function, you begin to establish the major spatial relationships in the landscape, as well as to define spaces and designate areas of major importance. By picking the form of plants, you may have overlooked the garden. You must now determine the type of character the garden will have, and this will be decided by additional characteristics of plants.

Slash pines, crepe myrtles, and magnolias became the major materials for the stark, treeless area in front of this new house. Careful planning puts the trees where they will do the most good.

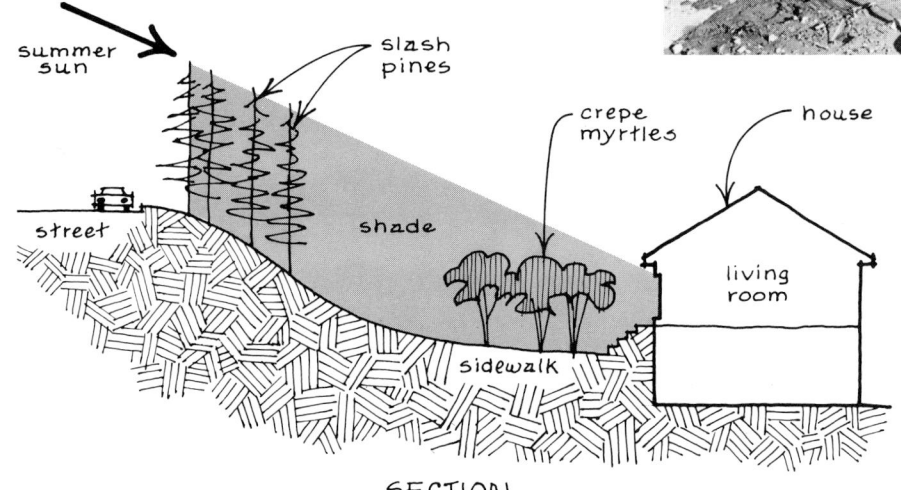

SECTION

Selecting Plants for Their Texture and Color

Texture and color are among the most appealing qualities of plants. Unlike form, which may vary with the maturity of the plant or with artificial shaping, such as pruning or shearing, the qualities of texture and color remain fairly consistent. Texture is perhaps the most consistent of these qualities since it involves foliage, size, and shape. Color, however, can vary with seasonal differences. Plants like nandina, the barberries, and some of the junipers demonstrate remarkable seasonal color shifts from their characteristic green; these color changes must be considered in your planning, since the plant will present an entirely different appearance at various times of the year. The color and texture of plants can be used for emphasis and accent, especially when they are combined with plants of contrasting textures and colors.

Texture

Texture is generally designated by three terms: coarse, fine, and medium. Coarse-textured plants usually have large leaves and stiff branches; white oak, Southern magnolia, Japanese fatsia, or rhododendron are typical examples. Fine-textured plants—like river birch, weeping willow, the spireas, or mondo grass—have small leaves and lighter, airier branches. Medium-textured plants fall in between these extremes; maple trees and the azaleas are good examples.

This Chinese photinia has been carefully pruned to encourage a more horizontal branching pattern. Frequent pruning will help keep the plant in scale with the container.

Specimen leatherleaf mahonias make a striking accent for this formal entrance. The irregular form and coarse texture of mahonia are displayed to excellent advantage in a container.

Designing with Plants

The play of different textures can help establish the mood and feeling of a garden. But arranging textures should not be haphazard; it must be well thought out. The shorter the distance from the plant to the observer, the easier it is to see the texture of the plant. At close distances, the actual size, detail, and elegance of the texture can be seen more easily. An example of this is in the use of finely textured ferns or finely detailed ground covers, like mondo grass, around sitting areas or where people walk and can study the plant's delicacy. Another reason for emphasizing fine texture in intimate spaces is that unless a coarse-textured plant is used specifically for an accent in a small garden, it can look harsh and out of context.

Coarse-textured plants are better used where they will be viewed from a distance— framing a garden or massed as a backdrop planting. If used singly, they will be accent plants; a good example of this type of planting is the use of a coarse-textured plant like loquat to designate a point of interest from across an expanse of lawn.

Medium-textured plants usually fill the garden and become the frame for fine-textured plantings, or they are used as a backdrop planting for coarse-textured accent plants. As mentioned above, certain plants have textures that help establish the mood of a garden. When selecting a plant, consider its appearance and the effect that the texture will have on the garden.

—Dense evergreens, like Fortunes Osmanthus, convey solidity and heaviness.

—Coarse-textured glossy foliaged plants, like holly and magnolia, have a stately appearance.

—Fine-textured, glossy foliaged plants, like yaupon and boxwood, appear gay and bright.

—Dull, medium-textured foliage, like that of ligustrum, looks somber and utilitarian.

—Fine-textured foliage, like that of spirea and river birch, gives the feeling of motion.

—Fine-textured foliage and open branches, like those of Japanese maple, have a soft and relaxed look.

—Pines with long needles feel soft, while those with shorter needles appear more rugged.

Color

All too often, the term *color* refers to flower color and does not include the prevalent foliage color associated with a plant during the growing season. After form and texture,

The plants in this design were pulled away from the front of the house to frame the entrance and provide a sense of separation between the house and street.

foliage color is the dominant element of a plant and a quality that may be used to create a variety of effects in the garden. Foliage color, seasonal changes, and flower color should all be considered when choosing a plant for its color.

Using color in the garden is complex, but gardeners can benefit from these two rules: mass plants of the same color for the best effect, and separate clashing flower colors with a green or neutral planting.

Located behind a winding planting of pine trees set in ground cover, the alignment of the new entry walk repeats the sense of movement. Windmill palms create a gate effect.

The planting areas were designed to surround the point where the walkways intersect, creating the effect of an open entry court.

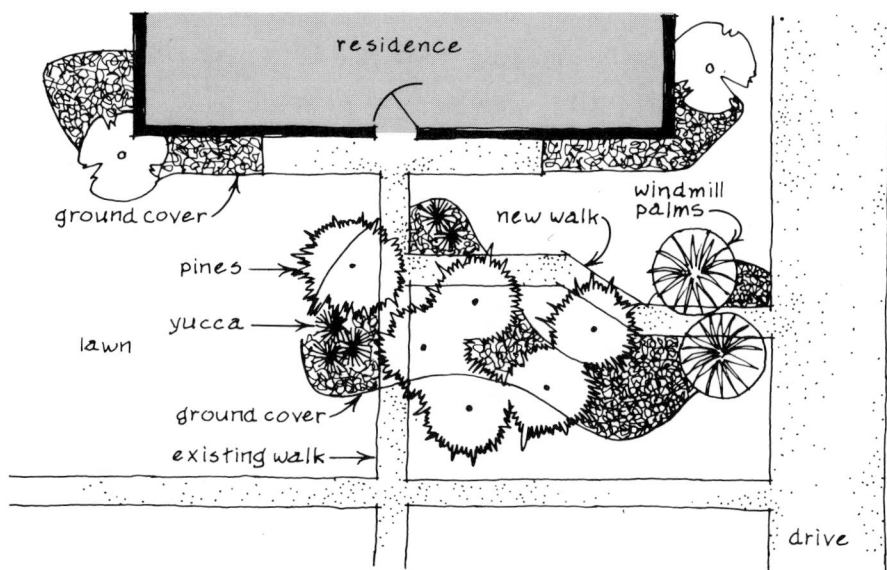

Designing with Plants

Color can be used as an accent. It is possible to use one white selection of redbud as an accent planting among several of the ordinarily magenta redbud species. Similar uses can be made of dogwood selections. The same effect can be achieved by combining flowering trees in unexpected ways; for example, the red flowers of red maple can be underplanted with white flowering plum. This type of planting will present a wall of pleasingly contrasting foliage and flower color year-round.

There are a few things to remember about pure colors. Reds and pinks are powerful; plants with these colors will stand out in the landscape. If viewed from across the garden, these plants will seem closer. Blues and violets are quiet colors and recede in the landscape. These colors bring a light-hearted feeling to the landscape. White flowers are either cloudlike or snowlike and visually lighten the garden when used as mass plantings.

The variety of foliage color seems endless. Each different hue has its special effect in the garden. For example, there is the silvery bronze Fruitland elaeagnus which brings a shimmering (visually lightening) effect to the plant. The light green of flowering dogwood also has a lightening effect in the shaded understory where it grows. Weeping willow with its bright yellow green and distinctive habit of growth makes a striking accent. White pine's blue green creates the feeling of depth and distance in the garden, while the deep green of Norway spruce and Southern magnolia yields a feeling of dignity and solidarity. The rugged black green of Japanese black pine and the reddish green of red cedar give a feeling of age and endurance. In contrast, the lighter, more neutral greens of sweet gum and winter honeysuckle create excellent backdrops for the display of light- or dark-foliaged plants. In many respects, green is the forgotten color in the landscape; yet, by varying the display with different hues of green, it is possible to create a landscape focus that will be effective through the comparatively "colorless" summer season.

Some plants are selected for special foliage color that is in marked contrast to the parent plant. Crimson King Norway maple, Bloodgood Japanese maple, many of the junipers, and Crimson pigmy barberry are good examples of the rich foliage variation that is readily available. Care should be taken when using these strongly contrasting colors in the landscape, though. Because of their contrast to the surrounding plants, these special selections will immediately be perceived as accent plants. Keep this in mind when

The clean, crisp foundation planting accents the architecture of the house without overpowering it. Two common boxwoods frame the front steps, while specimen crepe myrtles flank each side of the house and provide year-round interest.

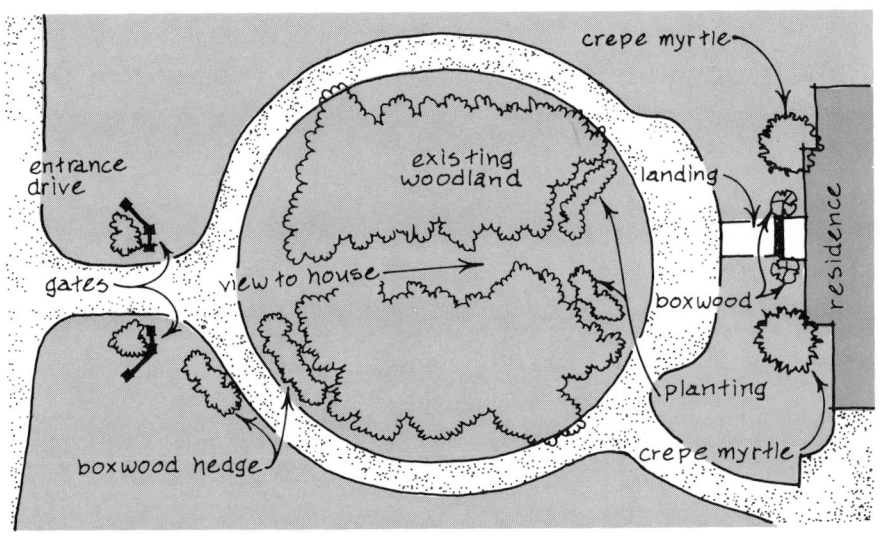

choosing a selection with color variation—it will be prominent in the landscape and should be used in a location that will emphasize this distinctive quality.

Autumn offers the opportunity for the widest range of color variation. And the fall color display that nature puts on is worth studying for its application to the home landscape. Visitors to the mountains witness a carnival of color where steeply sloping land glows with the characteristic gold of the dominant oak forests and is sprinkled with a rich diversity of upland red and orange. Fall color is not just red; it is enamel red, scarlet, crimson, and puce. It is not just yellow; it is butter yellow, lemon, ocher, and gold. The Piedmont South comes alive with the bright red of the black gums set against a backdrop of pines and the purple bronze of sweet gums. Even the Coastal South expresses fall with galled cypress—these trees cover the ground and dark waters with featherlike, reddish gold needles. The crepe myrtle also gives up its colorful blooms with its subtle display of yellow, rust, and gold. What gives fall its special impact is the immense color change; every deciduous tree and shrub discards its green for a characteristic hue. Unlike spring, when the change from bare branches to leaves will take at least a month, and when there is continuous bloom from February until May, fall color appears in a brief span. The peak effect may only last from 10 days to 2 weeks.

With a little planning, it is possible to orchestrate year-round color interest that ends in this grand foliage display.

—If you have a heavily wooded lot or one with a substantial number of shade trees, look for smaller understory ornamental trees to complement the color show of the existing canopy. For instance, a lot canopied predominantly with hickory and tulip trees, which have yellow fall coloration, would be an excellent backdrop for displaying the clear orange of sassafras.

—A neutral backdrop, such as a lot full of pines, offers unlimited choices—from the maroon red of dogwood to the scarlet of sourwood. Even a seemingly random color selection can work well beneath the green shelter of pines.

This foundation planting was designed to emphasize the architectural detailing of the house. Here, dwarf horned hollies and English Ivy ground cover frame a bay window.

A few well-placed plants were all that was needed for the foundation planting on this cottage-style house. Small, slow-growing plants, such as edging boxwood, dwarf yaupon, and mondo grass, were used.

Designing with Plants

—If you are shopping for your first few trees to install on a treeless lot, select shade trees that complement the basic color of the facade.

—If the initial planting is to be the fast-growing shade trees that will canopy the house, pick a single species, such as tulip trees, to give a dominant color. Then plan around this color when selecting ornamental trees and slower-growing, medium-sized shade trees which may provide more brilliant color.

Selecting Plants for Their Flowers

Landscape plants have a certain appeal throughout each season of the year, but the flowering trees, shrubs, vines, and ground covers reach their zenith when they bloom. But it is important to remember that this seasonal expression is also the shortest period of show in the year-round performance of a plant. When selecting plants for their flower color, there are two important things to consider: the color of the flower and the seasonal time of bloom. Beyond these, there are other important characteristics of flowering plants that determine the character of the display and in many ways the character of the plant.

The shape of the individual flower and the way it is carried on the plant determine a great deal about a plant's character. For example, the massive terminal flowerheads of snowhill hydrangea create the impression of a great wavering mound of white—a landscape look that is far from delicate. By contrast, the fragile blossoms of Yoshino cherry on tiny pedicels are set away from the limbs; they create a gentle, cloudlike display. Sourwood and Japanese andromeda drape panicles from the ends of the branches in one of the most graceful flower shows possible. The flower clusters of the native azaleas hover in midair, supported by almost invisible woody growth of the previous year.

Redbud flowers ride closely along the branches and turn the tree's appearance into a magenta etching of line in the landscape. Even the spireas, all members of the same genus, take on outstandingly different characteristics just by the shape and arrangement of the

This 4-year-old planting makes a good use of just a few plants in the right location. A shrubbery border that weaves along one side of the lawn frames the front landscape. The remainder of the front is trees and turf.

A canopy of loblolly pines screens this nicely tucked-away residence. The entrance walk, a series of brick landings, leads from curbside parking in a slightly wandering path to the front door.

flower clusters—from the exquisite Thunberg spirea to the heavier and mounding Reeves or the sculptural and perfectly formed clusters of bridal wreath. And perhaps nowhere does the flower change the plant's character so boldly as in the complex viburnum group, for here the plants can be delicately layered with blossoms or be boastful mounds of fragrant snowballs, each having a different impact on the landscape. By varying the selections, the variety in the garden can be increased and the effectiveness of a flower show prolonged.

Color selection calls for moderation and careful coordination and planning. This is true of trees, shrubs, vines, and ground covers. Your zeal for one type of flower, azaleas, for example, may be so overwhelming that it overrules some simple design principles, resulting in a garden becoming a hodge-podge of bloom. Similarly, if a flowering plant in a certain color is poorly located in the garden, its intended effect is destroyed. The very popular Hinode-giri azalea is frequently planted in the wrong location when it is used as a foundation planting in front of red brick structures. The competing and conflicting colors caused by this type of planting diminish the effectiveness of the plant's flowers as well as the planting design.

If your objective is to provide different colors in the garden, it is best to vary the season of bloom over a period of time. This will mix more colors into your planting scheme without resulting in distracting combinations. Too many gardens actually flower only one month out of the year; varying time of bloom can make the garden exciting year-round. Here are some suggestions.

While the exact time will vary according to seasonal conditions, the flowers of various plants will usually appear in a regular sequence. The flower season can begin in the garden as early as January and February with shrubs like flowering quince, winter honeysuckle, and winter jasmine; with small trees such as star magnolia; and with large trees like red maple. These are probably the earliest blooming plants for the Southern garden.

March brings the eagerly anticipated opening of the flowering cherries, peaches, and

Since the slope is a long, gradual grade, several single-log walls were used. They are spaced evenly up the slope, creating patches of ground cover in areas difficult to mow.

This simple firewood retaining wall is holding well-tilled soil back long enough for the roots of the ground cover to become established.

Designing with Plants

plums, along with the buoyant yellows of forsythia and the native azaleas. Redbud will also begin to unfold its characteristic magenta flowers.

Dogwoods and the hybrid azaleas bring the most renowned spring show into the landscape in late March and early spring and are closely followed by the flowering crabapples and Japanese andromeda. Tulip magnolia also blooms during this spectacular April period, as do many of the very fragrant viburnums.

In May, leucothöe colors the landscape, as do the rhododendrons with their great clustered trusses of flowers. Kousa dogwood consistently blooms in late May and early June, giving another show. The late-blooming Gumpo azaleas offer one more opportunity for azalea lovers in June.

July is a comparatively quiet month for flowers, highlighted by hydrangeas, which prolong their show for a month. This is also the month for crepe myrtle, the fragrant

The wooded entrance drive to this residence is framed by a pair of Chinese Chippendale gates, each punctuated with a single common boxwood.

gardenias, and the flowers of sourwood. Goldenrain tree and chaste tree's purple flowers also thrive well into August.

September is perhaps the most inactive month for flowers, but the landscape is highlighted by fragrant elaeagnus.

In October, the foliage dominates the landscape. Sasanqua opens late in October and starts the camellia season, which continues through November and December.

The season ends in December with the soft flowers of rosemary, a surprising color that lasts through the winter.

There is, of course, an overlap in the blooming periods; many other shrubs and trees in this text can supplement this small list. Obviously, a garden with year-round flowers is possible. Do not plant your garden for one quick season of bloom, but spread the color around and enjoy a full year's display.

This compact motor court design creates a major landscape impact. The simple expanse of paving accommodates visitor parking and creates a foreground for the house.

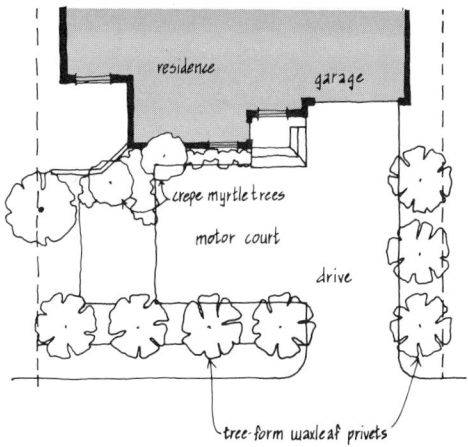

Gumpo azaleas take on a graceful, cascading form when used in an elevated container. Late-spring flowers are a bonus.

Designing with Plants

Planting and Transplanting Ornamentals

There is an old saying that if you are going to spend $15 for a new tree or shrub, $5 should go for the plant and $10 for the hole. And there is a certain amount of truth to that statement.

Planting trees and shrubs is a special part of gardening, much more than simply digging a hole and dropping in a plant. Successful planting involves choosing the proper planting-time, preparing the planting hole, the actual planting, and protecting the tree or shrub from wind and sun damage after planting. Transplanting established specimens deserves just as much attention. Using the techniques that follow will ensure your success.

New Trees and Shrubs

Planting at the correct time is essential to the success of any tree or shrub. In the South, that means during the dormant season (fall and winter) for most specimens; dormant planting is always recommended for deciduous plants.

Ornamentals set out during the dormant season are easier to establish, as there is time enough for new roots to develop before young leaves appear in the spring. And since dormant-planted trees and shrubs will be well on their way to being established before warm weather, they will be less subject to the stresses of summer—heat, drought, and severe sunscald.

A properly dug planting hole and correct planting are the keys to the success of any newly planted ornamental, and the requirements differ to some degree with whether you purchase the plants bare-root, balled-and-burlapped, or in a container.

Bare-Root Plants

Do not delay planting bare-root specimens, as their exposed roots are easily damaged when subjected to drying. For best results, soak the roots in cool water for 24 hours before planting.

Using a garden spade or round-point dirt shovel, dig a well-rounded hole that is deep and wide enough to accommodate the root system without crowding. Avoid making the hole too deep; about 12 inches deeper than the length of the root system is recommended.

Thoroughly mix peat moss into the backfill, especially in heavy clay soils. Bone meal may also be added to the backfill; this material is slow acting and safely stimulates the growth of new roots. Use at the rate of ¼ pound for a 4- to 6-foot plant, ½ pound for an 8- to 10-foot specimen, and ¾ pound for larger ones. Do not use inorganic, high-nitrogen fertilizers at plantingtime, as they easily burn young roots.

Place 6 inches of amended backfill into the prepared hole, thoroughly tamping it down; over this, form a firm cone of soil. After trimming away any broken roots, position the roots of the plant over the soil cone, spreading them evenly so that none are crowded.

At this point, check to be sure the plant will be set at the same depth it grew in the nursery; a dark-brown line on the lower trunk indicates its original planting depth. Planting too deeply may lead to future problems and is one of the major causes of decline in newly established ornamentals.

Holding the trunk of the plant steady, lightly sprinkle backfill over and around the roots, filling the hole to within 3 to 4 inches of the soil line. Periodically shake the plant gently to eliminate any air pockets that may have formed in the soil.

Water the plant thoroughly before completely filling the planting hole, and allow it to drain; then backfill to ground level, tamping firmly to eliminate air pockets. Mulch newly planted specimens with a 4- to 6-inch layer of pine straw or other organic matter.

Remove one-third of the branches of newly planted bare-root ornamentals at plantingtime. While this may seem severe, compensation for root loss when the plant was dug will ease establishment. Do not simply lop off the top third of the plant. Instead, carefully

In the South, the correct time to plant most trees and shrubs is during the dormant season (fall and winter). This allows the plants to be well on the way to being established when new growth begins in the spring and before the stresses of summer.

Planting and Transplanting Ornamentals

prune away individual branches, selecting weak or poorly placed limbs first; never cut out the main stem or leader, as the overall form of the tree may be destroyed.

Balled-and-Burlapped Plants

With few exceptions, balled-and-burlapped specimens should be planted much like bare-root plants. As the name implies, balled-and-burlapped plants are dug from the nursery with a ball of soil around the roots and then wrapped in burlap.

Immediate planting is also recommended for balled-and-burlapped ornamentals, although it is not quite as critical as with bare-root plants. If there is a delay, wrap the root ball with damp towels, tarps, or moist mulch until the plant can be set in the ground.

Dig planting holes twice as wide and 12 inches deeper than the root ball. Amend backfill with peat moss and bone meal as recommended in bare-root planting; then add enough backfill to the planting hole to make the hole as deep as the root ball.

Like bare-root ornamentals, plant most balled-and-burlapped specimens at the same

depth as they grew at the nursery. When properly planted, the top of the root ball should be at ground level. (Azaleas, rhododendrons, camellias, and daphne should be planted slightly higher.)

Gently set the plant into the prepared hole, grasping it by the root ball rather than the trunk; otherwise, you may break small feeder roots growing close to the soil surface.

Untie the cord from the burlap, and discard it; fold the burlap back from the root ball (do not remove it); gradually fill the hole three-fourths full of soil. Tamp the soil firmly several times during the filling process to remove any air pockets. Water thoroughly, and

Plant bare-root specimens as soon as received (adjacent); if you delay, their exposed roots may be damaged from drying. For best results, soak the roots in cool water for 24 hours before planting (above).

Planting holes for bare-root ornamentals should be large enough to accommodate the root system without crowding; about 12 inches deeper than the root system is recommended. Form a cone of soil in the planting hole, and spread the roots evenly over it before backfilling.

Planting and Transplanting Ornamentals

allow to drain; then finish filling the hole, bringing it up even with ground level.

Selectively prune one-third of the top growth of newly planted specimens in the manner described for bare-root plants. Also apply mulch as you would for bare-root plants.

Container-Grown Plants

Plant container-grown ornamentals just as you would balled-and-burlapped specimens. Container-grown plants are generally available in vinyl, metal, or plantable pots in sizes that range from 1 gallon to 7 gallons. With the exception of plantable pots, always remove the container prior to planting. Turn the plant upside down, and give the edge of

When planting any tree or shrub, firmly tamp the soil after backfilling to remove air pockets.

the container a sharp rap to loosen most of the root system; then remove the container. Metal cans can be cut down the sides at the nursery and tied together with twine until plantingtime.

Plantable pots are thick, cardboardlike containers made of papier-mâché and may be planted right along with the root system. Check with the nurseryman to make sure the container is plantable and biodegradable; if it is not and you plant it, the plant will soon be potbound or choked by girdling roots. Just remember always to bury plantable pots completely, as any exposed portion will act as a wick and draw valuable water away from the plant roots.

Transplanting Trees and Shrubs

Often considered a difficult job by many gardeners, transplanting does not have to be. Here are some pointers.

Mulch all newly planted and transplanted ornamentals to insulate the soil against temperature fluctuations and conserve moisture. A 4- to 6-inch layer of leaves, pine straw, or other organic matter is sufficient.

Planting and Transplanting Ornamentals

Before you begin to dig the plant, make sure it is a job you can handle. The root ball of large shrubs and medium to large trees will be heavy and often impossible to transport without professional equipment. A ball of moist soil 18 inches across and 1 foot deep usually weighs over 150 pounds, too heavy to be moved by an individual.

If a tree or shrub is over 5 years old (except dwarf plants), chances are it is too large to be successfully transplanted without the help of experienced workmen and special lifting equipment.

Ornamentals are most successfully transplanted in cool weather: November 1 through March 15 in the Upper South, December 15 to March 1 in the Middle South, and December 31 to February 15 in the Lower South.

Ideally, the digging process should begin two years before the plant is actually moved. Each fall, the roots of the specimen are severed close to the trunk by forcing a spade into the soil around the plant. The process is called root pruning and encourages the growth of new roots close to the plant, which you will be able to dig with the soil ball. Root pruning is usually too time consuming for home gardeners. Instead, most plants are dug and moved in a weekend or less; but with a little extra care, even this type of transplanting can be successful.

How To Transplant

Despite careful attention, a certain number of roots will be lost any time a specimen is transplanted. To compensate for this loss, selectively remove one-third of its total branch structure and 50% of the foliage. Prune carefully to avoid destroying the natural form of the plant, removing poorly developed or diseased limbs first. Tie remaining branches with twine to limit additional limb loss when the plant is moved.

Avoid digging plants if the soil is not moist; if dug dry, the soil ball may fall apart and expose tender roots to dehydration. Water thoroughly two days before you plan to dig if the soil is not sufficiently damp. When digging the plant, save as much of the root system as possible. The larger the soil ball, the better. As a general rule, plants with a shallow, fibrous root system require a wider, shorter ball than those with taproots. Plants with taproots require deep, very large soil balls.

Begin the digging process by making a trench around the plant equal to the desired size of the soil ball. Specimens with a trunk diameter (measured 1 foot above ground) of 1 to 2 inches need a soil ball about 20 inches in diameter; trunks 2 to 3 inches in diameter, a soil ball 24 inches in diameter; a 3- to 4-inch trunk, a 33-inch soil ball; a 4- to 5-inch trunk, a 43-inch soil ball.

Dig to a depth just below the root system, severing the roots around and beneath the soil ball. Be sure the trench is wide enough to work in so the plant may be easily removed. Grasping the soil ball, not the plant, lift the plant from the ground; set it on a tarp or piece of burlap so it may be securely carried to the new site. Replant immediately as you would a balled-and-burlapped specimen.

Protect Trees and Shrubs After Planting

To become well adapted to their new surroundings, many newly planted or transplanted specimens require protection from sunlight and high winds. Excessive swaying of small trees may delay the growth and establishment of new roots; tender bark may be damaged by direct sunlight if not protected.

Wind Protection

Whether newly planted or transplanted, trees and top-heavy shrubs from 3 to 20 feet in height should be staked to prevent wind damage. One or two strong stakes 6 to 8 feet tall are recommended. Carefully drive the stakes 2 feet into the ground, 6 to 12 inches from

Container-grown trees and shrubs are available in a variety of plantable and nonplantable pots. Dig planting holes twice as wide and 12 inches deeper than the root ball; except for plantable pots, always remove the container before planting.

Be sure to bury plantable pots completely, as any exposed portion will act as a wick and draw water away from plant roots.

Planting and Transplanting Ornamentals

Guying is a good way to protect newly planted trees, especially large ones, from wind damage. Be sure to thread the wires through pieces of garden hose, as bare wires will easily tear tender bark.

the trunk. This is usually easier if done before the planting hole is completely filled and also results in less root injury.

Depending on the number of stakes used, thread a length of wire through a piece of garden hose; twist it in a figure-8 around the tree, being sure no bare wire touches the trunk. Fasten the wire to the stake so the trunk is held firmly in place. The hose is essential for protecting tender bark; bare wire may girdle or scrape newly established plants, providing an entryway for insects and diseases.

Trees, especially larger specimens, may also be supported by cabling or guying. This should be limited in high-traffic areas, however, as the wire is often difficult to see and may be dangerous.

Drive three 6- to 8-foot-tall sturdy stakes into the ground in an equilateral triangle around the plant. Using three lengths of wire, thread each through a piece of hosing; loop each around the plant, halfway up the trunk; then secure a length of wire to each stake. Periodically check all wires wrapped around plants to be sure no girdling or other damage has taken place. Wires that seem tight should be loosened to prevent damage. Staked or guyed plants should be allowed to remain undisturbed for about one to two years; then remove the supports, and let the plant grow naturally.

Sun Protection

Wrapping the stem or trunk of newly planted trees and shrubs is recommended for protecting the bark from sunscald, especially in areas of intense sunlight. Use a commercially-available tree wrapping made of two layers of paper with asphalt sandwiched in the middle.

Beginning at the top just below the first shoot, snugly wrap overlapping layers of paper all the way to the bottom of the trunk; secure both top and bottom with cotton cord. The wrapping, which may also help prevent insects and rodent damage, may be removed after two years.

Ground covers add texture, color, and richness to the landscape. This group of comparatively low-growing plants contributes substantially to the effect that a garden imparts, whether it be the formal impression that Japanese spurge creates or a frisky, casual appearance that a plant like shore juniper suggests. Many ground covers are bright and cheerful, like St. John's wort, and can be deliciously fragrant, like Asian star jasmine. A ground cover can be any type of plant—a shrub, a perennial, or a vine. The term ground cover is actually a landscape use classification; and as the name implies, these plants are used to carpet part of the ground as an alternative to a lawn or a mulch.

While ground covers may be used to create particular visual effects, such as a blue rug juniper trailing over the top of a retaining wall, they are usually selected to supply special definition and character to the garden. This is, perhaps, the most important function of

Ground Covers
Carpets for the garden

English ivy, page 44.

Carpet bugleweed, page 39.

35

Cape plumbago, page 42.

Big blue liriope, page 54.

ground covers—they provide unity and pattern to a variety of plants. A wide variety of shrubs and trees can be planted within any ground cover planting, and the garden's unity will still be retained.

Similarly, a seemingly chaotic planting of shrubs can be pulled together into a functional landscape planting merely by unifying the entire bed with one plant material underneath. Planting a ground cover in a specific pattern to link disparate elements in the garden can provide a simple solution to a problem that appeared solvable only by drastic measures, such as removing all existing plants from the landscape.

To develop a plan for ground covers requires planning for a large mass of plants which will significantly affect the appearance of the landscape. For this reason, it is important to balance three factors: the plant's appearance or character, the purpose of the planting, and the horticultural requirements.

The plant's appearance and character create the feeling that a plant contributes to the landscape. For example, both Japanese spurge and English ivy are shade-loving ground covers; but they convey distinctively different characters in a garden. Japanese spurge is formal and elegant, creating a feeling of great care and deliberation; while English ivy is lush and verdant, evoking a sense of timelessness and weathered appeal that may be less formal than spurge. Each ground cover will project its distinctive qualities into the landscape, so it is best to carefully study each selection to ensure that it will harmonize with the overall garden effect.

The purpose of the ground cover planting will also determine the plant selection. If the planting is to stabilize the soil on a steep embankment, then a rapidly spreading, easily rooting ground cover like common periwinkle or Asian star jasmine will be needed; erosion would not be stopped with a slower-growing plant. If the planting is eventually intended to take the place of a lawn and eliminate the need to mow, then a stoloniferous-spreading plant, like mondo grass or carpet buglewood will work best, since these plants will spread and gradually cover any available suitable soil.

Perhaps the most important factor in selecting a ground cover is the amount of direct sunlight that the planting will receive. Even in excellent soil, a ground cover will not look its best if planted under the wrong conditions. For example, the extremely durable junipers are sun-loving plants and can take the severest summer sun and heat, developing a thick carpet of ground cover. But, if planted in shade, junipers will become leggy and spindly as they reach for light and will never achieve even coverage over the planting bed. Conversely, shade-loving plants, like holly fern and cast-iron plant, will burn if they receive almost any direct sun.

Fortunately, this does not severely limit ground cover selection in the South. Included here are a number of plants that will adapt to the wide range of horticultural circumstances throughout the region. In addition, the selection is varied enough to provide a plant that will fit a range of demanding functional and aesthetic needs as well as the diverse horticultural requirements.

Since every garden has its own characteristics, it is impossible to say which ground cover is best for a given location. Selecting a plant can become exasperating when you must choose from several which are acceptable. Each of the ground covers that follow will do certain things well in the landscape; keeping these things in mind could make selecting one an easier process.

—Carpet bugleweed creates a low-growing mat of tough, wide leaves that will thicken and spread into the surrounding soil. A purple-leaf selection has ruby-colored foliage and spikes of purple flowers in early spring. Both selections work very well at filling in small crevices and the interstices of rockwork or paving.

—Japanese ardisia is a rapidly spreading ground cover with a coarser texture than pachysandra that naturalizes well in the Lower South. It will cover large areas, spreading under the leaf mold and through finely tilled soil.

—Sprenger asparagus fern creates a plumelike, lime green cover that is finely textured and delicate in appearance in the gardens of mid- to lower Florida.

—Cast-iron plant is one of the tallest ground covers, as it reaches a height of 30 inches or more. The deep-green, swordlike foliage is hardy throughout the South and prefers deep shade.

—Holly fern makes an excellent accent plant or a ground cover for semishaded plantings.

—Blue and red fescue are clumpy, fine-textured grasses that bring unexpected colors into sunny locations. They are particularly adapted to small courtyard uses, although they can be successfully used in broad masses in the landscape.

—The ivies are the most widely used ground covers. Although vines, they are hardy, durable, and dependable plants, carpeting shady landscapes in a patterned green.

—Junipers are widely varied and grow very well in full sun. Sargent Chinese juniper is a low-spreading creeper, while shore juniper is plumelike, profuse, and especially salt tolerant. The andorras are upright and spreading, turning bronze purple in the winter—a color that should be anticipated. Blue rug is a deep blue green plant with a low-spreading

Mondo grass, page 55.

Shore juniper, page 53.

Carpet bugleweed, page 39.

Majestic liriope, page 54.

Cast-iron plant, page 43.

Holly fern, page 47.

habit of growth that makes it easily recognized. Bar Harbor stays low to the ground and has silvery green blue coloration that will change to bronze in cold temperatures. Parsons has silver blue foliage, a twisting, spreading habit of growth and is taller than the mat-forming selections.

—Big, blue liriope is tall, upright, and grasslike and can be depended on to endure a wide variety of horticultural conditions. It flowers in August with spikes of blue purple or white flowers.

—Mondo grass is indispensible for the appearance of a well-maintained lawn. It is short and very grasslike, requiring little care.

—Cape plumbago brings color to the gardens of Florida and the Gulf Coast. It is sometimes considered a shrub because of its tall mature size.

—Prostrate rosemary is an evergreen herb that tolerates a wide variety of sun and soil conditions. It is wild in appearance and flowers in winter.

—The lavender cottons thrive in blazing hot sun and have a mounding habit of growth. They flower in late summer with a profusion of yellow color.

—The periwinkles are loose and casual ground covers that will tolerate shade or partial sun. They look good with formal plantings or in naturalized landscapes.

—Wedelia brings a rapid growth habit as well as bright, daisylike flowers into the full sun of the southern Florida and Gulf Coast landscape.

Many of these ground covers will do well only in specific portions of the South since they are limited in their tolerance of cold. Most, however, can be used throughout the region and can be depended on to maintain a steady appearance in the landscape year-round. It is important to check local nurseries to see what is available in your area. An investment in a ground cover planting is usually a substantial undertaking—be sure that the plant will do well before you purchase. In addition, know all of the plant's effects before you plant; for example, the sudden foliage change of the junipers in cold weather is a factor which must be taken into consideration since the plant will significantly affect the appearance of the landscape during that season.

Rosemary, page 59.

English ivy, page 44.

Ajuga
Accents for shady garden corners

The dense, spreading growth habit of carpet bugleweed (*Ajuga reptans*) makes it an excellent ground cover for the Southern garden. In addition to its even, carpetlike appearance, carpet bugleweed provides a show of bright-blue flower spikes in early summer. Known to many gardeners simply as ajuga, carpet bugleweed has frequently been used to supplement the seasonal effects of garden borders. The dark, glossy-green foliage, which is evergreen, turns bronzy green in winter. This change of foliage color plus the appearance of the blue flowers later in the year provides three very different landscape effects.

Carpet bugleweed is a very adaptable plant that can be grown in almost any soil. But since it spreads by means of creeping stolons (a slender stem above or just below the surface of the ground which makes a new plant at its tip), a rich, well-drained, slightly sandy soil will encourage faster growth and more even coverage.

Although ajuga can be grown in sun or partial shade, a shady situation is preferred for gardens in the Lower South. Excessive heat and sun exposure tend to burn the leaves, so plant ajuga where it will be shaded during the hottest portion of the day. Because ajuga will tolerate a fair amount of shade, it makes a good border plant for use beneath large

AT A GLANCE
Light: sun to partial shade
Water: moderate amount
Soil: prefers well-drained, slightly sandy soil; will tolerate other soils
Growth Rate: rapid
Size: 4 to 12 inches in height

The bright-blue spikes of flowers of carpet bugleweed (above) appear in early summer.

Carpet bugleweed (left) is tucked into these rock crevices; it works better when massed in a small area rather than a large one.

Ground Covers

The glossy-green foliage and dense growth habit of carpet bugleweed makes an interesting contrast to the darker green of plants like this irregular boxwood hedge.

shrubs. It is also used to fill in shady corners of courtyards or along the north side of a wall.

Carpet bugleweed is sometimes affected by a fungus disease known as Southern blight or crown rot. Entering the plant through the roots and foliage, the disease cuts off the plant's water supply, causing it to wilt and quickly die. Fertilization during hot weather seems to aggravate the problem. The fungus can be controlled, however, by drenching the soil with a dilute solution of Terraclor®; follow directions on the label exactly. Even though crown rot can be treated in ajuga, it tends to be a recurring problem, especially in the Lower South. For this reason, it is advisable to use ajuga as an accent plant rather than a large-scale ground cover. This would help minimize the visual detraction of a widespread infestation of the disease.

Ajuga's trailing habit of growth makes it useful in rock gardens or along the upper edges of retaining walls. When planted along walkways, the stolons tend to grow across the paving for several inches, creating a soft, irregular effect along the edges. Since the plant is easily crushed, this use should be reserved for areas of lighter traffic.

Carpet bugleweed is also available in a number of selections developed for their distinctive foliage or flower colors. These variations can provide the garden with additional variety and interest. The selections most commonly available are Alba—like *A. reptans* except flowers are creamy white; Atropurpurea—known as bronzeleaf carpet bugleweed, has bronzy purple foliage year-round and dark purple flowers; Multicoloris—known as harlequin carpet bugleweed, has green leaves mottled with red, white, and yellow with flowers like *A. reptans*; Giant Bronze—has large leaves that are a metallic bronze with crinkled edges and flowers like *A. reptans*; Purpurea—has purplish green foliage and deep purple flowers; Rosea—like *A. reptans* but has rosy pink flowers; Rubra—like *A. reptans* but has purplish red flowers.

The dense, trailing habit of carpet bugleweed can be used to fill awkward garden spaces like the one between this terrace and an outcropping of rock.

Asian Star Jasmine
A sea of small leaves

Asian star jasmine (*Trachelospermum asiaticum*) takes the heat better than almost any other ground cover. This decumbent, evergreen vine from the Far East has become the most widely used nongrass ground cover in Texas and in much of the Gulf Coast area. Some of the reasons for the popularity of Asian star jasmine include its tolerance of poor soil, its rapid rate of establishment, and its tidy, easy-to-maintain growth habit. In the Lower and Middle South, Asian star jasmine is hardy as far south as central Florida and as far west as Dallas and Austin.

Asian star jasmine is ideal for covering large areas as an alternative to lawngrass. Vines twine around each other, quickly forming a dense mat of foliage 12 to 15 inches high. Once established, Asian star jasmine requires only an occasional trimming to keep it in bounds. Planted in masses, this vine creates an illusion of depth and distance, especially in a small garden. Asian star jasmine can also be used as an accenting border for a lawn. Used as a foundation planting, Asian star jasmine makes a superb underplanting for flowering bulbs or dwarf shrubs. Occasional trimming will keep the vines from climbing the shrubs. Because it spreads by surface stems, this vine can be used to cover rocky areas. The fragrant flowers, which appear in late spring, have creamy white petals twisted in a pinwheel shape.

Grow Asian star jasmine in either full sun or partial shade. Nearly any soil will support this moderate to rapid grower, but results are best if you add compost or peat moss to each planting hole when setting out the vines. Snip out the end of each stem to encourage branching. New plants also will form where the vines come in contact with the soil, speeding up the complete coverage of the bed.

Asian star jasmine is hardier than its cousin, Confederate jasmine (*Trachelospermum jasminoides*). Like Confederate jasmine, Asian star jasmine will also climb. If trained on a support, it will climb to nearly 60 feet and form a thick screen.

AT A GLANCE
Light: full sun or partial shade
Water: moderately drought tolerant when established
Soil: nearly any; best in improved soil
Growth Rate: moderate to rapid
Size: 12 to 15 inches as a ground cover; 60 feet or more as a climbing vine

Asian star jasmine is a good ground cover in sunny locations in the Lower South where the effect that English ivy gives is desired.

Asian star jasmine may also be used as a vine in selected situations.

Cape Plumbago
Summer-long bloom for ground cover

AT A GLANCE
Light: full sun
Water: moderately drought
resistant once established
Soil: light, sandy,
well-drained soil
Growth Rate: rapid once
established
Size: 3 to 4 feet high with a
spread of 10 to 12 feet

Cape plumbago (*Plumbago auriculata*), a summer-long bloomer, is a subtropical shrub from South Africa that has taken to gardens of the Lower South. More aptly described as a subshrub, cape plumbago is neither a true shrub nor a true vine, but something between the two. Planted near a trellis or similar means of support, cape plumbago can be tied up and grown like a climbing rose. Unpruned and unsupported, the long stems crawl along the ground, and the plants bunch up into spreading mounds of evergreen foliage and tufts of light-blue flowers. Because of this growth habit, cape plumbago makes an ideal ground cover.

Although it may seem to start slowly, cape plumbago is a rapid grower. The low, arching stems may become 8 to 10 feet long, bearing oblong leaves about 2 inches long and with terminal clusters of flowers that resemble wild blue phlox. Cape plumbago grows well in the Gulf South from south Texas to Florida and sometimes as far up the Atlantic Coast as Charleston. In areas of marginal hardiness, plants should be given a protected location during the winter. If winter damage does occur, cape plumbago can be rejuvenated by pruning.

In open, sunny areas, such as on banks or sloping rocky terrain, use cape plumbago as a rambling ground cover. Cape plumbago is a good choice for a confined area (for example, such as in a foundation planting), seldom growing taller than 3 or 4 feet. However, regular maintenance will be necessary to keep the plant in bounds. Situated along the top of a rock wall or in a patio tub, the arching cascade of foliage and flowers makes cape plumbago a pleasant addition to the garden. The selection Alba produces white flowers and is available in nurseries, particularly in Florida.

Plant cape plumbago in full sun and in well-drained to almost dry soil. If pruning becomes necessary, do it in early spring before the new growth begins. Flowers are borne on the current season's new wood, so pruning between midspring and late summer will remove flower buds. To encourage continuous growth and flowering, fertilize twice a year—once in spring after the new growth has begun and once in early to midsummer. In excessively limey soil, leaves may yellow, indicating mineral deficiency.

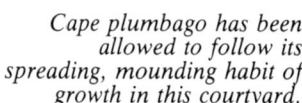

Cape plumbago has been allowed to follow its spreading, mounding habit of growth in this courtyard.

Cape plumbago is often seen as a foundation planting in Florida.

Cast-Iron Plant
Foliage for the shadows

AT A GLANCE
Light: full to partial shade
Water: moderate to light
Soil: rich, well-drained soil
Growth Rate: moderate to slow
Size: to 3 feet

Cast-iron plant (*Aspidistra elatior*) may derive its common name from the cold, almost clammy, feeling of its foliage—like that of an old cast iron lamppost. Or perhaps the name comes from its exquisite sculptural form: a form that has the line and elegance of an art nouveau drawing—simple, upright, and broad leaved. Whatever the derivation of its name, the plant is indispensable to gardeners of the Piedmont, Coastal, and Lower South; the cast-iron plant fills a void that few plants can. It survives in virtual absence of light and with low water.

Cast-iron plant should not be overlooked for garden spaces where few other plants can grow. It tends to grow in a large, leafy clump that makes cast-iron plant unsurpassable as a sculptural planting. This characteristic makes it very effective beneath the dense shade of magnolias and the mottled shade of live oaks as a texturally outstanding ground cover—its deep-green, glossy plumage ascending to as much as 3 feet above the ground.

Its principal landscape attribute, indeed the only landscape feature that the cast-iron plant brings to the garden, is the foliage. The plant sends up new, tightly whorled leaves as it spreads into the surrounding soil. The young, already deep-green shoots, that project like tiny drinking straws, unfurl into 4-inch-wide evergreen leaves that may be 12 to 18 inches long atop a 6- to 8-inch-high stalk (actually part of the leaf). Thus, mature clumps are tall, exotic-looking fronds of foliage.

With a primarily coarse texture, cast-iron plant is a good backdrop planting for low-growing flowering plants with a delicate texture or color. Even the lighter-green ground covers, like asparagus fern, are beautifully displayed against the color of cast-iron plant. Since the foliage is smooth to the touch, the plant is frequently used to edge garden walkways, where it will lean and encroach over the path only knee high.

The simple criteria for growing cast-iron plant successfully include low sunlight (full to partial shade); deep, rich, well-tilled and drained soil; and protection from freezing winter winds. It is successfully used in Charleston; and cast-iron plant will grow as far north as Raleigh, but only if sheltered from winter winds. In exposed locations, it suffers severe freeze damage from inadequate moisture during the colder months. The damaged foliage (which will appear dried and brown) may be easily removed with scissors. Most gardeners prefer to remove all the foliage each spring to have a fresh mass of leaves every year.

In addition to its excellent landscape properties, cast-iron plant is an almost infallible specimen for indoor potted use. When it is indoors, cast-iron plant will signal water loss by a pronounced drooping of its foliage.

Since the foliage is smooth to the touch, cast-iron plant is frequently used to edge garden walkways.

Cast-iron plant tends to grow in a large, leafy clump that makes it unsurpassable as a sculptural planting.

Cast-iron plant's deep-green, glossy foliage can ascend to as much as 3 feet above the ground.

English Ivy
Aging the garden gracefully

AT A GLANCE

Light: partial shade in Upper South; partial to full shade in Lower South
Water: needs moisture during dry weather
Soil: moist, fertile, well-drained soil
Growth Rate: moderate to rapid
Size: ground cover 10 inches high; vines to 75 feet
Remarks: numerous variations give different textural effects

English ivy cascades over these walls easily.

The elegance of English ivy increases with age. Perhaps the most widely used vine in American gardens, English ivy (*Hedera helix*) has established itself as a versatile ground cover and climbing vine in Southern gardens, where it has been used since colonial days. Despite the old-world connotations of ivy, this timeless vine can lend a contemporary feeling to a modern garden, depending on how it is used.

Native to Europe, English ivy is hardy throughout the South and as far west as Dallas and central Oklahoma. Grown solely for its evergreen leaves, English ivy produces three-lobed leaves with smooth leaf margins and prominent white veins. Leaves may be as much as 5 or 6 inches across on older selections to as little as 1½ or 2 inches across on newer dwarf selections.

English ivy climbs by aerial roots, sometimes called "feet," and consequently does not strangle host plants by twining around them. Ivy-covered tree trunks are a common sight in Southern gardens, and this is a good use of the vine provided that vines are confined to the trunk area by occasional trimming. Allowed to completely permeate the crown of a tree, ivy can shade leaves to the point where they are deprived of necessary sunlight.

Ivy makes a superb cover for stone and masonry, but do not use it to cover wooden walls, especially clapboard siding on houses. The vines soon grow under the clapboards, causing them to separate. If left unchecked, vines also grow under boards near eaves and under shingles. As with other vines, keep English ivy out of rain gutters and downspouts. If you are considering growing English ivy on a stone or masonry wall, be sure the vine will enhance the wall and not just obscure it. Stone walls are expensive and beautiful and should not be completely covered with a vine. Use ivy sparingly in such a location so that the plant embellishes the wall. Cinder block walls, on the other hand, may benefit from a cloak of ivy; but here, too, caution must be exercised. Use ivy on the broad faces of the wall, for example, and let the buttresses or corners remain uncovered. Remember, though, when you remove English ivy from any surface, the aerial roots always remain and are very difficult to remove. Old vines may become very heavy, and the weight of the vine may damage mortar or, in extreme cases, pull apart sections of the wall. If a complete cover is desired, consider using a lighter, more finely textured vine, such as climbing fig.

The most problem-free use of English ivy is for ground cover. An ideal grass substitute for rocky or shady areas of the garden, English ivy is easy to establish and gives complete coverage in two to three years. Because it is easy to confine small plantings of ivy, you can use it as a foundation plant where shrubbery is not appropriate but some greenery is desired. In either large or small plantings, ivy makes a good cover for naturalized bulbs, such as daffodils, or as an underpinning for shrubs. Used for ground cover, English ivy forms a thick mat of leaves and stems 6 to 10 inches high.

Dwarf English ivy, with its diminutive leaves, is often used as an edging plant and will cascade gracefully when grown in hanging baskets, planter boxes, or pots. Because of its compact habit, slow growth rate, and delicate, unusual leaves, dwarf English ivy provides contrast and definition when used as an edging in beds of annuals or perennials.

For erosion control, few vining ground covers are superior to English ivy. Remember to lay a 4- to 6-inch layer of pine straw, wood chips, or similar mulch to hold the soil and plants in place until the coverage is complete.

Grow English ivy in partial sun to deep shade. In the Lower South and Florida, (even in dense shade) the intense heat of summer may slow the establishment of new plantings and damage the established ones; it is best to use ivy in partial to complete shade. English ivy, in fact, is so well adapted to shade that you should consider using a different plant, such as Asian star jasmine, in a location exposed to direct sun all day. Ivy thrives in moist, rich, well-drained soil; but, at plantingtime, you need only improve the soil in individual planting holes to get plants off to a good start. Pinch out tips of vines to stimulate early branching.

Regular fertilization and watering will help plants through their first year. Once established, English ivy is fairly maintenance-free since the leaves shade out most weeds and retard evaporation of moisture. Trim English ivy at any time of year to keep it in bounds. Pest problems are minimal, but you may have trouble with spider mites during dry years.

Propagate English ivy from tip cuttings or by layering. If you have neighbors with large established plantings of ivy, you may be able to do them a favor by pulling up some of the vines where they have outgrown their location. Water newly transplanted vines generously until they become established.

For easy reference, the over 100 types of English ivy are divided into three large groups based on branching habits and coloring. The first group consists of those selections of English ivy that produce many lateral branches. Maple Queen, a selection with waxy dark-green leaves, and Meagheri, a selection with tiny five-lobed leaves, are two that belong in this group. The second group consists of those types of English ivy that produce very few lateral branches. The ivies in this group usually have a reddish purple tint in the fall but remain green the rest of the year. Selections such as Erecta, known for its upright form; Manda's Crested, which has curly leaves; Baltica, known for its hardiness; and Pedata, whose leaves are shaped like a bird's foot, are part of this group. The third group of English ivy contains types with variegated leaves. It includes selections such as Gold Dust, which has mottled green and white leaves; Gold Heart, which has green leaves that contain a yellow and cream center; and Heise-Denmark, whose leaves are edged in cream.

English ivy is a popular ground cover for traditional homes where partial shade is available.

When purchasing English ivy, check the size of the leaves, as this varies with each selection.

Fescue
Colorful, ornamental grass

AT A GLANCE
Light: full to partial sun
Water: moderate to light; drought tolerant when established
Soil: any soil; will tolerate poor locations
Growth Rate: slow to moderate
Size: to 10 inches

The finest texture in ground covers belongs to the fescues. The two species—blue fescue (*Festuca ovina* Glauca), sometimes called sheep's fescue, and red fescue (*Festuca rubra*)—are similar in growth characteristics but markedly different in coloration. These wiry, tufted grasses, native to Europe and now naturalized throughout the South, are two ornamentals that bring a clumpy but extremely delicate texture into the garden. The fine foliage of these grasses makes either of them a prominent ground cover planting in the landscape.

The fescues are extremely hardy and will grow well throughout the entire South. The durability of the groups extends their landscape usefulness, for these tough, wiry plants can tolerate excessive sunlight and heat. In fact, they are one of the few ground covers that can thrive in the reflected heat and light that sometimes occurs alongside the wall of a structure. In addition, these plants may be used in containers or as the ground cover in elevated planters.

The characteristically clumpy growth may be handled in a similar manner to mondo grass; that is, the plants may be easily divided and set out to cover a wider area than would be possible by planting individual clumps. However, unlike mondo grass, the small divisions of larger clumps will retain their clumpy fountainlike habit of growth; and when the planting of the bed fills in, the individual clumps will still be distinguishable.

Because of its color, blue fescue looks best in sunny locations; in fact, if planted in too much shade, the plant will lose part of the distinctive silver blue cast that makes it so attractive. Caution should be used, however, when planting blue fescue; the color and growth habit are so eye-catching that they could easily dominate other important features in a planting. Use these plants sparingly—as color accents in a garden border, for example, or to secure the soil on an eroding bank.

Because of its growth habit, fescue can be the backdrop planting for a display of bulbs planted between the individual plants. Crocus make an stunning display emerging from between the clumps, and bright-yellow daffodils combine handsomely with blue fescue.

Mature plants rarely reach over 10 inches tall, making it one of the lower-growing ground covers available. Fescues flower attractively in late May through July, depending on their location in the garden. The small flowers are delicate and fine. When the plant is in flower, its overall size may exceed 1 foot; and in fact, the small spikelets add greatly to the ornamentation of the plant.

When crocus are interplanted with clumpy tufts of blue fescue (far left), the gray of the foliage intensifies the crocus color.

Red fescue is easy to establish on banks and good for erosion control.

Holly Fern
Little plant, big effect

AT A GLANCE
Light: filtered shade
Water: moderate; needs humidity
Soil: moist, fertile soil
Growth Rate: moderately rapid
Size: 1 to 2 feet in height

The Japanese holly fern (*Cyrtomium falcatum* Rochfordianum) is a bit unusual as far as ferns go. It has a very coarse texture, and the rich-green foliage is dark and lustrous. Holly ferns can be grown as far inland as Shreveport, Louisiana, and Birmingham, Alabama, and as far up the Atlantic Coast as Raleigh, North Carolina.

Delightful accent plants for use along a walk or path, holly ferns make an excellent ground cover as well. They can be naturalized under tall shrubs or low-growing trees to great advantage. Used in a courtyard or near a terrace, holly ferns add a rich, graceful carelessness to the landscape.

Growing conditions are similar to those for most ferns: moist, fertile soil high in organic matter; light, filtered shade; and plenty of humidity during those warm summer afternoons. Relatively fast growing, a typical holly fern will get to be 2 feet high and wide in a single growing season.

Dark-green fronds and a gently weeping form are the holly fern's best features. The individual fronds are made up of 18 to 20 deeply serrated pinnae (leaflets) arranged alternately along a central rachis or stem. The new fronds are a very attractive yellow green—a striking contrast to the deep green of the mature foliage. As the tightly curled fiddleheads unroll, the entire frond takes on the graceful arching form characteristic of the plant.

Shown (above) is an excellent use of holly fern, tucked next to these porch steps.

Holly fern is often found massed under a tree-form crepe myrtle (left) as in this courtyard in the Lower South.

Ground Covers

Japanese Ardisia
Berries and flowers for naturalizing

AT A GLANCE
Light: full to partial shade
Water: moderate amount
Soil: well-drained, acid soil
Growth Rate: rapid
Size: to 18 inches

Japanese ardisia (*Ardisia japonica*) rambles and spreads across the landscape, creating a thick, dense covering of handsome leathery evergreen leaves. This makes it one of the best ground cover plants for the Lower South. It is a plant with a twofold character, combining an upright crown like that of Japanese pachysandra with a coarse-textured foliage that strongly resembles the leaves of lenton rose. This combination gives the plant a naturalistic appearance; and, accordingly, it is an appropriate choice for shaded woodland landscapes.

The plant has other properties that commend it for garden selection. In late spring—an unusual time for understory color—it bears upright terminal spikes of flowers. The flowers quickly ripen to bright-red berries that adorn the clusters of foliage at the top of the woody stemmed growth. In addition to being ornamental, the berries are valuable food for wildlife. Mature plants rarely exceed 18 inches in height.

Another feature of the plant is that it reseeds itself rapidly and grows into a vigorous clump. In a shaded portion of the landscape where rapid cover is needed, these attributes make Japanese ardisia a good choice.

Japanese ardisia looks best in a natural or naturalistic garden. The informal character of the plant makes using it in formal bedding patterns awkward; although it could, for example, provide a strong textural contrast to a formal planting of edging boxwood. The plant is an excellent ground cover for the glossy smooth foliage of native plants like sweetbay magnolia and Florida anise.

Its ability to cover large areas makes it suitable for ground cover use in the Lower South in a fashion similar to the way English ivy is used in the Upper South—it covers broad expanses of shaded ground where lawn maintenance is difficult.

Hardiness is variable with Japanese ardisia. It is reported to be hardy up into the Upper South but should not be relied on for steady performance. Generally speaking, it is more successfully used in the Lower and Coastal South. Perhaps with a sheltered location and adequate protection from wind chill, Japanese ardisia could be used more successfully in the Piedmont South.

This ground cover of Japanese ardisia looks very naturalistic massed in small clumps in front of these shrubs.

The red berries of Japanese ardisia are a bonus feature of the plant in summer.

Japanese Pachysandra
A lush ground cover

AT A GLANCE
Light: prefers shade, but will tolerate full sun
Water: moderate amount
Soil: rich, acid soil
Growth Rate: rapid
Size: 6 to 10 inches in height

For the take-care-of-itself area in the garden, Japanese pachysandra or Japanese spurge (*Pachysandra terminalis*) will do the job. This low, evergreen subshrub prefers the shade but can grow in full sun.

Japanese pachysandra looks best if used in borders or beds that are contained by a walk or some sort of edging material. The plants spread by underground runners that will compete for space with other plants. The ideal situation for a ground cover is in areas where it can grow by itself or under large trees with deep root systems that will not compete for nutrients. Also, this makes an ideal mass planting to reduce maintenance under groups of trees.

The plant has dark-green leaves that are from 2 to 4 inches long. The leaves form on the end of stems that may reach a height of 10 inches in full shade. In sunny areas the stems will reach a height of only about 6 inches. During the summer months, pachysandra produces rather inconspicuous fluffy spikes of fragrant white flowers followed by small white fruit.

Spring is the best time to establish a pachysandra ground cover. Set individual plants in rich, acid soil (which is common throughout most of the South). Space plants from 6 to 12 inches apart. While the plants are getting established, supply plenty of water and carefully cultivate the soil around the plants. Cultivation will make it easier for the runners to spread through the soil. Once the plants are established, it may be necessary to prune occasionally to keep them off walks or from covering other material. For best leaf color, fertilize with a complete fertilizer, such as 8-8-8, just prior to spring growth.

Japanese pachysandra (above) adds distinction to confined landscape situations, as in this planter around the tree.

Japanese pachysandra (left) is an excellent ground cover to mass under shallow-rooted trees, especially in the Upper South.

Ground Covers

Juniper
Green and graceful

AT A GLANCE
Light: full to partial sun
Water: moderate to low; drought tolerant when established
Soil: light, well-drained soil; suited to poor soils
Growth Rate: varies with species; most are moderate to rapid growers
Size: under 2½ feet; will spread to at least 8 feet

The juniper family provides us with an astonishing number of useful landscape materials. There are junipers for almost every use: shrubs, ground covers, and a variety of tree-form plants. All have similar cultural requirements, but the different colors, textures, and individual shapes distinguish them for landscape design.

In fact, the junipers are among the most varied of plants; thus, there is an array of plants available in the nursery trade. The selection of a particular type almost becomes a matter of individual preference; for some of the selections are remarkably alike in appearance, and, in fact, only a few offer significant landscape differences. Obviously, it is impossible to present all the selections that are currently available. Those included below have met a wide range of horticultural conditions and are proven performers across the South.

Depending on the selection, junipers can be spiny, sleek, or densely matted, or they can be tumbling and rambling masses of fine-textured foliage. Keep the individual growth habits in mind when selecting the plants, because even though the selections listed are all ground covers, there is a marked difference in their landscape character. For example, the larger mature selections, Andorra and Parsons, have substantial height to work as a free-standing mass in the landscape. In fact, shore juniper will reach as high as 2 feet in good horticultural conditions, although it tends to flop over onto itself in a loose, irregular tumble. The lower mat-forming junipers are good selections for rocky locations, and to visually soften the edge of a driveway, or to creep over the top of a retaining wall.

Because the juniper has a piney texture, some unusual foliage contrasts may be created—for example, shore juniper can be used as the underpinning for an evergreen planting like holly osmanthus or Nandina. And, at seashore locations, where the junipers

Andorra juniper (above) is noted for its attractive rusty purple winter color.

Andorra juniper (right) is the tallest of the creeping junipers.

are among the most durable and dependable plantings, the spiny texture can offset the rounded foliage of Indian hawthorn.

There are some cautions with junipers, though. Most of them are susceptible to red spider, which will cause the plants to become ragged looking and unhealthy. None of them can tolerate wet soil or heavy clay that retains water—the plants will quickly drown. In addition, it is very difficult to use junipers near Bermuda grass. Bermuda grass is so invasive that escaped shoots or seeds will soar above the mat of the juniper; and once a juniper plant is infested, removal can only be accomplished by laborious hand weeding.

Certain qualities unite the junipers as a group in spite of selection variations. They are universally hardy, durable, drought tolerant, even pesky in their persistence to thrive. They are all considered low-maintenance plantings; yet, except for the large selections (Andorra and Parsons), their landscape life is comparatively short. The plants tend to spread and shade themselves out, becoming ungainly as they age.

Their tolerance of poor soil, direct sun, and low water has made them excellent choices for problem locations. Often the dilemma with junipers is not whether to plant them but which selection to use. In fact, junipers may very well be overplanted; yet they offer a

Shore juniper will rapidly spread into a free-form tumbling mass of foliage.

Parsons juniper is the largest of the ground cover junipers.

Ground Covers

satisfaction and landscape texture that make them worth using in any sunny garden location. Their vigor and spreading habit make them a bargain planting for the amount of space that they will cover in a short time. But remember that most junipers will not grow taller if planted too close together—3 to 4 feet apart is basically good spacing for most selections.

Creeping Juniper

The selections of creeping juniper (*Juniperus horizontalis*) are among the best and most varied selections for the home landscape. Creeping juniper is native to the northern United States, but the plants are extremely hardy all across the South.

Andorra juniper (*J. horizontalis* Plumosa) is the tallest of the creeping group. It has a very compact habit of growth. The branches tend to stand erect or have a slightly arching form. A mature Andorra is 18 inches high and as much as 10 feet in diameter. If used as a ground cover, a spacing of 2½ to 3 feet between plants will ensure complete coverage of the planting area. Its bright-green foliage of early spring darkens to a medium green in late summer. After several days of cool weather in the fall, the green color changes rather dramatically to an attractive rusty purple. There is also a compact selection of Andorra (*J. horizontalis* Plumosa Compacta) which exhibits the same landscape characteristics yet grows much more slowly—to only about 2 feet tall.

Bar Harbor creeping juniper (*J. horizontalis* Bar Harbor) was selected in Bar Harbor, Maine. The plant grows extremely close to the ground, with a pronounced horizontally-spreading habit (8 to 10 inches high). It forms a dense, thick mat of bluish green foliage and is extremely slow growing.

Blue Rug creeping juniper (*J. horizontalis* Wiltonii) was appropriately named. Growing flat along the ground, the blue rug seldom gets to be more than 6 inches high. Space individual plants about 3 feet apart to ensure a dense ground cover. This juniper is truly blue—not robin's-egg blue, of course, but it is a silvery blue with just a touch of green underneath.

Waukegan creeping juniper (*J. horizontalis* Douglasii) grows close to the ground and covers an area with a thick, vigorous expanding mat of bluish gray foliage. In cold

Blue rug juniper easily trails over this wooden border (above).

The color of this Bar Harbor juniper massed under this holly (right) emphasizes the multistemmed feature of the holly.

Shore juniper prevents soil erosion on this bank in addition to providing a beautiful mass of greenery.

weather, the foliage turns from its characteristic steel gray to a handsome purple hue. The height of this plant is around 1½ to 2 feet.

Parsons Juniper

Parsons juniper (*J. davurica* Expansa) is the largest of the ground cover junipers, reaching to just 2½ feet tall in a sculptured mass of steel gray foliage that has a silver blue sheen. Mature species may spread as much as 6 feet and make excellent specimens as well as border plantings. In addition, the plant has powder blue fruit.

Sargent Chinese Juniper

Sargent Chinese juniper (*J. chinensis* Sargentii) is one of the old garden standbys that lost some popularity to the newer introductions. Sargent juniper is gray green in color and will spread 6 to 8 feet across and around 3 feet in height.

Shore Juniper

Shore juniper (*J. conferta*) is probably the most widely distributed ground cover juniper. It is exceptionally hardy and will rapidly spread into a free-form tumbling mass of foliage. Its growth rate is so vigorous that eventually it will shade itself out, developing open patches and brown foliage. Shore juniper is a good choice for poor soils and seaside plantings. These plants are generally seen spaced 18 inches apart in a ground cover planting; but this is overplanting, as a single specimen can cover a 3-foot square easily in 2 years.

The selection Blue Pacific (*J. conferta* Blue Pacific) is one of the best of the low-growing plants. The foliage is deep blue green and its growth habit is more controlled than that of the parent plant.

Junipers are excellent plants to use on steep banks to prevent soil erosion.

Sargent juniper is one of the old garden standbys.

Junipers are a natural complement to the rock gardens of the South.

Liriope
More than just an edging

AT A GLANCE
Light: full to partial shade
Water: irrigate first year;
established plants
moderately drought
resistant
Soil: nearly any
well-drained soil
Growth Rate: moderate
Size: 10 to 20 inches

Variegated liriope (above) massed in large quantities creates a bold ground cover accent and should be used carefully.

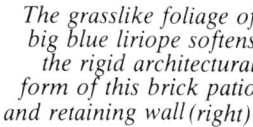

The grasslike foliage of big blue liriope softens the rigid architectural form of this brick patio and retaining wall (right).

Big blue liriope, or monkey grass (*Liriope muscari*), is one of the most familiar plants in the Southern garden. Even nongardeners can recognize this broad-leaved grasslike plant that is so often used as an edging, winding its way along sidewalks, driveways, and flower borders. Not to be confused with mondo grass (*Ophiopogon japonicus*), leaves of liriope are generally ½ inch wide, and the clumps may grow 10 to 20 inches tall, depending on which selection you choose. Liriope produces small blue flowers in summer which turn to black fruit, which is not particularly attractive and should be removed.

Like hybrid azaleas and camellias, liriope is native to the Far East but has been adopted by Southern gardeners. Liriope is hardy in all regions of the South. In Florida, liriope is reliably hardy in the northern half of the state but may not tolerate summer sun and heat south of the Orlando area, unless it is in dense shade.

The uses of liriope go far beyond the wormlike borders to which it has traditionally been relegated. Liriope can be massed on banks for erosion control or for foundation plantings. If you do choose liriope for a border plant, avoid the wormlike effect by staggering the plants in masses. A large, curling bed of liriope along a wooded area of the garden produces a natural contrast between the trees and shrubs and the lawn area. Because of its tolerance of shade, liriope can be a problem solver in sections of the garden where grass will not grow and shallow-rooted trees prohibit digging large planting holes for shrubbery. Liriope is also a choice plant for rock gardens.

Plant liriope in partial to full shade. In the Upper South, liriope will tolerate more direct sunlight, but plants will quickly brown at the tips and die from heat stress if planted in full sun in the Lower South. Liriope can be planted in almost any soil, but plants become established and spread more rapidly in fertile, well-drained soil. Established liriope is moderately drought resistant.

If you buy containers of liriope at a nursery, be sure to divide them before you set them out. Pull plants apart from the clump or use a sharp knife to cut through tangled roots. Space divisions 6 inches apart in all directions for coverage in two to three years. If you space divisions 12 inches apart, coverage will be slower, but you will not need to divide overcrowded clumps for four or five years.

To maintain a tidy appearance, raise the blade of your lawn mower to its highest position and mow liriope to the ground in late winter. When new growth resumes in spring, the bed will not be a mixture of healthy new leaves and scrawny, winter-burned old leaves. Liriope spreads by means of underground rhizomes and plantings and should be thinned every three or four years to keep it orderly. Discard overcrowded clumps or give them to friends to start their own liriope plantings. A single clump that measures 6 inches across at the base may be divided into a dozen or more plants.

Several selections of note are available commercially, including Majestic, which grows 15 to 20 inches tall; Munroe White, which has white flowers; and Variegata, whose leaves have narrow, white margins and also is somewhat tolerant of sun.

Mondo Grass
That marvelous ground cover

AT A GLANCE
Light: sun or shade
Water: moderate amount
Soil: will tolerate most soils
Growth Rate: rapid
Size: 6 to 15 inches
in height

A handsome little grasslike plant can be found growing in the gardens of the South from Texas to Virginia; but if you ask somebody what it is, chances are they will give you any one of at least a dozen common names.

But it does not really matter if you call it monkey or mondo grass, border grass, or lilyturf. When you are talking about *Ophiopogon japonicus* (ask for it by name), you are talking about one of the finest ground covers for the Southern garden. Mondo grass has so many desirable characteristics to recommend it, there is no wonder it is one of the most popular plants of its kind. Mondo grass is free of any serious insects and diseases; and it is durable, dependable, and evergreen. It also requires the barest amount of attention to keep it looking its best.

But there is something else you should know about mondo grass—it really does not grow in rows. Even though it is frequently used for borders and edgings, the professional garden designer will usually insist on using it as a ground cover. This insistence, however, is based on something more than a professional whimsy.

Mondo grass is, by its very nature, a ground cover plant. Spreading by means of shallow, underground rhizomes similar to those of St. Augustine, centipede, and Bermuda grass, mondo grass will form a low, irregular mass that becomes increasingly dense as the planting matures.

When mondo grass is planted along the edge of a walk or drive, it creates a separation between the sections of the garden, reducing its sense of unity. The usual intention of a border planting, particularly along the edge of driveways, is to minimize or soften the edge of the paving. Covering the edge with a narrow strip of greenery, however, does not really help to reduce its visibility. If anything, it may even exaggerate the situation. You can achieve a more satisfactory effect by widening the strip of planting to create a more appropriately proportioned space between the paving and the remainder of the garden.

The most successful uses of mondo grass take advantage of its characteristic color, texture, and adaptability. Mondo grass can withstand all sorts of physical abuse with an amazing amount of stamina. Prolonged periods of drought and periodic inundations seem to have no serious effects on its performance. This makes it a particularly useful plant for areas that receive irregular amounts of rainfall or occasional periods of standing water—under eaves, on steep banks, or in secondary drainage ways. Mondo grass can even tolerate a certain amount of trampling, a quality that makes it desirable for areas of heavy traffic such as entrance courts, service yards, and areas between sidewalks and curbs.

In addition to its extreme durability, the color and texture of mondo grass make it an effective substitute lawn where traditional lawn grass would be difficult or impossible to maintain. In areas of irregular topography, dense shade, steep slopes, or heavy root competition from surface feeding trees like beeches and magnolias, mondo grass may be the only solution when the effect of a lawn is required.

If it is planted exactly the way you find it in the nursery (usually sold in 1-gallon cans), mondo grass can be a rather expensive item in your landscape budget. It is not really necessary, however, to plant the entire clump in one location, unless, of course, you want

When mondo grass is planted as individual sprigs, it gives an even, lawnlike effect as the plants mature. It also makes an excellent contrast to the coarser textures of other plants.

to create a mounded or lumpy effect in the landscape. A gallon can of mondo grass can usually be divided into 15 or 20 individual plantlets or sprigs; by planting these sprigs 4 to 6 inches apart, you can create an effect that is quite satisfying even before the planting has matured.

If you would like to add a bit of seasonal interest to a planting of mondo grass, you might try an underplanting of perennial flowering bulbs. Set against the background of the deep hunter green of mondo grass, the colors of narcissus, jonquils, paper-whites, and rain lilies become even more pronounced. When the flowers have begun to fade, the mondo grass helps conceal their waning foliage.

Mondo grass should be available in most nurseries and garden centers; many nurseries even carry a variegated type. But if you should have some trouble finding it, just remember, it is probably hiding behind a sign with one of those other names.

Mondo grass is tough enough to withstand being trampled on occasions, but stepping stones are advisable if there is a lot of traffic.

As many as 20 individual plantlets may be taken from a single, 1-gallon nursery container of mondo grass. Spaced about 4 inches apart, the sprigs will give an even coverage in about two years.

In this contemporary application, a dense planting of mondo grass is used architecturally to create an asymmetrical arrangement with a specimen plant.

Ground Covers

56

Periwinkle
A sparkling ground cover for sun and shade

Common periwinkle (*Vinca minor*) is one of the best all-round ground covers for the South; in fact, it may be unsurpassed because of its adaptability to landscape uses and to horticultural conditions. Unlike many ground covers that are either distinctively informal or formal in landscape character, common periwinkle can be used either way. Not only does common periwinkle look splendid with edging boxwoods in a formal garden setting, but it is equally successful when used as the ground cover planting under the light and airy form of native azaleas in a naturalistic planting. Common periwinkle may either be confined to formal beddings edged with brick or may be turned loose to ramble and cover an expanse of garden where the deep evergreen blue green color is desirable. It is an exceptionally good cover for hard-to-fill locations, such as under the shade of a beech tree; it is also superb as a backdrop planting for a display of seasonal color, such as the spring emergence of daffodils.

Adding to the desirability of this ground cover is its tolerance for diverse horticultural conditions. Common periwinkle can tolerate full sun if adequate moisture is available and if the soil is friable and not a heavy clay; but it prefers shade or partial shade, attaining its best growth under the filtered light of canopy trees. In the Piedmont and Middle South, the plant will perform better in cooler shaded regions; in the Upper South, common periwinkle may be used in almost any location. This plant likes a rich, sandy loam that is high in organic matter; so till the planting bed well and work in bark and peat moss.

AT A GLANCE
Light: shade or full sun in Upper South; partial sun best elsewhere
Water: moderate amount
Soil: well-drained, friable soil
Growth Rate: rapid
Size: to 18 inches

Common periwinkle (above) does well in a small space if the runners are kept pruned.

Common periwinkle is an exceptionally good cover for areas in partial shade (left).

Above is a close view of the flower of bigleaf periwinkle.

The selection Variegata of bigleaf periwinkle has cream-colored leaf margins.

When fertilized and watered to a very dense cover, common periwinkle becomes prone to "blight"—a fungus disease. This does not occur in stands that have had no care for generations. Apparently, there is a limit to how thickly common periwinkle can be grown.

The hallmark of the plant is its glossy-green evergreen foliage and the tangled, rapidly spreading habit of growth. There is a spring bonus, however; bright-blue flowers appear as pinpoints of soft color hovering above the leaves. The five-petaled flowers are distinctive and can carpet the already dense covering with a fresh, beautiful look.

Common periwinkle's first cousin, bigleaf periwinkle (*V. major*) is a larger and far more coarsely textured plant that is more tolerant of heat. It may be successfully used in the Coastal Plain without fear of heat damage; it is not hardy in the Upper South. While somewhat more drought resistant than common periwinkle, bigleaf periwinkle still needs good soil and adequate moisture to ensure a fresh look. Bigleaf periwinkle will not grow as dense as common periwinkle. There are several selections available: (*Vinca minor*), Alba—white flowers; Bowles—dark blue flowers; Flore Pleno—double purplish blue flowers; (*Vinca major*), Variegata—cream leaf margins.

Both of these plants spread rapidly and are frequently overplanted. In good soil, they will fill in a planting bed when set as far apart as 18 inches. Older clumps are easily removed and divided. This makes the plant an excellent selection for erosion control or for planting in locations where soil retarding is necessary. Plant the clumps; then spread the runners out in a circle. Follow the runners until you find a section of stem where there are either leaves or roots. Bend the stem at that point, and bury the leaves or roots in the soil. This small section of periwinkle will produce roots and establish a new plant, helping to fill in the bed quickly.

The bright-blue flowers of common periwinkle provide an interesting combination (above) with the gray rocks.

Rosemary
An herb for the landscape

While herb gardening has long been considered a special pursuit and the plants relegated to culinary use alone, many gardeners have discovered the versatility of some herbs for general landscape plantings. One of the best and most durable of the herbs is the old-time seasoning favorite, rosemary (*Rosmarinus officinalis*). Not only does the plant have a vigorous, almost erratic growth habit, but it brings an unusual evergreen bluish gray foliage and softly scented wintertime flowers to the landscape throughout the South. Rosemary is disease and pest free; it is a good plant for tough locations, where a garden surprise is welcome.

Rosemary has a unique look in the landscape. It is thick and wild looking, almost like leggy shore juniper. This carefree habit of growth, with the plant sending out 12- to 16-inch leaders of foliage in free-form, scroll-like patterns, makes it an attention-getting plant in the garden. Combined with its tolerance, indeed, almost preference for difficult growing conditions, rosemary becomes exceptionally desirable. It can turn a throwaway garden location, where few plants would survive, into a thriving area. Its tolerance for tough horticultural conditions makes it a good plant for a seaside planting as well as for a hot, sunny southwestern garden. But rosemary's usefulness is not confined merely to sunny plantings. The plant can be perfectly at home under the filtered light of pine trees, where it is a surprising contrast to garden favorites like dwarf gardenia and the popular azalea.

While associated with formal plantings, rosemary looks equally at home in naturalistic locations that play up its free-form growth habit. This plant is a powerful accent to stonework, where the leggy stems will droop over the edge of the rock and then arch gracefully upwards. Mature plantings can reach 4 feet in height and will spread vigorously, since the drooping branches are likely to take root where the stems touch the ground. This ability to spread laterally, combined with a strong root system, makes the plant useful for hard-to-cover, eroding locations.

Rosemary is also an exceptional potted specimen or can be used to fill narrow, hard-to-fill planters, where crowded conditions would cause root damage in other plants.

One attractive added bonus of the plant is the soft purple or bluish flowers that appear in winter and sometimes persist through the coldest months of the year—a nice touch for the comparatively quiet winter garden.

The vigor that makes the plant so desirable can create some problems, especially if the plant is located in fertile soil. Here, rosemary will become almost ungainly in a short time and may expire under high fertility and moist conditions. Fortunately, it responds well to pruning (the clippings can, of course, be dried and used in cooking), and the plant will rapidly return to a more uniform appearance. In addition, there is a another selection (*R. officinalis* Prostratus) that has an even more pronounced cascading form of growth, which is particularly attractive in elevated plantings but is slightly less cold hardy.

Prostrate rosemary is a popular ground cover for planters, especially in arid regions of the South.

AT A GLANCE
Light: partial shade to full sun
Water: moderate amount; drought hardy when established
Soil: any soil; does well in poor soil
Growth Rate: moderate to rapid
Size: to 4 feet
Remarks: must have well-drained soil to become established

Rosemary does well in any soil and seems to have a preference for difficult growing conditions.

Santolina
At home in the heat

AT A GLANCE

Light: full sun to filtered shade
Water: moderate amount
Soil: well-drained soil
Growth Rate: rapid
Size: 1 to 2 feet

Prized for its blue gray foliage, santolina or lavender cotton (*Santolina chamaecyparissus*) is hardy in every region of the South. Also, this 1- to 2-foot shrublike perennial is evergreen in the South and bears masses of small yellow flowers during most of the summer. A green-leaved form (*S. virens*) is also available. Green santolina is generally lower growing and more compact in habit than the gray-leaved species.

Because of its low, spreading habit, santolina is most often used as a ground cover; but it also makes a good edging plant for a sunny border where its color tones and leaf texture contrast pleasingly with other plants in the border. Santolina is particularly at home around rocks, either near a stone building or in the rock garden. It also makes a striking show growing out of a riprap wall, where the plants seem to thrive even in a soil-starved situation. Santolina is also a good accent plant for the herb garden.

Among the most commendable traits of santolina are its ease of culture and ability to survive hot, dry weather. Planted in full sun or light shade, santolina will grow in nearly any soil if drainage is good.

To keep santolina at its best, prune the plants annually in late summer after flowers fade. Cut plants back to about 12 inches high to promote a compact, bushy form. Cut stems have a pleasing lavenderlike fragrance, and both flowers and foliage are used for indoor flower arrangements, either fresh or dried.

When planting santolina in a massed bed, set 1-gallon plants about 2 feet apart. To plant in a wall crevice or other constricted area, remove most of the soil from the root ball and wrap exposed roots in damp sphagnum moss; then stuff the wrapped roots into the crevice with a hammer handle or other dull object. Water plants regularly until they are established.

Lavender cotton can provide masses of bright-yellow flowers for several weeks during early summer.

Santolina is a popular rock garden plant.

Sprenger Asparagus
Fine, feathery foliage for ground cover

One of the best reasons for using ground cover plantings is to create contrasts with plant textures. Sprenger asparagus (*Asparagus sprengeri*) is one of the finest textured plants and can be used as a delicate accent plant among shrubbery and coarse ground covers. Its feathery plumes provide a striking, soft-textured mass in the landscape.

Although commonly thought of as a tropical plant, sprenger asparagus can be grown throughout the Gulf Coast area and as far up the Atlantic Coast as Charleston, South Carolina. Grow sprenger asparagus in partial shade and moist, well-drained soil. It will require watering until the plant is established, and then sprenger asparagus will need only minimum care. Sprenger asparagus may die back to the ground each winter, but the roots survive and send up new top growth in the spring. Repeated winterkill, in fact, helps control the plant naturally so that it does not become tall and unsightly; simply cut off the dead stalks at ground level each winter.

In south and central Florida, sprenger asparagus remains green all year, reaching a height of 2 to 3 feet. In cooler areas (northern Florida and the Gulf South) where this asparagus is grown as a perennial, plants reach a height of 1 to 2 feet in a single growing season before cold weather kills them back. Grown under optimum conditions, sprenger asparagus bears sprays of pinkish white, fragrant flowers in early summer, and these produce red, three-lobed fruit about ½ inch in diameter.

Situated in beds of other ground covers, such as English ivy, Asian star jasmine, or mondo grass, sprenger asparagus becomes a good accent plant. It is not recommended for covering large areas, except in south Florida. Because the plant spreads by arching stems and not by underground growth, thick coverage is seldom obtained. Also, the extremely fine texture of the plant discourages its use as a mat-forming ground cover. Sprenger asparagus is really at its best in planted boxes and parterre gardens, where the limited space accentuates the plants. If grown in hanging baskets or pots, plants will need to be brought indoors during the winter.

AT A GLANCE
Light: partial shade
Water: needs moisture
Soil: rich, loamy, well-drained soil
Growth Rate: moderate to rapid
Size: 2 to 3 feet

The textural contrast of agave and sprenger asparagus (shown above) is a popular combination in Florida landscapes.

The light-green foliage of sprenger asparagus (left) creates a tropical effect in almost any location.

Wedelia
A winner in the heat

AT A GLANCE
Light: full sun to filtered shade
Water: tolerant of most conditions
Soil: prefers fertile, sandy soil; will tolerate most types
Growth Rate: rapid
Size: 1 foot in height

Ground cover plants that tolerate intense heat and prolonged drought are not always easy to find, especially in the Lower South where exposure to full sun can result in ragged, brown leaves. One plant that seems to love the driest, most torrid conditions is wedelia (*Wedelia trilobata*). Native to the tropical regions of the Americas, wedelia is rapidly finding its way into gardens of south Texas and the Lower South. Not only is wedelia tolerant of glaring sun and dry weather, it also thrives in the salt air and inclement soil conditions characteristic of the Coastal South from Brownsville, Texas, to Charleston, South Carolina.

Valued for its low, mounding habit of growth, wedelia produces small, yellow, daisy-like flowers during most of the year. Reaching about 1 foot in height, wedelia spreads by surface stems that root where they touch the ground. Planted in full sun or in light, filtered shade, wedelia will grow in nearly any soil, even alkaline soil. Performance is best, however, in sandy soil that is moderately fertile. Set plants about 12 inches apart in all directions for complete coverage in two years. Keep beds weeded and mulched to encourage rapid spread of plants.

Because wedelia is easy to propagate either by layering or by rooting tip cuttings, it makes a quick landscape cover. Insert tip cuttings directly in the soil where plants are desired. Because of its spreading, above-surface habit of growth, wedelia is useful as a ground cover in rocky or hard-to-dig soil. You can cover banks or large expanses with wedelia, or use it as an edging.

The yellow daisylike flowers (shown above) bloom sporatically throughout much of the year in the warmer regions of the South.

Wedelia is popular in the Lower South because it tolerates heat, spreads rapidly, and thrives in the salt air (right).

Vines are the landscape's tracery. They are evocative plants and, as a group, contribute to the mood of a garden. They can be bouyant, like yellow jessamine tumbling airily across a trellis; or they can be somber and dignified, like Boston ivy climbing venerably up a granite wall or column.

Since they climb or can be trained to grow up the side of buildings, vines are used on structures more than other groups of plants. Historically, they were the link between the planting of the grounds and the architecture, serving to soften the harshness of a structure. Vines were invariably planted to pull the green appearance of the ground plane upward. Used this way, vines can smooth and visually soften abrupt changes in texture, materials, or elevation in landscape composition. In fact, vine plantings can cover architectural mistakes, discolored stone, or poor workmanship, and make the broad surfaces of a

Vines
Tracings and linkings
for the garden

Chinese wisteria, page 80.

Henryi hybrid clematis, page 69.

Coral vine, page 71.

building recede and blend into the landscape. Their best contribution to the garden, however, is that they can add an aged appearance to a building or ground quite rapidly.

As vines make a structure appear more aged, they can also add character—yielding a rustic and weathered look like wisteria; a delicate and sculptural look like climbing fig; or a dignified and eternal appearance like smilax. This two-fold ability of vines to contribute a settled-in appearance to a building and to generate special feelings in a garden makes selection and placement in the garden extremely important. As a rule, except where used for strongly functional purposes (such as retarding erosion or screening a view), vines should be considered accent plants and used with restraint to provide the best effect. Careful placement of a vine can complete a landscape composition, while poor placement or selection can turn a garden into an unkempt, overgrown-looking planting.

Types of Vines

One important key to using vines in the landscape is to understand how the vines climb. There are four basic ways and vines are grouped accordingly.

—Vines climb by twining. These plants wind around a supporting structure or tree, using the object for support. Yellow jessamine, trumpet honeysuckle, Confederate jasmine, wisteria, and silver lace vine climb this way.

—Vines climb by tendrils. Tendrils are long, slender, coiling extensions of a stem that wind around objects and provide a means of support for the vine. Coral vine and smilax climb with tendrils.

—Vines climb by leaf petioles. Clematis is the best example of this type. Basically, the leaf stalk, or petiole, acts as a tendril to provide support.

—Vines climb by clinging. There are two basic clinging mechanisms: aerial roots (rootlike hold-fasts) and small discs. Both of these line the stem of the plant and adhere to minute variations in the surface of a material. Some of the clinging vines are cross vine, Virginia creeper, Boston ivy, creeping fig, and trumpet vine.

Yellow jessamine, page 75.

Lady Banks rose,
page 76.

The vines in the first three groups must have structural support for climbing. They are generally used on trellis work, lattice panels, or arbors. If one of these vines is to cover a building wall, then it must be trained up a wire or a wood frame.

Vines in the last group can climb almost any vertical surface. Because of their method of adhering, they can cause maintenance problems if allowed to cover surfaces that must be painted. In addition, the small, rootlike hold-fasts will trap water against wood siding or wood trim and hasten deterioration. These vines are best used on masonry or stone surfaces.

The growing habits of vines should be combined with their form, foliage, and flower to get the most effective use from a vine planting. For example, a deciduous clinging vine (Boston ivy, Virginia creeper, or trumpet honeysuckle), planted on the south or southwest wall of a building, can help reduce the heat absorption during hot summer months by blocking the sun with its foliage. In the winter, when the heat is needed, the vine will not interfere with the radiant energy. Deciduous twining or tendril vines are also useful for arbors since they provide shade during the summer but allow the sun to penetrate during the winter. A small, deciduous vine-covered trellis that shades sliding glass doors would be an effective energy-saving device as well as appearing to bring the foliage indoors.

Evergreen twining vines, like smilax, yellow jessamine, or Confederate jasmine, can be used to cover a trellis or lattice frame to provide an effective privacy screen for the entire year. Used in the same manner, these vines can also soften the appearance of link fencing, such as around a tennis court. These same vines are equally effective on overhead arbors. They can provide shade the entire year and, importantly, create a green canopy that has the appearance of an outdoor room. Evergreen vines are also useful as a ground cover to prevent erosion. Since most vines are vigorous growers with rapidly spreading root systems, they can retain the soil even on steep banks. English ivy (see "Ground Covers") is frequently used in this manner.

Use a favorite vine to carpet the base of a pedestal or garden ornament, or to drape the panels of a brick and pillar wall. Clinging vines are best for this effect. Confine a clinging vine on one column of a porch or on the pillar of a fence. This makes the planted column special and softens the rigid look of masonry. However, if you use a twining or tendril vine, provide small hooks in mortar joints for support. Instead of hugging the wall like a clinging vine, these vines will ramble across the top and sides—a relaxing contrast to the

Chinese wisteria, page 80.

Virginia creeper, page 67.

Trumpet honeysuckle, page 73.

Lady Banks rose, page 76.

geometry of the wall. If a vine is not used to solve a landscape problem, then enjoy it for its subtle effects—it is one of the finest finishing touches in landscaping.

Special Uses for Certain Vines

Following are some specific examples for using vines in special ways.

—Climbing fig is successfully used to cover the risers (fronts) of stairs in green.

—Yellow jessamine rambles through the tops of trees in naturalistic plantings, adding bright color to the landscape twice a year.

—Both Boston ivy and Virginia creeper turn vivid red in the fall and, upon dropping their leaves, reveal their stems' filigree. On a stucco or stone wall, these stems appear as veinage, which gives the stone a natural weathered look. Virginia creeper also climbs the trunks of trees to produce a bowery effect.

—The spring flamboyance of Japanese wisteria is surpassed only by the reserved bold musculature of the vine in winter. Old wisteria looks rugged, indomitable, and timeless.

—Trumpet honeysuckle and clematis twine and wind, erupting into a show of flowers. They are unquestionably two of the boldest flowering vines and appear loose in their growth habit—use them on freestanding posts or lattice panels.

—Confederate jasmine looks sleek and grows profusely in the garden, but its special characteristic is its fragrance which can perfume an entire landscape.

—Hybrid trumpet creeper is a bold, vigorous mass of finely cut green foliage—a vine for fence posts. It also attracts hummingbirds to the landscape.

The vines discussed in this book are a cross-section of plants that will do well in at least two-thirds of the Southern states. In addition, the character and use of the vine was considered so that there are vines for formal landscapes, naturalistic plantings, for use up close or at a distance, and for a variety of horticultural conditions. Some vines with a limited area, or vines that grow rampantly and are hard to control, are not listed. Bittersweet, for instance, is good a vine in the Upper South, but it can become unruly and hard to control in a short period of time. Special categories of plants are also excluded, such as the climbing roses. While these plants are frequently used to cover trellises or arbors, they are not strictly vines; nor are they considered as maintenance-free and durable as the perennials listed here—one exception, however, is Lady Banks rose.

Confederate jasmine, page 74.

Yellow jessamine, page 75.

Trumpet honeysuckle, page 73.

Boston Ivy and Virginia Creeper
At home in the South

Boston ivy (*Parthenocissus tricuspidata*) and its close relative, Virginia creeper (*Parthenocissus quinquefolia*), are familiar deciduous vines in the South. These cousins share many desirable traits, including the brilliant scarlet fall color for which this genus is noted. Virginia creeper is native to North America and can be found throughout the woodlands of the eastern United States. Boston ivy was introduced to North America from Japan and central China.

Another ornamental feature of these vines is the character of their branches during winter when the plants are leafless. Against a white brick wall or a stucco wall, the branching pattern lends interest to an otherwise empty space. Since Boston ivy and Virginia creeper grow rapidly once established, they are both excellent covers for ground or walls, providing a rich, dark background for any setting. Each gives an especially effective naturalistic display when growing up a tree trunk. And the fall color of each against the bark produces an exceptional accent. Because of their rapid growth, it may be necessary to periodically cut these vines back.

The leaves of Boston ivy are three-lobed and coarsely toothed near the tips; Virginia creeper has compound leaves, each made up of five leaflets fanned out like the fingers of a hand. Both produce blue black berries in the early summer, but these are mostly concealed by the foliage and are not highly ornamental in themselves. They do attract birds, however.

Boston ivy and Virginia creeper climb by attaching their tendrils (clinging shoots that grow along the branches) to whatever support is provided. The rapid growth rate of the vines, plus their superb clinging qualities, allows them to cover large areas in a relatively short time. Do not grow Boston ivy or Virginia creeper on wooden buildings. A vine-covered wall dries out slowly after rain, promoting decay of the wood; and, if grown on a clapboard wall, the stems will soon begin to grow up under the individual boards, posing a threat to structural stability.

Both Boston ivy and Virginia creeper should be planted in full sun or partial shade. Rich, peaty soil is preferable for the best growth. When planted in poor soil, especially soil with iron or other nutritional deficiencies, these vines tend to look ragged and off-color and may be prone to attack by insects. While Boston ivy does not grow well in hot, dry sites, Virginia creeper is more tolerant of drought and heat. Both Boston ivy and Virginia creeper, once established, will withstand most city conditions.

AT A GLANCE
Light: full sun to filtered shade
Water: moderate amount
Soil: rich, peaty soil
Growth Rate: rapid
Size: will climb to 60 feet

Boston ivy is often used to cover brick or stone structures as it generally softens the architectural lines.

The fall color of the foliage of Virginia creeper is brilliant scarlet.

Virginia creeper (far right) is a familiar vine of the South, but it oftentimes is mistaken for poison ivy.

Vines

AT A GLANCE

Light: sun to partial shade
Water: moderate amount
Soil: fertile, light,
well-drained soil
Growth Rate: rapid
Size: depends on species
Remarks: roots must be
kept cool, so important to
mulch base; requires
support to climb

Clematis
The showiest vine

You must see a hybrid clematis in bloom to believe that such a magnificent display could arise from a small, almost spindly, vine. From soft pastels of lavender and pink to vibrant burgundy and numerous bicolors, the flowers of clematis present a varied portfolio of colors. But of all the hybrid clematis available, none are more magnificent than the white selections—flowers as large as 9 inches in diameter and as delicate as snow. Based on where they are often planted, hybrid clematis could be called the lamppost plant. However, there are many other landscape uses for this spectacular vine. Let it climb walls and fences; take advantage of its light weight, and use clematis to color latticework, a gazebo, or pergola.

The most critical consideration when selecting a planting site for clematis is that the root system must be kept cool, while the rest of the plant must be exposed to sunlight at least 5 hours a day for best flowering. A sunny location where the roots will grow under the house, a terrace, walk, or other cool location would be ideal. Always apply a heavy layer of mulch around the base of the plant. If you buy small packaged plants, plant according to the label directions. Clematis needs a well-prepared planting hole about 2 feet in diameter and 2 feet deep. Amend the soil with compost, leaf mold, or other organic matter to make it loose and friable. All newly-planted clematis vines should be pruned the first year to 6 to 12 inches above the ground; thereafter, pruning practices depend upon the bloom period and vary according to grouping. Because of their climbing habit and very rapid growth,

The selection Henryi softly blends a gazebo into the landscape. This is one of the most popular clematis hybrids, producing flowers up to 8 inches across.

Hybrid clematis is most often used on a lamppost, but it is equally spectacular when grown on a fence, trellis, or latticework (far right).

clematis vines need training—a vine can grow 4 inches on a warm spring day. After planting, stake small plants and guide the vine in the direction you want it to grow. Fertilize in spring and summer with ¼ pound of 5-10-10 broadcast around the base of the plant; water well. You may prefer to use a soluble fertilizer and apply it more frequently, perhaps every two or three weeks. Water plants frequently during dry periods.

Since clematis is such a large and varied genus, the species have been classified into 10 major groups based on flowering characteristics and pruning practices. Five groups comprise the large-flowered hybrids so popular in Southern gardens: Florida, Jackmanii, Lanuginosa, Patens, and Viticella. The selections in these groups vary in flower size, color, and blooming period (spring or summer).

After flowering (left), the fruit clusters appear and persist through the winter.

The creamy-white blossoms of Henryi are a handsome contrast to a rustic wooden lamppost.

Florida Group

Double and semidouble flowers are characteristic of selections in this group. They flower on short growths from the old wood in late spring and need no pruning. They will occasionally produce single flowers in late summer on new wood. Florida selections include Kathleen Dunford (rich rosy purple), Mrs. Spencer Castle (heliotrope pink), Duchess of Edinburgh (double white), Belle of Woking (double silvery mauve).

Jackmanii Group

Like the Lanuginosa selections, these clematis bloom continuously throughout the summer. However, they produce blooms only on new wood and need pruning every year. Prune in late winter or early spring, cutting plants back to 3 or 4 inches above the ground. Popular selections include Comtesse de Bouchaud (mauve pink), Ernest Markham (petunia red), Jackmanii (dark velvety purple), Hagley Hybrid (shell pink), Star of India (reddish plum with a red bar).

Lanuginosa Group

This is the largest group of clematis. They bloom throughout the summer, flowering on new and old wood. Pruning is not necessary, but may be done if desired. Well-known selections include Crimson King (crimson red), Henryi (creamy white), Mrs. Cholmondeley (lavender blue), Ramona (lavender blue), Violet Charm (rich violet).

Patens Group

These selections produce very large flowers in late spring on short stems of the previous year's growth. Prune after the main flowering period, but only if necessary to control growth. They may bloom again in the fall on new wood. Popular selections include Barbara Jackman (petunia mauve with crimson bars), Kathleen Wheeler (plummy mauve), Nelly Moser (pale mauve pink with deep carmine bars), Lincoln Star (cochineal pink with paler edges), The President (deep purple blue), Gillian Blades (pure white).

Viticella Group

These clematis also bloom on new wood but later in the season, with most flowering from July to October. Prune the same as those in the Jackmanii group. Flowers of these clematis are smaller than the other hybrids. Included in this group is the very vigorous Huldine (pearly white with pale-mauve bars), along with Madame Julia Correvon (deep wine red) and Venosa Violacea (violet blue).

Vines

Climbing Fig
Clothing the garden in green

AT A GLANCE

Light: full sun or partial shade
Water: moderate amount; likes high humidity
Soil: rich, well-drained soil
Growth Rate: slow to moderate
Size: will climb to 15 feet or higher

Climbing fig is a popular substitute for English ivy in the Lower South because of its tolerance of the sun.

Climbing fig (*Ficus pumila*) covers walls and chimneys in a thick cloak of small green leaves, sometimes in just two to three years. The stems, with their clinging "feet," search their way up the wall in irregular patterns and eventually form a complete cover of greenery. Climbing fig may be one of the neatest and most inviting vines that is available. The tiny leaves lay over one another and hug the surface; the visual effect is more that of a green wall treatment than the cloaking by a plant. In addition, the young spreading branches fan out to create beautiful fernlike patterns as they ascend. Not only is the plant a pleasure to look at when its growth is completed, but it also has a refined, elegant look in adolescence. Best of all, the plants are easy to maintain in their naturally compact form with an occasional trimming when they spread beyond their intended bounds.

Climbing fig is a hardy evergreen in the Middle and Lower South; but in the northern reaches of its hardiness zone, climbing fig may die back severely each winter. This trait is not necessarily a negative one, however, as growth resumes from the roots in spring, and the spread of the plant is thereby controlled by the climate. The vines can be confined in small areas, such as building foundations in the Middle South; but, used in similar locations, they would grow too rampantly in areas of the Lower South such as Jacksonville or New Orleans. Young plants often grow slowly at first; but, as the vines mature, they become more vigorous.

In places where it can grow to its maximum length, climbing fig may reach 15 or more feet. Eventually, the vine develops thick branches that grow out from the support and produce leaves three to four times the size of those borne by the main stems (mature foliage). In the warmest areas of the South, the vines bear 2-inch-long oblong fruit that is inedible. The juvenile leaves of climbing fig are 1 inch long and heart shaped with conspicuous veins. Aerial rootlets along the stems stick to wood, masonry, and other structural surfaces as well as tree trunks. The vines are easy to establish and thrive in hot, humid climates. Very little space is required for the roots, so you can plant climbing fig in small pockets of paved terraces and patios, in cracks between steps, and in hanging baskets. If planted in containers, climbing fig should be brought indoors in winter.

Plant climbing fig in full sun or partial shade and in moist, well-drained soil. Add peat moss to excessively sandy soils to promote moisture retention, and break up hard clay soils by adding compost or ground bark. Pinch out the tip of each vine to encourage branching. During the first year water the vines, both roots and foliage, every three or four days unless it rains. As the vigorous roots become established, they become increasingly drought resistant. Prune climbing fig, if necessary, in early spring as new growth is beginning. In areas where the vines die back to the ground, clip off old stems at ground level. In warmer areas, cut off winter-damaged parts to a live portion of each stem.

Coral Vine
Not just a weed

Some consider coral vine (*Antigonon leptopus*) to be in the same noxious category as runaway honeysuckle in the Lower and Middle South, but the plant has great merits in the landscape when you know its growth habits and where to plant it. It is difficult to find a faster growing, more dependable, prettier pink-flowering vine for trellises, fences, pergolas, or arbors in the Lower South. Coral vine is a native of Mexico and Central America, where it performs as an evergreen as it does in parts of south Florida. Also known as Queen's-Wreath and Chain-of-Love, this vine has a very luxuriant appearance as it climbs. However, coral vine is deciduous in most of the South; so you can use it in summer for shade in a location such as on an arbor over a sliding glass entry, and in winter, it will allow the sun to pass through. During summer, coral vine grows into a dense mass to provide medium to heavy shade or form an effective screen.

Reaching 40 feet in length, coral vine is a very fast-growing climber with alternately arranged, light-green, heart-shaped leaves about 4 inches long. The vines climb by tendrils and must be supported by a fence, arbor, or other structure. Every winter coral vine foliage is killed by frost (except in south Florida) and should be cut back to the ground. In spring, it will rapidly grow back to full size and will flower during summer and fall. Blooms are small but numerous in long, drooping racemes. One selection which has white flowers is not as hardy as the pink-flowering type. The fruit has small brown seeds surrounded by the dried flowers and is not very conspicuous.

For best growth and heavy flowering, plant coral in a sunny location. It will also grow in light shade, but it will not be as dense or flower as well. Coral vine is tolerant of most soil types. Small seedlings that may sprout from fallen seed underneath coral vine should be pulled up if you wish to limit its growth and range.

AT A GLANCE

Light: full sun to light shade
Water: moderate amount
Soil: tolerant of most soil types
Growth Rate: rapid
Size: will climb to 40 feet
Remarks: requires some support

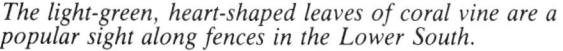

The light-green, heart-shaped leaves of coral vine are a popular sight along fences in the Lower South.

The pink flowers of coral vine give a colorful display all summer and into the fall until the frost comes.

Cross Vine
A rugged native favorite

Allowed to climb, cross vine
(left) will produce runners up to
25 feet long.

In its native habitat, cross vine (right)
climbs similarly to English ivy; and
its yellow red flowers are spectacular
in early spring.

The feature of the hardy, native cross vine (*Anisostichus capreolatus*) which gives it its name is not in an obvious position. In fact, it is a marvel that the vine ever retained this name, for the cross is found only when a stem is cut; then, the cross-shaped pattern of the pith inside the woody shoots is clearly visible. But perhaps early botanists, who had to struggle through tangles of this plant, noticed the feature. There are few vines in the Southern gardens that will give the rapid growth and quick cover of cross vine.

Cross vine is a vigorous, bold plant. Slightly coarse-textured in appearance, it will wind and climb its way to rapidly cover any structure, adhering in a most peculiar manner. Unlike most vines with tendrils that wind themselves around guy wires or other structural supports, the tendrils of cross vine are equipped with tiny adhering discs. These discs allow the vine to climb into locations that lack support for the tendrils.

The evergreen foliage is slightly coarse and lanceolate (shaped like a lance head), occurring in groups of even-numbered whorls at regular intervals along the semiwoody vine. The tendrils that enable the vine to ascend also emanate from the leaf center. Thus, groups of ordered leaves look suspended along the stem as though somebody attached them with a particular determination to space them evenly.

The vine has long been valued as an ornamental, having been authenticated as one of the original native plants widely used at Williamsburg. In early spring, this primarily evergreen vine comes to life with a covering of tube-shaped yellowish red flowers that appear in clusters along the length of the vine. The flowers are strikingly unusual and call attention to the vine, which blends quietly into the landscape the remainder of the season.

Another bonus of the vine is its adaptability to conditions all across the South. Only in the Upper South will the plant occasionally suffer a dieback; although because of its rapid growth, it can be expected to recover quickly. Cross vine prefers a good soil, and it performs well in either full sun or in the shade where it grows naturally. However, it will bloom more heavily if allowed some direct sunlight. Once planted, cross vine will be a steady and durable grower for years.

Honeysuckle
A vine to save

Trumpet honeysuckle (*Lonicera sempervirens*) brings lush evergreen foliage; delicate, trumpet-shaped flowers; and a loose, irregular habit of growth into the landscape. While a vigorous grower, this native plant does not spread out of control like Hall's Japanese honeysuckle (*Lonicera japonica* Halliana), which covers woodlands throughout the South. Like other honeysuckle vines, trumpet honeysuckle climbs by twining and is perfect for use on a section of fence or on a mailbox or lamppost. Because of its loose, floppy character, it has a softening visual effect on architectural features. In fact, if properly trained to a wall, it will tumble and race across the top without hiding the wall beneath a mass of foliage.

Flowers of trumpet honeysuckle are borne in clusters at the end of stems in midsummer. Their shape is striking—the corolla is almost 2 inches long and shaped like a delicately tapered trumpet. Color is generally a deep pinkish red with a yellow center. After the initial flowering, trumpet honeysuckle may continue to flower sporadically throughout the remainder of the season.

Another unusual feature of this vine is the foliage. Frequently, the last pairs of leaves on the stem will be connate, or joined together, with the stem growing through the center of what appears to be a single leaf. The remainder of the leaves on the plant are oppositely arranged along the stem and are highly variable in shape. All the leaves of this vine, however, maintain the dark, deep-green coloration.

Trumpet honeysuckle is hardy and durable. In the Lower South, it is evergreen, while in the Upper South it may die back during a severe winter. It tolerates direct sun and poor soil but prefers slightly acid soil with a moderate amount of humus. In the Upper South, the vine may bear fruit during the winter months. The small, red fruit appears in clusters at the end of the stems.

Several selections are available. The selection *L. sempervirens* Sulphurea has bright-yellow flowers; another selection, *L. sempervirens* Superba, has flowers that are deep red. Another similar plant that is worth noting is *Lonicera* x *heckrottii*. Its flowers are pinkish purple on the outside and yellow on the inside.

AT A GLANCE
Light: full to partial sun
Water: moderate amount; will tolerate drought
Soil: any moderately fertile soil
Growth Rate: rapid
Size: will climb to 15 feet

Trumpet honeysuckle (left) climbs by twining and is perfect for use on a mailbox or lamppost.

While a vigorous grower, trumpet honeysuckle (right) will not spread out of control.

Jasmine
For a privacy screen

AT A GLANCE

Light: sun or shade
Water: moderate amount
Soil: tolerant of many soil types
Growth Rate: rapid, once established
Size: will climb to 30 feet or more

The white flower clusters cover this vine in summer and are delightfully fragrant.

With the exception of fast-growing vines, plant materials that make attractive screens for privacy usually take a long time to develop. But, though slow to start, star or Confederate jasmine (*Trachelospermum jasminoides*) does extremely well as a fast-growing screen, once it is established. Its lustrous dark-green growth is dense, providing plenty of foliage for screening. Mature leaves develop to 3 inches long; new leaves are glossy light green. An added bonus is an abundance of white flower clusters that have a delightful sweet fragrance in summer.

To start a star jasmine for screening purposes, you need plants that have been staked at the nursery. A support for the twining vine can be a metal fence, a trellis, or your own specially designed support. You must be careful not to pinch the tips of the jasmine, or you will end up with a sprawling shrub from 1½ to 2 feet tall instead of a climbing vine for the screening effect desired. Established star jasmine screens require yearly pruning. Cut back jasmine one-third each year to prevent excessive woody growth and any bare spots that might otherwise develop. This pruning also encourages summer flowering.

In addition to developing into protective screens, star jasmine makes a good ground cover under trees and shrubs where grass will not grow. The plant can also be used in raised beds, entry gardens, and as an edging along walks or drives.

Because it has been thinned, Confederate jasmine provides a tracery effect on this lattice screen (above).

Confederate jasmine climbs and then cascades over this structure (right) to provide a handsome screen.

Jessamine
Turn yellow jessamine loose

You may have never noticed the delicately foliaged vine of yellow jessamine until the spring woods ripple with treetop golden yellow flowers. Blooming from February through April, yellow jessamine (*Gelsemium sempervirens*), also called Carolina jessamine, is one of the most prolific flowering perennial vines native to the Southern states. There is also a double-flowering type, called Pride of Augusta.

The vine climbs from ground level up to 20 feet high, where it can wind its way into the limbs of a supporting tree. The woods seem to glow with the color of the deep-throated, trumpet-shaped flowers; and when the bloom is over, the vine disappears again into the foliage of the woods. But the show does not end in spring. In fall, yellow jessamine puts on another, more sporadic, flower show, making it one of the few vines with a recurring bloom. And even though it is an evergreen, the foliage will turn a subdued bronze color that lasts until spring.

Fortunately, the vine has almost limitless home landscape uses. It can be set in a naturalistic planting similar to its native habitat, or it can climb and twine through the top of an arbor where it will provide summer shade and the fragrant blossoms can be enjoyed. Yellow jessamine is an excellent plant for covering chain link fences that enclose a yard or a tennis court. Planted at the foot of a brick wall and trained to the top, yellow jessamine will grow and spread, spilling flowers and foliage over both sides and softening the hard edges of the masonry.

Yellow jessamine need not climb to be attractive. It is handsome as a ground cover on steep banks or weaving among the stone or railroad-tie construction of retaining walls. When used as a ground cover, it will cover large areas of the landscape. Another use for yellow jessamine is in an elevated planter where it will tumble over the container's edge.

Part of the plant's versatility is its ability to adapt to varying horticultural conditions. It will grow in full or partial sun (although it will flower much better in full sun). In fact, it can be planted in shade and be expected to climb to available light for flowering. Yellow jessamine prefers rich soil, similar to the friable loams of its native woodland habitat; but it will adapt itself to a variety of soil conditions from slightly acid to slightly alkaline. Once planted, yellow jessamine requires little attention except for occasional thinning.

AT A GLANCE
Light: full or partial
Water: moderate amount
Soil: rich, well-drained soil
Growth Rate: moderate
Size: will climb to 20 feet
Remarks: seldom gets out of hand; requires little attention—flowers, leaves, and roots may be poisonous to animals

The tube-shaped yellow flowers are prolific in the spring and may appear sporadically again in the fall.

Tumbling over a brick wall, this yellow jessamine brings bright-yellow color and lustrous, rich foliage into the landscape.

Lady Banks Rose
Looks better with time

AT A GLANCE
Light: full to partial sun
Water: moderate amount; drought tolerant when established
Soil: any medium fertile soil
Growth Rate: rapid
Size: will climb to 25 feet
Remarks: needs space and training when young

The tumbling show of the cream yellow flowers of Lady Banks rose is frequently seen along fences throughout the South.

Few plants have endured the test of time better than Lady Banks rose (*Rosa banksiae*), and few plants provide the fine show in the landscape that is the hallmark of this rambling and determined plant. Lady Banks rose has the distinction of being one of the remaining rose species that is still widely used as a landscape plant. Most of our ornamental roses are hybrids, but Lady Banks rose is virtually unchanged after years of garden use. There are double- and single-flowering forms, and two different colors; but mention Lady Banks rose and inevitably the pictures that spring to mind are the soaring ambitious runners, the fine-textured semievergreen foliage, and the tumbling show of yellow, late springtime double flowers that cover as softly as a snowfall.

The show is a toast to springtime in the South, and it is not unusual to see this prolifically flowering vine running freely in treetops or tumbling across the roofs of garden structures. Lady Banks rose is a vine that needs to be turned loose to look its best, and it must have room to grow. The plant can easily ascend to 25 feet in a mounding style of growth that can look unkempt. Unlike most vines that twine, adhere to structures, or climb by tendrils, Lady Banks rose ascends on sheer vigor alone. Lacking the mechanisms of other vines, Lady Banks rose must have structures or supports to keep it aloft. Generally speaking, in its first few years of growth, the vine must be tied until it gains the necessary height. Once it climbs to the upper location, though, it will remain as a tumbling fountain of flowers.

The vigorous growth habit and relatively thornless stems make the plant a good problem solver. In just a few years, the plant can completely cover a trellis or arbor, thus providing screening from either the sun or privacy from neighboring locations. One splendid landscape use is to turn the rose loose on a wide expanse of rooftop that needs visual softening, such as on the roof of a garage that faces the street. The weight of the rose will keep it up on all but the most steeply pitched roofs, thus providing a covering that can mollify the harsh expanse of a shingled roof for years. In addition, the plant can also be used as a free-mounding ground cover or as a large shrub.

Lady Banks rose is not particular about soil or heat. It is a plant that thrives in direct sun and will grow vigorously in every Southern state. In the Upper and Piedmont South, though, the plant will be semievergreen. Lady Banks rose has few, if any, of the debilitating diseases or insect pests that most hybrids possess, making it a long-term plant that can be added to the garden. Selections include Alba Plena—double white flowers; Lutea—double yellow flowers; and Lutescens—single yellow flowers.

Silver Lace Vine
A fleece of late-summer flowers

August can be one of the quietest months for flowers in the Southern garden, but not if your plantings include silver lace vine (*Polygonum aubertii*). This herbaceous vine climbs by twining to 20 feet or more, draping its support with foliage and, in late summer, with masses of slightly fragrant white flowers. Tumbling from arbors and trellises, silver lace vine can be a pleasing adornment during a time when few other garden plants are making a show. Silver lace vine, a native of China, is hardy in the Upper and Middle South but not in the Lower South.

Silver lace vine is deciduous. The distinguishing spade-shaped leaves are 1½ to 2½ inches across, and tiny flowers are borne in erect clusters up to 6 inches long. Despite its delicate appearance, silver lace vine is a rugged garden plant, tolerating wind, drought, urban pollution, and neglect. Untended vines, however, will eventually find their way into nearby shrubs and trees where they will detract from the overall good looks of the garden. Grown over a fence or trellis, the vines are not only easy to maintain, but their flower clusters take on a graceful drooping habit. On a chain link fence, silver lace vine can conceal the fence as well as screen unattractive areas. It is a very rapid grower but can be easier to control than most twining vines since it can be pulled up in locations where it is not desired.

Because this vine climbs by twining, you will need to provide some form of support. Transparent fishing line run between two eye hooks makes an adequate and unobtrusive support for this vine to use for climbing on walls, solid fences, and other flat surfaces where the vine cannot twine. Grow silver lace vine in full sun or partial shade. It flowers best in full light. Any garden soil will support this easy-to-grow vine; but it grows most vigorously in loamy, well-drained soil. Only in the most depleted soil does silver lace vine require fertilizer. Flowers are borne on new wood, so light pruning in early spring can encourage bushier plants. Once established, silver lace vine will weather both cold and heat, but keep newly planted vines watered and mulched the first year.

AT A GLANCE
Light: full sun to partial shade
Water: moderately drought resistant
Soil: almost any; best in improved soil
Growth Rate: rapid
Size: 20 to 30 feet

Tiny greenish white flowers are borne in delicate panicles on the current season's growth. They are mildly fragrant.

Grown on a chain link or lattice fence, silver lace vine provides a late-season flower display and helps screen unwanted views.

Smilax
Catbrier tamed for the garden

AT A GLANCE
Light: full or partial sun best
Water: moderate amount
Soil: any well-drained soil
Growth Rate: rapid
Size: will ascend to 20 feet
Remarks: climbs by tough tendrils and prefers some support—once established, it will climb on its previous growth

Any woodland walker knows the tenacious vines called the catbriers (*Smilax sp.*) or the greenbriers. They are perhaps the most vexing native vines around, with countless sharp thorns and a tough, durable stem that seems unbreakable. So strong is the stem that, in many areas of the South, members of this large family are called bullbrier—a testimony to the force needed to walk through a forest that is draped or tangled with them.

But one species has been tamed for the garden—greenbrier smilax (*Smilax lanceolata*). It has become an almost indispensable ornamental in the Lower and Piedmont South; and at Christmastime, it comes indoors. Bowers of greenbrier smilax are cut each season to adorn balustrades and provide the greenery for centerpieces. The foliage will retain its dark-green luster, and the leaves will remain unfurled long after cutting. As an added bonus, because of the plant's ordinarily rapid growth, it can be expected to withstand severe seasonal cuttings each year and still recover its lush look by the mid-growing season of the following spring.

Smilax is a vine to plant for shade. It rapidly covers trellises or arbors with its clinging tendrils. In a short time it will layer over itself to create a dense sunscreen that is surprisingly light and airy in appearance. Guaranteed to gain almost 10 feet in a single season, the vine is appropriate for hard-to-screen locations or for places where rapid sunshade is desired. Should it, of course, appear out of control, the yuletide clippings will bring it back into balance.

The flowers are inconspicuous; but the fruit is dull red changing to splendid blue black and abundantly covers the vine, bringing different ornamental looks to the steady evergreen appearance that is the plant's hallmark. Sadly, the plant has fallen out of fashion and with little reason. For a quick sunshade or as an ornamental vine to soften the architecture of a doorway or entrance way, smilax provides a durable evergreen covering that is available throughout all Southern states.

Greenbrier smilax is frequently used to frame doorways (far left).

Smilax must be pruned to be kept in bounds, and its popular indoor use as Christmas greenery helps to keep the vine under control.

The stems of smilax are lined with thorns which can be dangerous.

Trumpet Vine
A chorus of summer color

The trumpet vine (*Campsis radicans*) actually seems to thrive on neglect; it needs no cultivation and grows rampantly without benefit of human intervention. Trumpet vine is native to the Southeast and plays the dual role of weed/ornamental, depending on where you find it. Grown with some care in the garden, it is unmistakably a valuable ornamental. As an ornamental, trumpet vine displays bright-salmon to orange trumpet-shaped flowers during midsummer when few other vines are in bloom. Allowed to overtake fences, other plants, and buildings, it is a weed.

Hardy throughout the South, trumpet vine is not available in many local nurseries; but travel along almost any roadway in the South, and you can find a plant to pull up and put in your yard. Plant trumpet vine in full sun or partial shade and in nearly any soil, including clay. Growth is most vigorous in well-drained soil. Resistant to heat, drought, and pests, trumpet vine grows vigorously with no care at all. The chief maintenance consideration with this vine is restraining it; a single annual pruning is all it takes. Flowers are borne on new wood, so pruning should be done in early spring before new growth begins. The leaves of trumpet vine are compound, with 7 to 11 ovate leaflets. Flowers are borne in clusters at the ends of branches. The individual blossoms are 2 to 3 inches long and very showy. Seed capsules, which are 4 to 5 inches long, hang off the vines even after the leaves have fallen.

Trumpet vine is deciduous and therefore of limited use as a screening plant; but used in combination with an evergreen such as yellow jessamine, trumpet vine is an excellent plant for chain link fences. Trumpet vine can be grown on lampposts, mailbox posts, arbors, and trellises if pruned severely to keep it in check. Unpruned vines may reach 40 feet or more. Climbing by aerial rootlets, trumpet vine easily climbs stone or cement walls and other rough surfaces. Hardly any training is required to make the vines climb if they are planted close to their support. Tie up the vines their first year in the ground to ensure good establishment.

A popular hybrid, trumpet creeper (*Campsis* x *tagliabuana*), is available now in the nursery trade. The hybrid trumpet creeper is not as vigorous as the native, and it is much more suited for the average home garden. It is very easy to control, and the flowers are large and showy. Two selections are available: Madame Galen, which has orange red flowers; and Yellow Trumpet, which has orange red flowers. Of the two selections, Madame Galen has far superior flower quality.

AT A GLANCE
Light: full sun to partial shade
Water: moderately drought resistant
Soil: nearly any well-drained soil
Growth Rate: rapid
Size: to 40 feet

The flowers of Madame Galen (below, bottom) are bright orange red.

A rapid grower, trumpet vine may become a pest if not controlled.

The long pods of trumpet creeper (far left) may persist throughout the winter.

The hybrid trumpet creeper tends to be more controllable than its parent.

Wisteria
Wind into a tree

AT A GLANCE
Light: full or partial sun
Water: moderate amount
Soil: any well-drained, rich soil—slightly acid to alkaline is best
Growth Rate: rapid
Size: will climb to 30 feet
Remarks: needs to be supported

Wisteria's spring show of flowers can drape a tree or an arbor with racemes of color almost 3 feet long. Colors range from soft whites shaded with violet to rich, radiant pinks and full lavender blues, and the blooms persist for almost a month. The twining wisteria vines also bring a distinctive fragrance.

The mature plant gives the best show, especially if the wisteria winds into an existing tree and the flowers drift through the foliage. But wisteria is a vigorous, twining vine (it is a member of the pea family) and can actually kill its supporting plant. If you want wisteria in your garden, build a structure to support it. Wrought iron or metal is best; if placed on a wooden structure, wisteria will eventually crush it.

Training wisteria along a structure is not the only way to use the plant effectively. Wisteria can also be trained along a wall or up an embankment. The effect of flowers cascading over the top of a wall is exceptional. Wisteria can also be trained to wind into a tree form. Set out young plants and stake for support until the branches are strong enough to support the weight of the plants. Used in this way, the plant's sculptural form can be prominently displayed in the winter landscape. Another advantage is that the plant can be located anywhere that special interest is desired. The tree form is also effective for small courtyards or seating gardens.

Two species are commonly available, Japanese wisteria (*Wisteria floribunda*) and Chinese wisteria (*Wisteria sinensis*). Japanese wisteria offers the selections Alba (white flowers), Purpurea (purple flowers), and Rosea (pink flowers). Chinese selections include Alba (with extremely fragrant white flowers) and Purpurea (with deep purple flowers). Chinese wisteria has flower clusters that average a foot in length; it climbs by twining from left to right. Japanese wisteria may have flower racemes over 2 feet in length and climbs by twining from right to left. The Japanese selections turn yellow in fall, while Chinese species have little fall color.

Wisteria works well draped on a trellis or around an arbor.

Wisteria may be trained as an espalier.

Shrubs occupy an intermediate position in the garden—varying in size from knee-high dwarf azaleas to tree-size Burford hollies and wax myrtles, shrubs provide the garden with both structure and ornament. A hedge of waxleaf privet, for example, can be used to build a garden's walls, and the specimen camellia can set its mood. This interplay of ornamentation and structural use is a key ingredient when placing shrubs in the garden. Most of the plants included in this book are shrubs; and although the quantity does not determine one's appreciation for shrubs, the abundance of this type of plant is of importance to the creative gardener. The casual gardener, the landscape architect, and the landscape gardener tend to classify plants according to the way they are used—for example, function, space, and general aesthetics; and despite the varied soil types, topography, and climates of the South, it is possible to choose a shrub that satisfies both horticultural and design objectives.

It is difficult to use a plant effectively without understanding how it grows. Horticulturists usually classify plants as either deciduous—those plants that lose their foliage during some part of the year; or evergreens, the plants that maintain a consistent, full-foliage effect. Since this classification implies a simple visual characteristic of the plant, this is the best way to begin a discussion of landscape shrubs.

Deciduous Shrubs

Deciduous shrubs provide the garden with its most vivid reflection of the seasons. Their wealth of flowers, handsome summer foliages, and vibrant autumn colors express the full range of nature's process of regeneration and fulfillment.

Although they are secondary to evergreens, deciduous shrubs have their place in the creation of a garden's fabric. A hedge of large deciduous shrubs, for example, can be used to screen an area that is used primarily in summer, like a swimming pool or vegetable

Shrubs
The garden's structure and ornament

Border forsythia, page 114.

Hybrid rhododendron, page 147.

Florida flame azalea, page 91.

garden. In winter months, when separation is not necessary, the openness these plants afford will totally transform the overall appearance of a garden.

Deciduous shrubs can also play an important part in providing the garden with emphasis, variety, and ornament. Since their overall appearance changes so dramatically from summer to winter, large specimens of fringe tree, Mentor barberry, winged euonymus, or other shrubs with distinctive forms can be used as major focal points within a garden. Smaller shrubs like lesser-flowering quince, pinxterbloom azalea, or maple-leaved viburnum can be used to punctuate a border planting, bring variety and interest to an entrance court or terrace, or provide a sculptural accent for a fence or wall.

But the greatest value of deciduous shrubs is the way they emphasize the mutability of nature. Through flowers, fruit, and foliage, they capture all the subtlety and drama of the changing seasons. Deciduous shrubs give the garden a continual progression of new blooms. Starting in early spring with border forsythia and Thunberg spirea, the show progresses through mid-spring with native azaleas, fragrant snowball, red buckeye, and bridal wreath. Later, when spring seems nearly through, Vanhoutte spirea, Piedmont azalea, and the beautybush bloom into summer.

Although it is generally regarded as a time for annuals, summer can be filled with shrubs in bloom. Oakleaf hydrangea, which starts to bloom in early June, is joined midseason by its Gallic cousin, French hydrangea. Plumleaf azalea with its almost shocking touch of red in early summer is a delightful late-bloomer, as is Bumalda spirea, whose lacy blooms are rosy pink.

Autumn, of course, is the time for brightly-colored foliages, but peegee hydrangea is at peak bloom in autumn; and with a little luck, the flowers of chaste tree will linger, and the lesser-lowering quince will repeat its cycle. Finally, after the first frost has taken almost all the other flowers, winter jasmine, winter honeysuckle, and Japanese quince assure us that this cycle will begin again.

When flowers seem in short supply, deciduous shrubs provide us with delightful ornamental fruit. As early as late September there is color in the berries of rockspray cotoneaster and the applelike fruit of Japanese quince; at the same time, beautyberry offers us a spectacular vivid wine display. And later in winter, there is Japanese barberry, cranberry bush, cranberry cotoneaster, possum haw, and winterberry. They brighten up the winter day, provide us with decoration during Christmas, and offer a feast for birds.

Spectacular autumn color is another benefit of many deciduous shrubs—for example, oakleaf hydrangea, Japanese barberry, red buckeye, Mentor barberry, and bridal wreath add vivid autumn color. A few, like winged euonymus, make autumn their "seasonal debut." Quiescent through the winter months, almost anonymous in summer, the winged euonymus explodes into a brilliant, fiery red in late September; it persists in this exuberant display until the early days of winter.

Despite the many seasonal advantages offered by deciduous shrubs, some people are dissatisfied with them because they are inactive during the winter. The fault can frequently be assigned, not to the plant, but to the way it is used. The barren twigs and branches of deciduous shrubs have a beautiful sculptural quality during the winter; but to be appreciated, they must be properly displayed. Too many deciduous shrubs in the same area will have a tangled, overgrown appearance in the winter; but if they are interplanted with

Reeves spirea, page 152.

Common oleander, page 136.

evergreens, or set against a simple background like a fence or wall, the handsome lines of these plants will be presented to best advantage. When they offer their display of seasonal effects, a proper setting will help emphasize the qualities that make deciduous shrubs such an important part of the garden.

Evergreen Shrubs

Since they provide a full-foliage effect throughout the year, evergreen shrubs are indispensible in the creation of a garden. They are used to define space, establish privacy and enclosure, and create the framework for a garden's total composition. Evergreens are also valued for their diversity of shapes and sizes, the richness of their foliage, and their seasonal effects.

Large evergreen shrubs (those which grow to more than six feet in height,) are especially useful in the creation of a garden's structure. Planted along the property line, a perimeter hedge of large, dense shrubs—like waxleaf privet, thorny elaeagnus, or Japanese anise tree—defines the limits of a garden and creates its walls. In addition to giving privacy and spatial definition, such plantings also form a background against which the other features in a garden are displayed.

When complete enclosure is not necessary or desired, clusters of large evergreens can still be useful in creating balance or establishing a rhythm for the garden. A distinctive shrub like Fraser photinia, for example, can be planted at strategic points within a garden to focus the viewer's eye on the total composition. A pair of formal shrubs, like Chinese holly, can be placed at the corners of a garden to create a comfortable, symmetrical effect; when a specimen like Fortunes osmanthus is planted on axis with a door or window, or at the end of a garden walk, it provides a focal point for the viewer.

A well-placed group of shrubs can screen isolated views, like service yards and storage structures, or create privacy by blocking the view of a neighbor's terrace. Conversely, a particularly handsome evergreen, like a specimen camellia, can emphasize a smaller landscape feature like an ornament or a garden pool which may otherwise be overlooked. Large evergreen shrubs work well when used to reinforce or minimize the appearance of architectural features. A series of large shrubs planted on each side of a small residence, for example, can help extend its line and mass and reinforce its sense of scale and presence. An oversize shrub, however, will tend to dwarf the house and make it seem even smaller. A grouping of large evergreen shrubs can also minimize or counteract the out-of-balance look associated with houses built on steeply sloping lots. Planted at the lower end of these houses, a shrub like wax myrtle, sweet viburnum, or sweet olive creates an elevated visual effect, providing a more stable overall view.

Shrubs of intermediate size, those which grow from three to six feet in height, provide the gardener with a delightfully diverse array of ornamentals. Plants in this group are small enough to be used near the house without overgrowing their location, and yet large enough to have sufficient presence as free-standing specimens. Many intermediate-sized shrubs also lend themselves to massed effects—a massed planting concentrates the impact on the landscape and also gives a substitute for larger shrubs. Plants of this size are frequently associated with foundation plantings; when used with an appreciation for their ultimate size, plants like edging boxwood, Zabel laurel, Japanese andromeda, and Florida leucothöe do make a handsome complement to architecture—but these plants may find

Burford holly, page 118.

Banana shrub, page 92.

their greatest value in the garden proper.

Middle-sized shrubs are especially useful in completing a garden structure that has been established by trees and larger shrubs. They can, for example, soften the transition between a perimeter hedge and the lawn, or help extend the line of the hedge without continuing its height. An enclosure of intermediate-sized shrubs can also be used to give a sense of separation to garden areas without totally interrupting their view.

Intermediate-sized shrubs can also be used to unify what would appear to be a disparate arrangement of existing trees and shrubs. A group of unrelated plants along a property line or in the center of a lawn, for example, can appear more unified when the area between them is filled in with a consistent planting of Japanese pittosporum, laurustinus, leatherleaf viburnum, or Southern Indian hybrid azaleas. Aside from creating unity, such plantings can also offer a dramatic sense of movement when they are arranged in a free-flowering mass.

Evergreen shrubs which stay below three feet in height provide the finishing touches for a landscape composition. Their size makes them ideally suited for enrichment and detail effects, but they can also solve many landscape problems, especially in small gardens where space is limited. Low-growing evergreen shrubs can also help improve the sense of scale and overall proportions of a large landscape, too.

Since the gardener may overlook these plants for large-scale plantings, small evergreens are frequently reserved for spaces near the house or areas where they can be observed in more detail. Areas where people tend to linger, like an entrance court or a terrace, are excellent locations for small shrubs; but they also make effective, unexpected accents planted near a set of steps, a garden gate, or at the entrance to another portion of the garden. Set in front of a low window, compact evergreens like dwarf yaupon, coastal leucothöe, or Gumpo azaleas provide a visual foundation for the window without interrupting views; and such plantings can be enjoyed from inside the house as well.

Low-growing shrubs can define space without creating too much separation. Planted along the edge of a terrace, an entrance walk, or a landing, for example, an arrangement of dwarf gardenias, winter daphne, or Satsuki hybrid azaleas will reinforce the limits of the space without unduly separating it from the remainder of the garden. Small shrubs can also be used as a transition between larger, background shrubs and an area of lawn or ground cover. This technique can also be used to give a layered look to garden plantings, to add depth and reinforcement to an informal hedge or screen, or to provide a foreground for an accent tree or shrub.

When planted in a mass, low-growing shrubs can be used as ground covers, too. Shrubs with weeping or horizontal habits of growth, like rock cotoneaster, dwarf gardenia, or winter jasmine take on a greater importance when planted as a mass; the seasonal effects of fruit and flowers are also concentrated in such plantings. Compact, rounded shrubs like Hellers holly, rotunda holly, and dwarf pittosporum create an interesting, bunched appearance when planted as a ground cover. If the planting is installed in parallel rows or as a staggered grid, it will have a handsome, geometric pattern that is ideally suited for the formal garden. Small evergreens are especially effective when used singularly as accents. A specimen such as Oregon grape, Harlands boxwood, or Japanese holly planted near an entrance can emphasize its location.

Many small shrubs also lend themselves to container culture. When planted in a handsome pot or jardiniere, these plants take on particular importance. Check with your local nurseryman or county agent, however, to make sure the plant you choose is container hardy in your area.

Dwarf winged euonymus, page 110.

Sasanqua camellia, page 100.

Anise
A special plant for every garden

Japanese anise (*Illicium anisatum*) is the hardiest and largest of the two anise species grown in the South. In the Lower South, Japanese anise grows to 20 feet tall and about 8 feet wide; in the Upper South, its height is about 8 to 10 feet. The large evergreen shrub, which is native to Japan, has an open, rounded form that can be used in a foundation planting, as an unclipped hedge or screen, or in a shrubbery border. In the Lower South, large shrubs can be limbed up to form small trees. Anises are lighter colored than most evergreen shrubs, ranging from medium green to light-olive green. In spring, Japanese anise produces a small, light-green bloom less than an inch in diameter, which is followed by green fruit.

Florida anise (*Illicium floridanum*), native to the Coastal Plains from Florida to Louisiana, is smaller than Japanese anise, growing to only about 10 feet tall with bright maroon red flowers. Florida anise is less hardy than Japanese anise and should be planted only in the Lower and Middle South. It can be used in a foundation planting, as a clipped hedge, in a shrubbery border, and in smaller areas than Japanese anise.

Anise grows best in moist, fertile, well-drained soils. It grows well in full sun or shade. However, very dense shade is not desirable for good growth. Under healthy cultural conditions, anise can be considered relatively pest free except for general pests, such as mites and scale.

It is the foliage that makes anise different from any other shrub grown in the South. The distinct aniselike smell of a crushed leaf and the angle at which the young foliage is held immediately identify anise in the landscape. The younger leaves of anise are held at a 45-degree angle, pointing toward the sky; the foliage looks like it is folding up to lay flat against the stem. The leaves relax as they age and hang like a large leaf, evergreen rhododendron. The foliage of Florida anise is more relaxed than Japanese anise.

Anise is an excellent evergreen shrub to use as a tall unpruned hedge or screen. To appreciate its foliage and form, anise should not be drastically pruned, and never clipped. There are other plants, such as Japanese yew, yaupon, and Japanese holly, which are more suitable for clipped hedges. Once clipped, the large, thick, leathery leaves of anise look like pieces of leaves hanging on to an artificially shaped shrub. To keep the plant dense and low, plant in a sunny location and clip the longest branches near the base so that new branches will form from the bottom two buds.

AT A GLANCE
Light: sun or shade
Water: moderate amount
Soil: fertile, moist soil
Growth Rate: medium
Size: 10 to 20 feet high; 8 feet wide

Japanese anise is a good evergreen shrub for a tall, unpruned hedge.

The flowers of Florida anise are bright maroon red and bloom from early spring until summer.

Aucuba
Colorful, dependable, exotic

AT A GLANCE
Light: partial to deep shade
Water: moderate amount
Soil: moist, well-drained
soil
Growth Rate: moderately
slow
Size: 6 to 10 feet in height,
6-foot spread

*Japanese aucuba produces
bright-red fruit in winter.*

*Gold-dust aucuba is a
beautiful accent for shady
garden areas.*

Japanese aucuba (*Aucuba japonica*) has so many qualities to recommend it that you will definitely want to include it on your list of indispensable plants. The coarse-textured leaves may be the most noticeable feature; but adaptability to a variety of soil conditions, tolerance of deep shade, and a remarkable toughness (Japanese aucubas are hardy to 5 degrees F.) are what make the aucuba truly versatile.

The large, glossy-green leaves and bright-red fruit of Japanese aucuba give it a wonderfully handsome appearance; in the variegated form (*Aucuba japonica* Variegata), the effect is more exotic. Also known as gold-dust aucuba, this variegated aucuba will add a touch of brightness to a dark corner and relieve the monotony of too many evergreen plants. Put one by a door, and you can be assured of a cheerful welcome even on the gloomiest day.

Both Japanese aucuba and gold-dust aucuba have dwarf forms. The growth habit is more erect than that of the standard types, and the female selections bear a generous amount of fruit. In many cases, the bright-red fruit is more prominently displayed than the fruit of the standard types, because the clusters are above the foliage. The dwarf selections seem to be less tolerant of sun and cold temperatures than the standard selections.

An extremely good plant for deep shade, Japanese aucuba should be protected from direct sunshine. Too much sun in the summer will cause the leaves to burn, while the winter sun will bleach the leaves to a sickly green. Since Japanese aucuba will withstand severe cold, it is ideally suited for use at a northern exposure.

Japanese aucubas prefer a rich, sandy loam high in organic content, but they will adapt successfully to a heavier soil as long as the surface drainage is good. Although they like a fairly moist soil, aucubas do not perform well when they are planted in damp locations.

Mature Japanese aucubas may grow to 10 feet in height in several years. Moderately slow growing, an average Japanese aucuba gets to be about 3 feet high in four to five years. An irregular, multistemmed habit of growth makes Japanese aucuba a natural for informal plantings, while the dense, compact form makes it useful as a free-standing specimen as well.

Pruning is seldom required on Japanese aucuba if the plants are located where they can grow to their natural size and form. It may be necessary from time to time to cut back individual branches that have become elongated. Severe pruning is best done in March or April. Few insects and diseases plague the Japanese aucubas; see page 250 for this information.

Because Japanese aucubas are deciduous (flowers of only one sex are borne on a single plant), fruit production depends on the successful cross-pollination of male and female plants. Crotonifolia is the most widely recommended male selection. Recommended female selections include Longifolia, Nana, Serratifolia, and Picturata. If foliage, not fruit, is the main interest, however, plants of either sex will prove satisfactory.

Azalea
Southern gardener's favorite

If there is a group of plants that is synonymous with Southern gardens, it is the azaleas—probably the most popular plant in the South. While the name evokes an explosion of spring colors, the azaleas are actually a broad grouping of plants that vary extensively in form, color of bloom, and landscape use. Azaleas are the staple of the spring garden color, and this is their source of popularity. But all too often, other qualities of the plant are overlooked in the selection process, qualities that are characteristic of the azalea hybrid or species group. Studying these hybrid and species characteristics and carefully planning color coordination will give the best results with azalea planting.

Evergreen Azaleas

Without a doubt, the evergreen azaleas are the most popular group of landscape plants in the South. And making them a tour de force as a landscape planting is comparatively simple. The key is coordinating the color of bloom so that each planting (from different selections) is allowed to bloom without competing or clashing with other color displays in the landscape. In addition, as with any evergreen, the form, foliage texture, and foliage color will also determine how the plant is used in the landscape.

Generally speaking, azaleas are most effective when used in drifts of separate colors that create a sweep of bloom through the landscape. The plants are generally loose and irregular in shape—planting them in casual drifts not only reinforces the form of the plant but creates shapes and patterns that are comfortable in the landscape. In fact, except for some of the dwarf plants that have tight compact forms, azaleas look awkward in formal plantings or when planted in rows. When used formally or in rigid clipped plantings, they look artificial and contrived.

Color choice is a matter of personal preference, but color coordination is not; for example, a red brick house and red azaleas will create visual tension instead of harmony in the garden. Every effort should be made to separate plantings to avoid this type of visual distraction. In fact, azaleas rarely work well as a foundation planting since they vary in appearance so widely during the year.

One of the most effective ways to achieve this is to use selections that bloom at different times of the year; thus, only one color will be in the landscape at any given time during spring. Another very useful idea, but requiring a lot of room, is to separate the different colors with a neutral evergreen planting or masses of white azaleas. Also, selecting plants of one color and allowing them to be the only azalea plantings in the garden is very satisfactory. Be sure to consider the color of any flowering trees or bulbs already in your garden. Neither a planting of redbud and red or pink azaleas nor a planting of bright-red azaleas and bright-yellow, late-blooming daffodils may be successful.

The hybrid or species character of azaleas is another important factor in landscape use. Some hybrid groups like the Kurume hybrids, which are extremely popular for their color, look very poor during the winter months in the Piedmont and Upper South. The foliage discolors to a dark maroon, and the leaves shrivel and eventually drop. Thus, the plant should not be planted in a prominent location. It should be used where its flower show can be appreciated, and the plant can then fade gracefully into the rest of the landscape. The

AT A GLANCE

Light: partial shade is best; full sun may stunt growth and deep shade inhibits flowering
Water: medium wet—once established and well mulched, they can resist drought
Soil: moist, well-drained, acid soil; rich in organic matter
Growth Rate: rapid—2 to 4 inches of new growth per stem each year depending on selection
Size: varies from 2 to 10 or more feet
Remarks: it is extremely important to plant azaleas in a slightly raised bed—most dieback problems occur when azaleas are either planted too deep or are allowed to dry out

Massing evergreen azaleas according to color under trees produces a bold spring show.

The upright, stemlike habit of growth of native azaleas will provide a sculptural effect in most Southern gardens.

Satsuki azaleas produce flowers in late spring to early summer.

large Southern Indian hybrid azalea will grow large enough in the Lower South to make a screen planting. This is an effective landscape use, especially when the plant is allowed to develop its full, graceful mounding form. Pruning, done to correct overplanting or insufficient room for plant growth, will destroy the form of the plant. The Satsuki hybrid, which includes the low-growing Gumpo azaleas, is an exceptionally handsome plant. It has attractive foliage with a prostrate habit of growth and makes a beautiful ground cover. In addition, it is an excellent container plant. Some hybrid as well as evergreen groups and some of the most commonly available selections follow.

Delaware Valley White azalea (*Azalea mucronatum*) is an excellent white azalea with a loose, irregular growth habit that deserves mention in this species. It is considered one of the best white flower types and has the additional bonus of being fragrant.

Glenn Dale hybrid azaleas (*Azalea* x *glenn dale*) are large plants that are cold hardy to the Piedmont South. They will reach 3 to 5 feet in height and are extremely popular. The plants vary considerably in form, texture, and time of bloom. Some common selections are: Buccaneer—orange red flowers with a dark blotch; Copperman—brilliant orange red flowers; Evensong—rose flowers; Fashion—orange pink flowers; Geisha—white flowers which are flaked and striped with purple; Glacier—white flowers with chartreuse throats; Pearl Bradford—rose pink flowers; Treasure—upright white flowers with a pink blotch.

Kurume hybrid azaleas (*Azalea obtusum*) are the extremely popular hybrids. The color range is widespread—from white to pinks, reds, and salmons. They are generally considered dwarf plants but will actually reach 4 to 6 feet in height. These are some of the hardiest azaleas and can grow in the Piedmont and Upper South, although they will suffer

during severe winters in northern plantings. Some selections include: Christmas Cheer—brilliant red flowers; Coral Bells—coral flowers; Glory—peach pink flowers; Hershey's Red—bright-red double flowers; Hino-crimson—crimson red flowers; Hino Supreme—dark-crimson flowers; Hinode-giri—vivid-red flowers; Pink Pearl—salmon rose flowers; Sherwood Red—orange red flowers; Snow—white flowers.

Pericat hybrid azaleas (*Azalea* x *pericat*) are hybrids that were developed for greenhouse forcing and are considered as hardy as some of the Kurumes. They have rich, dark-green foliage. Some common selections are: Hampton Beauty—carmine rose flowers; Hiawatha—rose red flowers; Sweetheart Supreme—rose pink flowers with a dark blotch.

Rutherford hybrid azaleas (*Azalea* x *rutherfordianum*) are very similar to the Southern Indian hybrids and are reliably hardy only in the Lower South. Some common selections are: Alaska—white flowers with a chartreuse blotch; Dorothy Gish—orange red flowers; King's White—white flowers; Mother of Pearl—pale pink flowers; Pink Ruffles—violet red, semidouble flowers.

Satsuki hybrid azaleas (*Azalea* x *satsuki*) are low plants that spread (to 3 or 4 feet) close to the ground. They also bloom late, usually in May to early June. Of particular interest in this group are the Gumpos. These dwarf prostrate plants bloom late in the season, usually in May or June. Their foliage is dense; and unlike most azaleas, they have some tolerance to direct sun. The flowers are white, pale pink, pinkish red, and bicolor. Some of the selections are: Balsaminaeflorum—orange red, double flowers; Flame Creeper—orange red flowers; Macrantha—pink flowers; Waka-bisu—salmon pink flowers.

Southern Indian hybrid azaleas (*Azalea* x *indicum*) are the most evocative of the azaleas. They are loose and mounding in growth habit and produce a magnificent flower display. These were the first evergreen azaleas introduced into the United States in 1840. They are exceptionally good plants for naturalizing or for informal drifts and can be expected to reach 10 or more feet in height. They grow best in the Lower and Coastal South. Common selections include: Fielder's White—white flowers with a faint chartreuse blotch; Fisher Pink—light-pink flowers; Formosa—magenta flowers; George Lindley Taber—white flowers flushed violet red with a dark blotch, and an overall orchid effect; Judge Solomon—pink flowers, similar in form to Formosa; Mrs. G.G. Gerbing—white flowers; President Claeys—orange red flowers; Pride of Mobile—deep rose pink flowers; Prince of Orange—orange red flowers.

Native Azaleas

One of the greatest discoveries by homeowners in recent years has been the native azaleas—and with good reason. They offer an airy, sometimes highly perfumed bloom in a hardiness range that covers almost the entire South. Their colors range from whites and pinks to flaming oranges, even yellows. In addition, their season of bloom stretches from earliest spring to mid- and late summer.

These durable, carefree shrubs (many times called wild honeysuckle) present a peculiar landscape challenge to azalea lovers, because all species are deciduous. This is a surprise

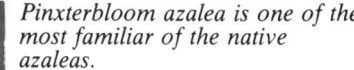

Pinxterbloom azalea is one of the most familiar of the native azaleas.

Shown here are the buds of flame azalea in winter.

Gumpo azaleas are among the few evergreen azaleas which flower late with a smaller mass of blooms.

Oftentimes, the flowers of native azaleas are referred to as wild honeysuckle.

Native azaleas are popular foundation plantings for rustic homes.

to gardeners, who associate the name azalea with the more popular evergreen types. But once native azaleas are seen and appreciated, they become a must in almost every garden.

The distinctive difference between the native and hybrid azaleas is in the growth and flowering habit. Unlike the evergreen hybrids, native azaleas are upright and stemmy, sometimes reaching the size of a small tree. The flowers appear in clusters borne at the end of the branches. The individual flowers are tube shaped and can be fragrant. Depending on the type, the flowers will emerge before or after the foliage. Importantly, the overall appearance in the landscape, even when the foliage is out, is one of line instead of mass.

Such a striking difference in appearance demands a different approach to landscape

use—and nature provides some excellent ideas to follow. In the wild, native azaleas are most often found at the edge of a woodland or a clearing. The branches seem to emerge in an irregular tangle that almost disappears into the backdrop of the woods, leaving the inflorescence suspended above the ground. This is especially true of the types that flower prior to the emergence of foliage. The plants that flower when the foliage is out hover with bursts of color underlined by the green base of the leaves—almost like individual landscape corsages. In some instances, native azaleas may be found in colonies; however, they are usually noticed as single plants—accents in a woodland vista.

Duplicating these natural plantings allows native azaleas to work easily in the home landscape. Plant them at the edge of a naturalistic border, or tuck them underneath the canopy of a grouping of trees. Smaller gardens without expansive borders can use native azaleas before a neutral backdrop, such as a fence or a wall. These structures will silhouette the flowers and the form of the plant. While native azaleas can look good emerging from other shrubbery, it takes a deft hand to plant them in this fashion. Generally speaking, native azaleas are most striking when planted in a low ground cover or as an accent among naturalized perennials. Above all, do not cover up the branching form of plants with evergreens—this is an easy temptation but one which will destroy the subtlety that a native azalea planting brings to the garden. Each species offers something a little different—here is what to expect.

Alabama azalea (*Azalea alabamense*)—fragrant flowers, usually white with a yellow throat; 3 to 6 feet tall; prefers drier soils; flowers after leaves.

Flame azalea (*A. calendulaceum*)—nonfragrant flowers; variable color—orange red to orange to clear yellow; large, spreading to 10 feet; flowers from mid-May to late June.

Florida flame azalea (*A. austrinum*)—fragrant flowers, golden or rich yellow in color; small, 3 to 6 feet tall; flowers before or with new leaves.

Oconee azalea (*A. flammeum*)—nonfragrant flowers, orange, red to salmon to pink; often confused with flame azalea but flowers earlier; medium height to 6 feet; flowers with leaves out.

Piedmont azalea (*A. canescens*)—fragrant flowers, white to light or deep pink; to 10 feet tall; diverse habitats; flowers before or with new leaves.

Pinxterbloom azalea (*A. periclymenoides*)—fragrant flowers, pale white to pale pink to violet; medium to 6 feet; cold hardy.

Plumleaf azalea (*A. prunifolium*)—nonfragrant flowers, orange red to deep red; to 10 feet; heavy flowering late in season—July to August.

Swamp azalea (*A. viscosum*)—fragrant flowers, white to creamy white; medium to 5 feet; dense plant; cold hardy; tolerates moist locations.

Note: The authors are well aware that botanists correctly use *Rhododendron* as the genus name for Azaleas. However, for reader clarity and to avoid confusion, *Southern Living*, like many other publications, uses *Azalea* as an acceptable name for the genus.

Southern Indian hybrid azaleas (top) are the largest and produce the biggest blooms of the evergreen types.

Kurume azaleas are popular because of their massive floral display, but they may look unattractive after flowering.

Banana Shrub
A one-of-a-kind scent

AT A GLANCE

Light: sun or partial shade
Water: moderate amount
Soil: fertile, well-drained, acid soil
Growth Rate: slow
Size: 10 to 15 feet

Banana shrub (*Michelia figo*) has endured the test of time. This fine plant, widely planted in gardens of the Lower and Middle South for many years, is still considered one of the most elegant and durable small members of the magnolia family. In some parts of the South, banana shrub is not as well known as it used to be, but professional landscapers rate banana shrub among the best of Southern landscape plants.

The slow-growing, evergreen banana shrub exhibits the same stateliness as the Southern magnolia. Growing from 10 to 15 feet high and 6 to 10 feet wide (depending on the region), banana shrub holds its rich-green, 3-inch-long, elliptic leaves on many smooth, gray brown branches. Characteristic of banana shrub is the dense, many-branching habit that sometimes gives it the appearance of having been lightly pruned.

Depending on its location, banana shrub will bloom in early or mid-spring; and the small flowers borne along the stem between the leaves will smell sweet, like a ripe banana. This is where banana shrub gets its common name. The blooms are creamy yellow, about 1½ inches wide, and edged in purplish red. They are typical of a magnolia bloom but are much smaller and less showy than other familiar magnolias, such as the star, tulip, and Southern magnolia. Banana shrub is a magnolia planted not so much for its flowering beauty, but for its foliage, form, and dependability.

Because of its large, stately character, banana shrub is successfully used alone as a specimen plant in the same way you might use common camellia. It also makes a good background plant for smaller shrubs or may be used to frame a house. Branching close to the ground and having a dense, irregularly rounded form, banana shrub should be allowed plenty of space in the landscape to grow into its natural form. In partial shade the plant is less dense, so it is easier to see its gray brown trunk and branches.

Banana shrub must be planted in well-drained, fertile, acid soil. To plant banana shrub in poor soils, amend the planting hole with organic matter such as compost or peat moss. If the soil is not slightly acid, the foliage will be a faded yellow green.

Banana shrub is often used in foundation plantings.

In the Lower South, banana shrub takes on an upright-arching form when mature.

The flowers are fragrant and smell like bananas, which explains the common name.

Barberry
A durable, formidable family

AT A GLANCE
Light: full sun best; will tolerate partial sun
Water: moderate amount; once established, they are drought hardy
Soil: well-drained, light soil preferred
Growth Rate: moderate
Size: varies with species

The barberries are a rugged and underused group of plants in the home landscape. And this is a loss to gardeners across the South, for this group of shrubs is hardy, basically disease free, and requires little attention. In fact, most barberries are used in institutional or commercial landscapes—a testimony to their longevity, durability, and tolerance of extreme horticultural conditions. Not only will they grow well in the Upper South, but they will also withstand the severe heat and unusual dry conditions that extend from the Lower South into Texas.

But the barberries have more to commend them as landscape plants than their horticultural tenacity; each plant or selection can bring its own individual look or usefulness to the garden. They may enclose a space, forming a dense hedge barrier against wind or unsightly views, or they may be used as a durable ground cover planting where foliage color or rugged character is desired.

As a group, the plants are rugged, almost foreboding, characterized by dense woody growth and sharp spines. For this reason, they must be used with care in the landscape—as a backdrop planting for annuals and perennials, to enclose a distant corner of a lot, to direct pedestrians, or to control access to and from a residence.

In addition to their characteristic habit of growth, barberries flower profusely in spring, filling the garden with a rich pollen scent, which may be unpleasant to some people. The flowers, which are yellow, white, or pink (according to type), are waxy looking and are borne on clusters along the stems. They eventually develop into red or blue black fruit.

The barberries are both evergreen and deciduous, but they may vary according to the climate. In the Upper South, even the durable wintergreen barberry may defoliate to some degree in a severe winter.

In the landscape, the large barberries create an effective mass planting where a dense, impenetrable mass is desired. The larger species—wintergreen, Mentor, and Sargent—are also frequently planted to create a tall, clipped hedge or to drift in mixed evergreen borders. The texture of the plant, which appears fine when viewed up close, is actually a twiggy tangle of foliage, thorns, and branches. Thus, the large barberries are an exceptionally good, though often overlooked, group of middle-size plants.

While not usually thought of as accent shrubs, barberries can bring an unexpected look to the landscape when used as single specimens. The weathered form and glossy foliage that covers the erratically spreading branches are at once intriguing and eye-catching. The spines alone give the plants a sort of "don't-touch-me" accent look. Also, the Japanese barberries are noted for their colorful foliage which is a strong spring and summer accent. If used as an accent, the plants would best be served by a neutral backdrop or as the visual punctuation in an unusual-looking bed of ground cover, such as wedelia or one of the low, spreading junipers.

The smaller barberries are more noted for their interesting foliage and dense habit of growth than for their screening capability. Many of these smaller plants reach a mature height of only about 4 feet and form brightly colored mounds of foliage. The characteristic burgundy—or wine-colored foliage of crimson pygmy—is one of the brightest colors in the

The colorful selections of Japanese barberry make beautiful accent plants.

Shrubs

One of the best uses of wintergreen barberry is as an unclipped hedge or as a barrier plant.

The flowers of wintergreen barberry are bright yellow and eye-catching in the spring.

Japanese barberry produces yellow flowers in spring.

Chenault barberry grows to 3 feet and works well in foundation plantings.

garden. Since crimson pygmy is exceptionally tolerant of heat and sun, it makes an excellent ground cover for plantings that need a brightly colored accent. The burgundy color is a beautiful contrast to the deep green of other popular full-sun plants like the junipers. Following are some of the recommended species and selections of this genus and a brief description of their distinguishing horticultural characteristics.

Chenault barberry (*Berberis* x *chenaultii*)—evergreen, to 3 feet, arching branches and glossy foliage, yellow flowers; Japanese barberry (*B. thunbergii*)— deciduous, dense, compact, to about 5 feet, tan stems, yellow flowers which need sun for maximum coloration, highly variable, selections include: Kobold green counterpart to Crimson pygmy, Argenteo-marginata—edges of new foliage silver, Atropurpurea—foliage dark purple, Atropurpurea Nana (crimson pygmy)—dense, rounded, dark with purple to red foliage, Aurea—yellow foliage; Mentor barberry (*B.* x *mentorensis*)—deciduous, very cold hardy, 4 to 6 feet, twigs bearing bright-red fruit, slightly open-branching habit, good fall color; Sargent barberry (*B. sargentiana*)—evergreen, 4 to 6 feet, bright-red new shoots, brown stems, bright-yellow flowers, blue black fruit; three-spine barberry (*B. wisleyensis*)—evergreen, to 5 feet, finer texture than most barberries, pinkish white flowers, generally pale-green foliage; warty barberry (*B. verruculosa*)—evergreen, to 3 feet, yellow flowers, warty, knotty branches, fine-textured foliage; wintergreen barberry (*B. julianae*)—evergreen, 6 to 8 feet, densely branched, mounded growth habit, shiny green foliage, yellow flowers, bluish black fruit, durable shrub, cold hardy.

Beautyberry
Plant beautyberry for the berries

Beautyberry (*Callicarpa americana*), or French mulberry as it is sometimes known, is not an easy plant to use. The dull-green foliage is rather ordinary, and the twiggy form can be a bit unruly; but the magenta berries are simply dazzling, offering a dramatic touch of color for the early weeks of autumn. Native to the woodlands from Virginia to Florida and west to Texas, beautyberry can be grown in every Southern garden. Since it is a forest plant, beautyberry performs best when given partial shade, even moisture, and rich organic soil. However, it can be grown in full sun and any soil type, including heavy clay and sand. Beautyberry is also tolerant of wet feet and prolonged periods of drought.

Despite its many attributes, beautyberry may not be appropriate for every garden situation. The upright, irregular form, combined with coarsely textured foliage, gives beautyberry a rather unkempt appearance; since the foliage tends to yellow in early summer, the plant appears to be somewhat unhealthy as well. For these reasons, beautyberry is best reserved for use in naturalistic landscape plantings.

The open shade of pine trees is an ideal situation for beautyberry. The simple form of the pines provides a striking contrast to the beautyberry's wild irregularity; the pine straw helps control weed growth, while its color complements the vivid-purple fruit of the beautyberry.

Since beautyberry tends to lose its foliage early in the season, a background planting of evergreens can help highlight the brilliant color of the fruit. Waxleaf privet, cherry laurel, and photinia provide a fine backdrop for beautyberry. Plants that have red or orange berries, such as holly and pyracantha, should be avoided since these colors tend to clash with the magenta of the beautyberry fruit.

Although it has a moderate rate of growth, beautyberry will eventually attain a height and spread of 6 feet or more. Plants can be kept below 3 feet, however, by removing the largest branches at the ground. Pruning should be done in autumn when the berries begin to fall.

A white-fruited selection of beautyberry (*Callicarpa americana* Lactea) is also available. Although the fruit is not as striking as the magenta of the species, it does avoid the possibilities of clashing color combinations. The white berries also seem to attract more birds to the fall garden.

AT A GLANCE
Light: partial shade best, but adaptable
Water: moderate
Soil: prefers rich, organic soil, but tolerant of most types
Growth Rate: moderate
Size: up to 6 feet in height and 6 feet in diameter

Although the tangled form and coarsely textured foliage of beautyberry may give an unkempt effect, the magenta berries in early autumn more than compensate for the plant's appearance in other seasons.

Beautyberry is a coarsely textured shrub.

Boxwood
Undeniably refined

AT A GLANCE
Light: full sun to partial shade
Water: keep evenly moist; most boxwoods do not tolerate drought or overly moist locations—mulch heavily during winter to prevent dehydration
Soil: very adaptable; acid or alkaline—prefers slightly acid, well-drained soil, rich in organic matter
Growth Rate: varies with type; typically slow
Size: varies with type; generally dense, compact shrubs

Common boxwood, framed here by a Chippendale fence, provides a stately entry to this home.

The boxwoods (*Buxus sp.*) are perhaps the most respected plants in cultivation; they have reigned supreme in Southern gardens for almost 300 years. They were considered indispensable in formal, historic gardens and set the standard for traditional refinement. But they are admired today also. Their handsome forms and foliages, plus their durability, let boxwoods fit into the scheme of almost every garden.

There are several types of boxwood on the market today; some of them are better suited to specific regions of the South than others. Although these plants may vary slightly in size, hardiness, and individual appearance, they all possess the qualities that make a boxwood special—handsome evergreen foliage, delicate texture, and a form that is substantial without heaviness. Following is a brief description of the boxwood types to help you choose the best one for your garden.

Common Boxwood

The common boxwood (*B. sempervirens*), the parent plant of edging boxwood, is second in popularity only to its offspring. Although it, too, should be regarded as a slow-growing plant, its rate of growth is not quite as slow as that of the edging boxwood. Common boxwood does, however, get to be much larger than its offspring, eventually attaining a height and spread of 20 feet or more. The cultural requirements of common boxwood are identical to those of edging boxwood; it, too, should be reserved for gardens in the Middle and Upper South.

Edging Boxwood

The edging boxwood (*B. sempervirens* Suffruticosa) was one of the first plants to be introduced to the colonies from Europe; it has played a major role in the evolution of the Southern garden. To many people, this is the ideal boxwood; it is the one to which the others are compared.

Sometimes known as English boxwood or Truedwarf boxwood, the edging boxwood is an extremely slow-growing plant, taking as long as 30 years to reach a height of 3½ to 4 feet. At maturity (anywhere from 75 to 150 years), a single plant may be as much as 6 feet tall and just about as wide. Even though it is frequently used to create an architectural hedge, the most beautiful form of edging boxwood develops without pruning. Only when it is allowed to grow untrimmed does it take on the mounded, almost billowy form of maturity.

Edging boxwood is a durable plant for gardens in the Middle and Upper South. It can be grown in sun or shade and almost any soil, but it performs best when planted in a semishaded location in a soil that is evenly moist and rich in organic matter. But in the Lower South and also in Texas, edging boxwood is not recommended; in these regions, the plant is highly susceptible to nematodes, red spider, and root fungus.

Harlands Boxwood

Harlands boxwood (*B. harlandii*) is a neat, compact shrub ideally suited to the gardens of the Lower South. It is not, however, considered cold hardy above central Alabama and the coastal regions of North Carolina. Seldom growing more than 3 feet high and 2 or 3 feet across, it has a dense, upright rounded form that is slightly broader across the top than at the ground. Easily distinguished from the other boxwoods by the size and color of its foliage, the bright-green leaves of Harlands boxwood may be as much as 1½ inches long, tapering just slightly toward the base. Richardii is a popular selection.

Japanese Littleleaf Boxwood

Japanese littleleaf boxwood (*B. microphylla* Japonica) is another popular selection for the Lower South. Along with Harlands boxwood, it tolerates the heat and high humidity associated with this area. Japanese boxwood is somewhat hardier, however, than Harlands boxwood, growing as far north as Tennessee and central North Carolina.

Perhaps the fastest growing of the boxwoods, Japanese littleleaf boxwood will gen-

Japanese boxwood is one of the best types of boxwood to grow in the Lower South.

English boxwoods are prized specimens for gardens in the Middle and Upper South.

These untrimmed English boxwoods have followed their mounding habit of growth.

Harlands boxwood is noted for its inverted wedge shape.

Shrubs

Single specimens of English boxwood are unobtrusive accents for many garden terraces.

Boxwoods may be shaped into almost any form, from sheared hedges to topiaries.

English boxwoods and dogwoods are symbols of the traditional Middle/Upper South landscapes.

erally attain its maximum height of 4 feet within 3 to 5 years. The dark, glossy green foliage of Japanese littleleaf boxwood tends to be more rounded than most other boxwoods. The leaves are usually ¾ to 1 inch long and ¾ inch wide.

Korean Littleleaf Boxwood

Korean littleleaf boxwood (*B. microphylla* Koreana) is considered to be the hardiest of all the boxwoods; it can be grown throughout the South from Maryland to Texas. Also, the smallest of the boxwoods, Korean littleleaf boxwood rarely grows to more than 2 feet high. A dense, slow-growing plant with extremely small, finely textured foliage, and an open, loosely rounded form, Korean littleleaf boxwood comes closer to the billowy, cloudlike form of edging boxwood than any other type.

Traditional clipped gardens at Williamsburg show how easily common boxwood may be shaped.

Camellia
Almost a native plant

AT A GLANCE
Light: partial shade
Water: damaged by drought
Soil: moist, well-drained, acid soil
Growth Rate: slow to moderate
Size: to 20 feet

Camellias are so much a part of Southern gardening that many people are surprised to learn that camellias are not native to the South. Valued for their dark, glossy, evergreen foliage and brightly colored, cool-season flowers, these handsome ornamental shrubs have become as much a part of our garden tradition as azaleas and jasmine.

Most camellias available from retail nurseries are hybrids of two principal species: the common camellia (*Camellia japonica*), and the sasanqua (*C. sasanqua*). The tea plant (*C. sinensis*), another handsome member of the genus, is also gaining popularity. The cultural requirements of these three camellias are nearly identical, but the plants vary greatly in their form, flower types, and period of bloom. This makes it possible to grow several kinds of camellias within a garden and still obtain a varied landscape composition.

Since camellias are an understory plant in their native habitat, they require protection from the hot midday and early afternoon sun of Southern summers. Camellias also need a rich, well-drained, slightly acid soil; consistent soil moisture; and protection from cold winter winds. When they are grown in areas of heavy clay or other poorly drained conditions, camellias are quite susceptible to root rot; to avoid this problem, plant camellias in a shallow hole and bank soil around the roots. Plants grown this way should be heavily mulched and watered frequently, however, to prevent dehydration.

Camellias are prone to nutritional deficiencies, particularly iron deficiency, which causes the margins of the leaves to turn yellow while the veins remain green. This problem, known as chlorosis, frequently occurs when camellias are planted in alkaline soils. You can correct iron chlorosis by sprinkling 2 or 3 tablespoons of Epsom salts around the base of the plant, or by applying iron chelate either as a leaf spray or in granular form to the soil.

Common Camellia

Common camellia (*C. japonica*), or japonica as it is often known, is usually selected for the kind of flower it produces. But flowers should not be the only consideration when selecting japonicas for the garden. Ultimate size, habit of growth, and cold hardiness are just as important as the color of the bloom. Since these qualities vary with individual hybrids, be sure to ask your nurseryman for the specific characteristics of each plant before you make your choice.

Hundreds of types of camellias are available through local nurseries and mail-order houses. If you are planning to plant several selections together, you may want to choose selections that will offer a succession of bloom. Also, flower forms vary from singles (a single row of petals) to semidoubles, doubles, peony form, anemone form, and rose form. Bloom period for japonicas may be fall, winter, or early spring. Most common selections bloom in February or March in the South; but during cold winters, bloom may be delayed until April. During mild winters, japonicas may bloom as early as January. Japonicas should be pruned as little as possible. Plants can quickly become disfigured if they are repeatedly sheared or pruned to control their size. Limit pruning to removing dead or damaged wood, unproductive branches, and disproportionately long shoots.

Given ample room, camellias can create an effective screen, particularly when they are

The open, airy form of tea plant gives it a more delicate appearance than its better-known cousins, the camellias and sasanquas.

staggered in an informal mass and not simply lined up in a hedgelike manner. Japonicas, because of their preference for shade and acid soils, make good companions for pines, magnolias, and other large, shade-casting trees. Camellias are ideal for planting at the edge of a natural area where their flowers and greenery accent the open spaces under the tree canopy. A single camellia can make a good accent for an entry, provided the plant has room enough to grow. Because of its upright, nearly columnar form, japonica is a candidate for formal plantings and may also be introduced to the shrub border if other border plants are proportionately large. Large hollies, Japan cleyera, or sweet olive would blend well with camellias in either a border or an informal screen.

Sasanqua Camellia

Sasanqua camellia (*C. sasanqua*) resembles common camellia only in flower form; the plants are considerably different. Sasanquas are generally less pyramidal in form, attaining a looser, more informal growth habit. Although they may reach 20 feet in height, most sasanqua selections grow to 6 to 8 feet tall. The leaves of sasanqua are about 2 inches long, obovate, and with serrated edges.

Because of its bushier form, sasanqua is a more versatile landscape plant. Sasanquas can be integrated with most other shrubs in a border or else used by themselves as specimens and accents. The off-season flowers (most sasanqua selections bloom in the fall) add interest to the garden during a time when other shrubs are inactive. Massed infor-

Sasanqua camellia blooms in the fall in the South.

Sasanqua camellia, when unpruned and allowed to grow loose and open, makes a handsome foundation plant.

mally, sasanquas can be used where a screen or informal hedge of medium height is needed. They also make good background plants for the perennial border or for low-growing shrubbery. Sasanquas are sometimes used as espaliers, although this treatment may require more maintenance than the average gardener is willing to undertake.

Tea Plant

Surprisingly, the plant that supplies the world with one of its most important beverages is also a camellia. The tea plant (*C. sinensis*) is the leading crop of commerce in India and Ceylon, but it can also make a valuable addition to your garden as an ornamental shrub. A handsome shrub with dark-green leaves and a rounded, yet open and airy form, tea plant makes a dependable evergreen for gardens in the Lower South and coastal regions of the Middle South. Further inland, however, tea plant will need protection from cold winter winds. Since it must be brought indoors during periods of prolonged freezes, tea plant is best reserved for container culture in the Upper South.

Rarely getting to be more than 5 feet high and wide, tea plant can be used in areas too small for camellias or sasanquas. Since it blooms in late September or October (several weeks before its more familiar cousins), tea plant helps extend the bloom season of camellias as well. Best of all, the 1-inch diameter white flowers of tea plant are mildly fragrant. Adding to the plant's ornamental quality is small, quincelike fruit that forms after the flowers fade.

The flowers of common camellia vary in form from single to semidouble to double blooms.

Because of its dark-green color, common camellia makes a handsome treelike foundation plant.

Common camellia is often used as a specimen plant.

Chaste Tree
Spikes of summer blue

AT A GLANCE

Light: full sun
Water: moderately drought resistant
Soil: nearly any soil; best in improved, well-drained soil
Growth Rate: moderate to rapid
Size: 15 to 20 feet

At maturity, the trunk of chaste tree is similar to that of dogwood.

The lavender flowers of the chaste tree bloom in early summer, when few other flowers bloom.

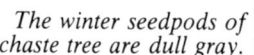

Some plants seem subject to the ebb and flow of fashion. One such plant that is currently regaining popularity is the chaste tree (*Vitex agnus-castus*), an old-fashioned deciduous shrub that used to lay easy claim to a place in most gardens. Native to southern Europe and western Asia, chaste tree grows well throughout the South, except in west Texas and south Florida where performance may be less than optimum. Valued for its spikes of light-blue flowers that bloom in early summer, chaste tree, also called lavender tree and butterfly bush, can be grown either as a large shrub or a small tree. Blooming just after the bigleaf hydrangeas and just before the crepe myrtles, chaste tree fills a brief lull in garden flowering with delicate color and pert, airy foliage. Several selections of chaste tree are available in the retail nursery trade, including Alba (white flowers) and Rosea (pink flowers), and they tend to have somewhat small foliage and mature heights.

Chaste tree is best used as a specimen or accent plant for seasonal color. In a shrub border, chaste tree makes a good companion for forsythia, bridal wreath spirea, and similar deciduous shrubs. If you choose to grow chaste tree as a small tree, plant it in a conspicuous place. Because of its unrestrained size and rapid growth rate, chaste tree makes a good specimen tree for a terrace or deck or beside a pool. The delicate arrangement of branches and leaves gives the plant a pleasing appearance even when it is not in bloom. An unpruned chaste tree may grow 15 to 20 feet high. When lower limbs are removed and the plant is trained to tree form, it develops an irregular, slightly spreading crown. The leaves are compound with five to seven lanceolate leaflets that are flat, green on the upper surfaces and nearly gray underneath. They have no significant color change in the fall.

Plant chaste tree in full sun. This durable plant will survive in most soils, including clay; but the best results are achieved when soil is improved by adding compost, ground bark, or shredded leaves. Regular fertilization during the growing season brings plants to a semimature size in four or five years. Chaste tree has no significant pests; and pruning, although it increases blooming, is rarely required except to remove suckers from the main trunks of tree-form specimens. Flowers are borne on new wood, so it should be necessary to prune the plant in late winter. Located where it can attain its full size, you should never need to prune chaste tree to control it.

The winter seedpods of chaste tree are dull gray.

Cotoneaster
Rambling plant—profuse with berries

The cotoneasters are a group of evergreen and semievergreen plants conspicuous because of their weeping to arching and many times prostrate growth habits. The wide variation in foliage and extravagant flower display give the landscape an added bonus. These plants are tolerant of severe heat and poor soils and in some cases can provide a profusion of berries that will cover the plant in winter.

The genus is large and diverse, ranging from tall, almost hedgelike plants, such as willowleaf cotoneaster (*Cotoneaster salicifolius*) to the prostrate miniature-leaved bearberry cotoneaster (*C. dammeri*). Many additional selections are available in the nursery trade since the genus is highly variable and highly adaptable across the South.

Each species or selection brings a variation of the beautiful show that is characteristic of the genus. In late spring the plants are covered with tiny red, white, or slightly pinkish flowers. Many of the plants quickly set fruit that becomes visible by late summer and remains on the plant throughout the winter or until the birds eat it. The flowers and fruit are borne either singly or in clusters along the stem. Although most types discussed here are considered evergreen, it is not unusual for the plants to shed foliage during severe winters.

The cotoneasters may be divided into two landscape use groups; the large or fountain-like plants like brightbead, willowleaf, Franchet, and cranberry cotoneaster; and the prostrate ground cover plants like bearberry and rock cotoneaster. Each group brings its own individual merits to the garden, though it must be used differently to receive the greatest benefits from the plant's attributes.

The large groups of cotoneasters generally reach a height no greater than 10 feet. Accordingly, they are most effectively planted as a medium level shrub in front of a background of evergreen trees or as the backdrop plant in a garden border. Since the plants look handsome all season, they should be considered for a slope or to frame one side of a garden, like an evergreen forsythia. While generally large and fountain shaped, the large cotoneasters do differ in plant character. Willowleaf (*C. salicifolius*) is graceful and arching but will create a dense cascading mound of foliage, flowers, and berries. The texture of the plant is slightly coarse, not unlike elaeagnus. Brightbead (*C. lacteus* Parneyi) is more upright and visually lighter than willowleaf. Franchet (*C. franchetii*) cotoneaster is very light and airy in appearance, almost as delicate as a spirea even though it is evergreen. Cranberry cotoneaster (*C. apiculatus*) is a vigorous, heavily berrying plant that forms a dense attractive tangle of foliage and fruit. It is a moderately fine-textured plant and is attractive in almost any landscape use.

The two cotoneasters which are ground cover plants, rock and bearberry, are most frequently associated with rock gardens where these vigorously spreading plants will cover as much as 4 to 6 feet of garden space each. The plants love direct sun and can grow in poor soil. Consequently, they are an excellent choice for a bank planting or for any slope that is difficult to maintain. Both rock and bearberry cotoneaster spread very low to the ground, and they will frequently root where branches touch the soil and thus spread even more rapidly. These plants are most frequently used as ground covers where an interesting form

AT A GLANCE
Light: full to partial sun
Water: moderate amount; moderately drought hardy
Soil: light, well-drained soil
Growth Rate: rapid
Size: varies with selection; large selections to 10 feet—ground cover types to 3 feet

Red fruit appears on many selections of cotoneaster by late summer.

Rockspray cotoneaster has foliage with a prostrate habit of growth which creates a tracery effect in the landscape.

The bearberry selections of cotoneaster do exceptionally well in the South due to their reduced susceptibility to fire blight.

and seasonal color are desired. Generally, the plants do not form a dense enough cover to prevent weed growth, something that can be a problem if they are planted near a vigorously spreading lawn like common Bermuda grass. Seasonal mulchings are recommended to reduce weed growth.

Unfortunately, the large selections of cotoneaster may be subject to fire blight in some parts of the Middle and Lower South. While the plants are dependable in Kentucky and South Carolina, fire blight may kill them in warmer areas such as the Piedmont, coastal Georgia, and Alabama. Smaller selections may suffer from lacewing damage, which will retard growth. While the plants will grow along the Coastal and Gulf South, they are especially susceptible to diseases in these areas.

Here is a guide to some commonly available cotoneasters: Bearberry cotoneaster (*Cotoneaster dammeri*)—semievergreen, to 3 feet, prostrate habit, roots easily, white solitary flowers, bright-red fruit, selections are Lowfast and Skogholmen; Brightbead cotoneaster (*C. lacteus* Parneyi)—semievergreen, to 10 feet, upright arching habit, white flowers in clusters, red fruit; Cranberry cotoneaster (*C. apiculatus*)—evergreen to 4 feet, mounding habit of growth, pinkish solitary flowers, scarlet fruit; Franchet cotoneaster(*C. franchetii*)—evergreen, to 10 feet, upright weeping habit, pink to white flowers in clusters, orange red fruit; Rock cotoneaster (*C. horizontalis* Rockspray)—evergreen, to 3 feet, prostrate habit, roots easily, pinkish to white flowers solitary or in pairs, bright-red fruit, vigorous grower; Willowleaf cotoneaster (*C. salicifolius*)—evergreen, to 10 feet, upright weeping habit, white flowers in dense 2-inch clusters, bright-red fruit, selection Repandens has a prostrate habit of growth.

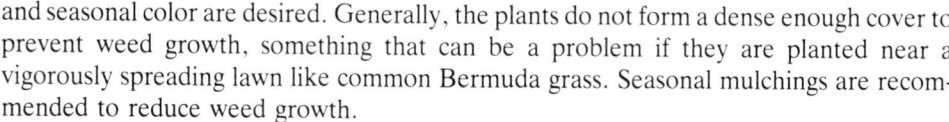

Willowleaf cotoneaster produces white flowers in spring followed by red berries in fall. It is one of the best large cotoneasters for the South.

Cotoneasters have an arching to weeping habit of growth.

Cycad
Slow grower for limited space

In terms of plant evolution, cycads are one of the most primitive seed-producing plants used in the landscape. Both the sago palm (*Cycas revoluta*) and queen sago (*Cycas circinalis*) are remnants from the ancient Mesozoic times when cycads and ferns were the predominant plants.

Palmlike in looks, cycads develop short, stocky trunks, which may not become apparent for several years because of their slow growth rate. The foliage is a dense crown of dark-green, long, shiny leaves, which are divided like pinnate palm fronds that whorl from the center of the plant and lie on each other to form a thick umbrella. The cycads have an eye-catching texture and should mainly be used as an accent in a prominent area, such as an entrance or by a frequently used patio or terrace, but be sure to allow for them to grow. They are definitely plants to place where they can be seen and appreciated.

Cycads provide an interesting, low, broad form for limited areas. Most sago palms are single trunked and have about a 4-foot foliage spread. However, with age, the plants may sucker from the base to form a multitrunked group, spreading 6 to 8 feet.

Cycads are deciduous, but the female blooms later than the male and develops cones of small bright-orange red fruit. Cycads grow best in a well-drained soil and sunny location. Because of their slow growth rate, fertilization should be limited to once or twice a year. For pest and disease problems, see page 246.

Sago palm (*Cycas revoluta*) grows in Florida and the Gulf Coast region; however, in the Middle and Upper South, it is not hardy. The leaves are 2 to 7 feet long and finely divided into many sharp pinnae that curve downward from the leaf midrib and terminate in a sharp tip. Forming a short, stocky trunk, the extremely slow-growing sago palm may reach a height of 8 to 20 feet in about 50 years.

Queen sago (*Cycas circinalis*) is dependably hardy only in south and central Florida and extreme south Texas. In north Florida and the Gulf Coast region, queen sago may be planted, but it may possibly be lost or the foliage may die back during a severe winter. In other parts of the South, it can be used as an indoor landscaping plant in locations where it receives bright light. Queen sago will grow to about 10 to 20 feet tall with long palmlike foliage up to 8 feet wide in tropical areas such as Miami. But towards the northernmost limit of its hardiness area, the plant may only be half that size because occasional cold may kill the foliage back to the trunk. Queen sago is also slow growing, but it is not as slow as the sago palm.

AT A GLANCE
Light: sun or partial shade
Water: moderate
Soil: well-drained soil
Growth Rate: slow
Size: revoluta, 8 to 20 feet; circinalis, 10 to 20 feet tall, 8 feet wide
Remarks: adaptable only to Gulf South

Queen sago is limited in outdoor use to Florida and the Gulf Coast region, but it may be grown indoors in other parts of the South.

Although limited to the Gulf Coast region, sago palm makes a lovely slow-growing entry accent.

Shrubs

Reeves spirea, page 152.

Common camellia, page 99.

Heavenly bamboo, page 135.

Shrubs

Chaste tree, page 102.

Southern Indian hybrid azalea, page 89.

Fruitland elaeagnus, page 109.

Edging boxwood, page 96.

Shrubs

AT A GLANCE

Light: partial to deep shade
Water: minimal; avoid planting in wet locations
Soil: must be well-drained soil; sandy loam is best
Growth Rate: slow
Size: to 4 feet
Remarks: can be difficult to grow

Daphne
The sweet fragrance of winter

Although fragrance in the garden is associated with spring, there are numerous landscape plants that will scent the landscape even in winter. One of the most fragrant is winter daphne (*Daphne odora*), an old-fashioned favorite that is regaining popularity. Widely planted in the early part of this century, winter daphne was replaced by easier-to-grow plants. But in the Lower South, the plant has always been prized for its incredibly fragrant small flowers, which some gardeners consider sweeter than gardenias. Winter daphne is hardy in the Upper South; but in the colder regions of the mountains, it should be planted in a location that is protected from any sudden changes in temperature.

Winter daphne is a dwarf evergreen shrub that grows slowly to a mature height of 4 feet. The mature form is mounded and slightly irregular. Leaves are 2 to 3 inches long and taper to a point, branching off the plant in a habit similar to that of Japanese andromeda. The flowers occur at the end of the twigs and appear to be set on top of the outermost cluster of leaves. They form a tight, attractive rosette and are short and waxy in appearance. Generally, the plant will begin to flower in February and continue through March.

Winter daphne is extremely sensitive to soil conditions and may be difficult to grow. It needs a well-drained soil, but can adapt to either alkaline or acid soil conditions. Plant it in an area that receives partial shade, as direct sunlight will burn the foliage. After the initial watering when planted, the plant requires very little attention in the way of moisture. There are several selections available: Marginata has leaves bordered with yellow; Rubra has wine red flowers; and Variegata bears pale-pink blossoms and leaves bordered with yellow.

The small rosettes of flowers are carried at the end of the twigs. Despite their small size, the blossoms are incredibly fragrant.

Winter daphne needs partial shade and deep, well-drained soil. This selection is Variegata, which has yellow-bordered foliage and pale-pink flowers.

A slow grower, winter daphne reaches a mature height of 4 feet and assumes a slightly irregular mounding habit of growth.

Elaeagnus
The fragrance of fall

Anyone who has ever mistaken the sweet autumn fragrance of elaeagnus (*Elaeagnus pungens*) for the scent of gardenia will soon want to grow elaeagnus in his or her own garden. Not only are the blooms of this large evergreen shrub fragrant, but elaeagnus has gained recognition as a useful landscape plant. Native to Japan, elaeagnus grows well throughout the South, except in western Texas and Oklahoma. Plants may also be subject to winter damage in West Virginia and northern Kentucky.

Elaeagnus is a fast-growing, upright, fountainlike shrub that may grow 15 to 20 feet tall with an equal or greater spread. The leaves are oval to oblong (about 2 inches long and 1 to 1½ inches wide) and range from silvery gray to brightly variegated. The tiny white flowers are inconspicuous but memorably fragrant, and the brownish silver fruit that appears in winter is quickly eaten by birds. The fruit, in fact, accounts for one of the common names of elaeagnus—silverberry.

In the landscape, elaeagnus makes a dense, but attractive, screen when plants are massed together. This moderate to rapid grower is prized for its natural arching character and should be located where pruning will not be required. A single plant situated at the edge of a woodland also makes a good year-round accent, and the scent of the flowers is strong enough that the fragrance can be enjoyed even at a distance. When rustled by a slight breeze, the silvery undersides of the leaves give an illusion of space and depth.

Plant elaeagnus either in full sun or partial shade. Tolerant of heat, wet areas, and nearly any soil, elaeagnus may be an appropriate planting for banks and other difficult landscape situations. Suckers arising from the base of the plant help fill spaces between plants with greenery. Among the best selections of elaeagnus are Fruitlandii (wavy, silvery leaves); Aurea (leaves edged bright yellow); and Aureovariegata (golden leaf centers and dark-green margins).

AT A GLANCE

Light: full sun, partial shade
Water: moderately drought resistant
Soil: nearly any soil—tolerates wet or dry
Growth Rate: rapid
Size: 15 to 20 feet, equal spread
Remarks: variegation is not as pronounced in shade

Aureovariegata is a popular, variegated form.

Expect elaeagnus to become quite large and arching with almost leafless runners. This plant needs room to grow but makes a nice large, unpruned hedge.

Euonymus
Ignites in autumn

AT A GLANCE
Light: full to partial sun
Water: moderate
Soil: any soil—grows slowly in wet locations or heavy clay
Growth Rate: moderate to rapid
Size: to 15 feet

The most striking color of the September landscape belongs to winged euonymus (*Euonymus alata*), which is rivaled only by the sumacs in intensity of color. Winged euonymus reaches its peak quickly and remains colorful for as long as a month. And since the color change comes two weeks before that of other deciduous plants, the fiery red euonymus is contrasted against the still-green backdrop of the landscape. Although the plants located in full sunlight will be the most brightly colored, those in a shaded area also will be vivid.

When the foliage drops, clusters of tiny fruit are revealed. As is characteristic of all kinds of euonymus, the true fruit is enclosed in a capsule that splits when the seeds are mature. The capsules remain on the branches, but you can see the orange fruit tucked inside. When the seeds fall to the ground, the capsules stay on the branches, extending the ornamental quality of winged euonymus into the winter. Winter also reveals the almost perfectly symmetrical growth habit of winged euonymus. As it matures, the plant assumes a vase or fountain shape, with branches arching over and almost touching the ground. Another characteristic of the plant which is easily visible in winter and also contributes to its common name is the "wings." They are the ½-inch-wide, flat, corky growths that project along the branches. The wings give the plant a sculptural look, and the cut branches are attractive in indoor arrangements.

In spring, the plant is draped with tiny flowers that produce the fruit while the bright-green foliage is emerging. In summer, the plant is rather unassuming except for its vase-shaped form. It remains this way until the spectacular show in mid-September.

Winged euonymus is durable, relatively pest free, and not particular about sun or soil. This flexibility makes it an excellent landscape plant as long as its mature height (to 15 feet rapidly) and fall color are carefully considered before planting. If size is a problem, there is a dwarf selection (*Euonymus alata* Compacta) that only reaches 6 to 8 feet tall. Although the wings are not as predominant on the dwarf selection, its fall color is even more vivid than the parent.

Remember that wherever winged euonymus is planted, it will be the dominant feature in the landscape for about a month, so this plant must be placed carefully. Above all, avoid planting winged euonymus in front of a red-brick structure or with other plants that may clash with its fall color. Generally, this plant is best used in evergreen borders or planted against a neutral backdrop, such as weathered redwood or pine fencing.

Almost overnight, this hedge of winged euonymus changed from summer green to fiery red, becoming a spectacular landscape feature.

The summer effect of winged euonymus is a fine-to-medium-textured foliage which is bright green.

Shrubs

Fatsia
Prized for its foliage

AT A GLANCE
Light: full to partial shade
Water: moderate
Soil: prefers rich,
well-drained loam
Growth Rate: rapid in the
Lower South, moderate in
the Middle South
Size: up to 8 feet in height;
diameter of 6 to 8 feet

Japanese fatsia *(Fatsia japonica)* is one of the most dramatic foliage plants you can find for use in the shady Southern garden. Large, deeply serrated leaves up to 1 foot in diameter and a deep-green color give Japanese fatsia a remarkably tropical appearance. Its effect in the garden is equally exotic.

Since the large, coarsely textured foliage is Japanese fatsia's most distinctive landscape feature, it should be used with a sense of boldness in the landscape. Japanese fatsia makes an excellent accent plant for the entrance of a house, or it can be massed along the edge of a terrace to create the effect of a tropical retreat. For a touch of dramatic contrast, try planting a single Japanese fatsia in a bed of finely textured ground cover such as mondo grass or periwinkle. But no matter how you use it, be sure to give fatsia a prominent location so that its special characteristics can be appreciated to the fullest.

A dependable plant for gardens in the Middle to Lower South (Dallas to Atlanta and as far up the coast as Columbia, South Carolina), Japanese fatsia really is not hardy farther north. Along the Gulf and Atlantic Coasts, however, Japanese fatsia is a rapid-growing evergreen that can reach a height of 8 feet and a diameter of as much as 6 to 8 feet.

Although it has a tough, leathery appearance, Japanese fatsia is not a plant for sunny locations. It can tolerate a certain amount of filtered light, but too much sun can burn the leaves; prolonged exposure will eventually kill the plant. Even the winter sun can damage the foliage of a Japanese fatsia, particularly if the weather is extremely cold and dry. Sunlight causes the plant to lose moisture through the leaves; if the ground is frozen or if precipitation has been limited, the plant can suffer from serious dehydration.

With the exception of specific sun requirements, Japanese fatsia is a very adaptable plant, particularly in terms of soil and moisture conditions. It grows best in a moist, well-drained soil that is rich in organic matter, but Japanese fatsia will perform quite satisfactorily in a heavier soil or a sandy situation. It can tolerate a short period of drought or an occasional flooding with no serious consequences. Best of all, Japanese fatsia is basically free of any serious insects or diseases. When selecting a Japanese fatsia in the nursery, look for a dense, well-developed plant with a number of healthy young shoots at the tip of the stem. If available, select a plant with several stems since this will produce a more compact, bushier plant.

Tucked here into an entryway corner, Japanese fatsia becomes a bold accent because of its coarse texture.

The lush, tropical appearance of Japanese fatsia (right) makes it an excellent accent plant for entrances or shady garden corners. The berrylike fruit appears after the flowers in early fall and lasts throughout the winter.

This large, irregular mass of fatsia (left) makes a striking contrast to the simple lines of a contemporary house.

Firethorn
The berries of fall

AT A GLANCE
Light: full sun
Water: moderate amount
Soil: prefers rich, fertile soil, but will tolerate most well-drained types
Growth Rate: moderately rapid
Size: depends on species; ranges in height from 3 or 4 feet to 15 feet or more

Firethorn needs plenty of room to grow and produce its spectacular berry show. These plants should not be espaliered.

Firethorn is the mainstay of the fall garden in the South; it is known and loved for its bountiful yellow, orange, or scarlet fruit which lasts from October to January. Firethorn (*Pyracantha sp.*), also commonly known as pyracantha, provides a blaze of rich color year after year. Native to southern Europe and western Asia, firethorn has selections that have adapted to the entire South. However, performance may be less than optimum in south Florida and west Texas.

In spite of its popularity, firethorn is a misunderstood plant. Too often, firethorn is planted where it must be cut back repeatedly to control its size. The result is a stubby-looking ball of sticks and stickers. Left to grow naturally, selections range in size from 3 or 4 feet to 15 or more feet at maturity, with an equal or greater spread. The irregular, open form of the plant is an asset when located correctly; as plants reach full size, they tend to become more and more treelike. Branches of old selections are thorny, but many of the new ones have smaller thorns or may even be thornless.

Firethorn is evergreen in most of its growth range but may lose some leaves during winter in cooler areas of the Upper South. Leaves of firethorn are narrow, elliptic, 1 to 1½ inches long, and about ½ inch wide. White flowers, borne in 2- to 4-inch clusters, appear in late spring and last one to two weeks.

The best location for firethorn is one in which the plant will need only occasional pruning to remove an elongated branch or two. This precludes setting plants (except the dwarf types) next to a house or too close to a driveway. Firethorn makes an outstanding specimen or accent plant. Textured architectural structures, such as stone walls or split-rail fences, accentuate the texture and color of the plants. It is also a good candidate for the sunny shrub border. A single large plant can screen a small area; but if you have a large area to screen, you should consider another evergreen shrub, such as elaeagnus or one of

Low-Dense is a popular dwarf selection which has a mounding habit of growth.

the viburnums. The impact of several firethorns might be overwhelming. Firethorn is also popular for espaliers, but this treatment requires more maintenance than most gardeners have time to spend. Do not espalier this plant.

Plant firethorn in full sun and nearly any well-drained soil. Plants prefer rich, fertile soil but will tolerate almost any soil except wet. Several insect problems are common to firethorn, but these often vary with the locale. See page 247 for control.

Good species for the South include: Scarlet firethorn (*Pyracantha coccinea*), with its selections: Kasan—red orange berries with spreading but rigid habit of growth to 20 feet; and Lalandei—orange berries with rigid upright habit of growth to 15 or more feet, very spiny and vigorous grower; Formosa firethorn (*Pyracantha koidzumii*), with its selections: Low-Dense—large orange red berries with mounding habit of growth to 6 feet, berries often hidden, texture appears fine and new growth light; Victory—large red berries with upright arching growth habit to 10 feet, very showy berries especially good for fall display; and Walderi Prostrata—large red berries, prostrate habit of growth to 4 feet, very good for bank covers and high ground cover plantings.

Note: New types are constantly being introduced to the market. The selections listed are those which have proven to be good performers in the South.

White flowers appear in early spring.

Many of the dwarf selections have distinctive flower shows in addition to their fruit show.

Shrubs

Forsythia
A welcome in gold

AT A GLANCE
Light: full to partial sun
Water: moderate amount
Soil: any rich, well-drained soil
Growth Rate: rapid
Size: 6 to 12 feet

Just about the time you begin to think the winter will never come to an end, the border forsythia (*Forsythia* x *intermedia*) explodes into bloom. Without the slightest warning, the tangle of leafless twigs and branches is transformed into a glowing mass of brilliant yellow flowers.

The forsythia is a desirable plant for several reasons. It will grow in almost any type of soil; it is highly resistant to insect pests and diseases; and it will tolerate an amazing amount of neglect and abuse. This includes the all-too-frequent attempt on the part of many gardeners to maintain the forsythia as a formal, sheared hedge. Careless pruning will destroy the form of the plant.

A gently arching form and spreading habit of growth make the forsythia an excellent choice for the naturalistic garden. Once the plant has become established, it requires little attention to keep it healthy. Every three or four years, the older branches may need to be removed to permit the younger, more vigorous shoots to develop, but this should be done only in the early spring, immediately after the flowers have faded.

Forsythia is a fast-growing plant, reaching a height and width of 6 to 12 feet, but it may take a number of years to develop its characteristic mounding habit of growth. The shoots of an immature plant will tend to grow straight up, giving the plant a spiky effect. Due to its rich-green foliage in summertime and its handsome, twiggy character during the winter, forsythia becomes an extremely useful plant for year-round seasonal effects.

Several forms are available today—*Forsythia* x *intermedia* Beatrix Farrand, a large, upright shrub with a dense habit of growth and vivid-yellow flowers; *F.* x *intermedia* Lynwood, a rather stiff, vertical plant with deep brassy-yellow flowers; *F.* x *intermedia* Spectabilis, which is similar in form and flower color to Beatrix Farrand but has larger flowers that appear in greater profusion; and *F.* x *intermedia* Spring Glory, which produces extremely large, soft-yellow flowers.

Border forsythia has one of the earliest spring shows.

Trailing over this brick wall, border forsythia makes a brilliant yellow spring show.

In summer, border forsythia grows rampant.

Fringe Tree
Old-fashioned favorite

AT A GLANCE
Light: full or partial sun
Water: moderate amount
Soil: any soil if well drained
Growth Rate: moderate; rapid in fertile soil
Size: to 15 feet

There is something old-fashioned about fringe tree *(Chionanthus virginicus)*. Blooming after the dogwoods, fringe tree is really a tall deciduous shrub, although it can be trained to be either a single- or a multitrunked small tree. The drooping, fringelike panicles of white flowers, from which the plant derives its common name, persist for two to three weeks during mid-spring. The flower panicles of male trees may be 4 inches across or larger. On female trees the flower clusters are smaller, but the plants bear prominent dark-blue berries in loose, open clusters in late summer. The fruit is quickly devoured by birds, another asset of this attractive plant. The leaves of fringe tree, which appear at nearly the same time as the flowers, are oval to oblong, 6 to 8 inches long, and turn translucent yellow in the fall.

Also known as old-man's-beard, grandfather graybeard, and gransir' graybeard, fringe tree is native to the southeastern United States and can be grown with ease nearly everywhere in the South except central and south Florida. Fringe tree makes a prized specimen or a surprising accent, particularly in the small garden where a showy, tidy tree is needed for a limited space or a garden border. Also, fringe tree is a striking accent plant for the edge of a wooded area or in a natural area of the garden.

In full sun or partial shade, fringe tree can be among the easiest plants to grow if the soil is deep and well drained and if moisture is readily available. Although established trees are moderately drought resistant, young plants should be watered regularly during dry weather. Pruning is seldom required; but if you need to remove excessively dense growth or train the plant, prune after flowering, as flowers are produced on the previous year's growth. Unfortunately, fringe tree, depending on the location, may be attacked by spider mites.

No named selections of fringe tree are available, but an imported species, Chinese fringe tree *(C. retusus)*, can sometimes be found in nurseries. The Oriental type is larger in size, and the flowers are borne on the new season's growth rather than on last year's.

Often called grandsir' graybeard, fringe tree is a native plant that provides a spring accent of white flowers and a yellow fall color display.

At maturity (after 20 years) fringe tree may exceed 15 feet in height.

Gardenia
Scent for the Southern garden

AT A GLANCE
Light: sun to partial shade
Water: even moisture
Soil: fertile, acid,
well-drained soil
Growth Rate: moderate
Size: 4 to 6 feet

Dwarf gardenia is an ideal ground cover plant for tight spaces, such as this planting bed along a brick wall.

One of the most fragrant plants in the Southern garden is the gardenia (*Gardenia jasminoides*). So delightful is this shrub that you need only a single plant to scent the garden for almost a month. Gardenia, also known as cape jasmine, is a compact evergreen shrub from China. It is reliably hardy in the Lower South and in much of the Middle South. Further north, gardenia is a greenhouse plant and should not be grown outdoors unless protected against temperatures below 20 degrees.

In most of the South, gardenias seldom exceed 6 feet in height with a 3- to 5-foot spread. In the Lower South, particularly in south Florida, plants may grow larger. The leathery leaves are a rich, dark green, elliptic to obovoid, and about 4 inches long. The flowers, appearing in late spring and early summer, are waxy white, 2 to 3 inches across, and extremely fragrant.

Gardenia is a superb choice for a sunny shrub border and requires the same moist, well-drained, acid soil as azaleas, camellias, and hydrangeas. Unimposing in appearance, gardenias can be subtle accent plants near an entry or a terrace where the scent can be enjoyed while they are in bloom. In areas where soil is too alkaline for gardenias, you can grow one or two in pots or in a large planter.

Few plants have the clean, lustrous-looking foliage of dwarf gardenia (*Gardenia jasminoides* Radicans), and this makes the plant a splendid ornamental for use in ground cover plantings. For some reason, it has been widely overlooked as a foundation planting—a use for which it is particularly suited. Dwarf gardenia affords the advantage of rarely exceeding 2 to 3 feet in height, spreading to create a shiny green mass almost 4 feet in breadth. This makes it an excellent evergreen planting for houses with low windows that might be covered by larger species. In addition, the fragrant flowers make it a superb choice for border plantings or plantings near an outdoor seating area as it will perfume the entire area with its characteristic scent. Use the fine-textured foliage of the dwarf gardenia as the underpinning for coarse-textured plantings such as rhododendron that are planted in shade, or for plants like Japanese viburnum that are planted in sunnier areas. A splendid and unexpected use is to mix dwarf gardenia in a planting of Gumpo azaleas—where the foliage texture contrasts year-round, and the flowers of the two plants will bring successive bloom to the same location in the landscape.

Protected from winter winds and cold, gardenias require relatively little care beyond mulching, routine fertilizing, and watering during periods of erratic rainfall. Pests may be somewhat of a problem—see page 248 for insect and control. Plant gardenias in full sun to partial shade and in well-prepared soil. Work generous quantities of leaf mold, rotted sawdust, or composted manure into the planting hole to ensure that the soil is acid; then replenish the mulch with fresh organic material once or twice a year to maintain the soil at the correct pH and to discourage weeds at the same time.

Gardenia, also known as cape jasmine, is one of the most fragrant of Southern garden plants when it begins to bloom in late spring.

Glossy Abelia
Six months of tiny white flowers

AT A GLANCE
Light: full sun, partial shade
Water: somewhat drought resistant in good soil
Soil: prefers loamy, well-drained soil; tolerates many soils
Growth Rate: moderate to rapid
Size: 3 to 8 feet; taller in warmest regions

Glossy abelia (*Abelia* x *grandflora*) combines some of the most desirable traits of a landscape shrub—evergreen foliage, small white flowers that last from spring to fall, controllable size, tolerance of neglect, and freedom from pests. One of the most useful plants for the Southern garden, glossy abelia can be used alone as a subtle accent or massed for screening purposes. It is hardy throughout the South, but in the Upper South, glossy abelia may lose some of its leaves during winter and may even partially die back during severe winters. But the plants respond to pruning and regain good form and vigor by the end of spring.

Glossy abelia grows from 3 to 8 feet tall, depending on the selection used and where it is planted in the South. In Florida, glossy abelia may reach 10 feet or more. With their open, arching branches, plants may spread 4 to 8 feet if they are not pruned. The small, white, bell-shaped flowers, which are borne on the current season's growth, begin to appear in mid-spring and continue throughout the summer, often lasting until the first killing frost. Leaves are ovate, 1 to 1½ inches long, and taper to sharp points. The margins are toothed. Although the leaves are deep, glossy green during the growing season, they often turn slightly bronze during cold winters. In addition to the common form found at nurseries, you may also want to try Edward Goucher for its pink flowers.

Abelia is not showy in a dazzling sense, but when used in combination with other shrubbery, abelia becomes a good anchor plant. With a background of hollies, camellias, or other large evergreens, the subtle colors of glossy abelia are accentuated. Because of its fountainlike form, glossy abelia is a good companion for plants of more static form, such as boxwoods or azaleas. The arching form may also be repeated in a shrub border with forsythia, elaeagnus, and deutzia. And abelia may be sheared and used as a formal hedge. Dwarf forms of abelia make good foundation plants or underplantings for tall shrubs. One low-growing selection, Prostrata, has a cascading effect when planted along the top of a wall or in a planter.

Plant glossy abelia in full sun or partial shade. Flowering is best when plants receive about four hours of direct sunlight daily. Loamy, well-drained soil is best for abelia, but plants will tolerate many soils. If pruning becomes necessary, do it in late winter or in early spring as new growth begins. Winter damage, which often necessitates pruning, can be reduced if plants are protected from winds and planted in a location that faces South.

Left unsheared, glossy abelia will grow in an upright, arching fashion up to 8 feet in length.

Glossy abelia makes a colorful hedge when sheared (as it often is) because its lovely mid-spring flower show extends through summer, and then its glossy-green fall foliage turns an attractive light bronze in winter.

Holly
Shrub for every garden

If Burford holly becomes too large for its space, one solution may be to prune it into a small tree.

A holly can be found for almost every landscape situation. One of the most varied and useful groups of Southern landscape plants, the holly group includes evergreen and deciduous shrubs (and small trees, see page 186) from 2 to 25 feet tall in pyramidal shapes; other shapes include low-growing, dense, rounded mounds; medium-sized, stocky irregular pyramidal forms which are often used as alternatives for boxwood; low-spreading types often used as ground covers; weeping forms; open-arching forms and others.

Before using holly, or any plant in the landscape, be sure you know its growth habit and ultimate size. Several holly types with similar foliage, but different growth habits, may be available where you purchase your plants; so be sure you know which one you are buying. For example, if you purchase an *Ilex vomitoria* Nana (dwarf) for a ground cover instead of the intended *Ilex vomitoria* Stokes (dwarf), you will end up with a 4-foot-high ground cover instead of a 2- to 3-foot one.

Most holly types grow well throughout the South, with some being native to the region. In general, hollies grow best in fertile, well-drained soil; but some, such as yaupon and dwarf Chinese holly, tolerate poorer soil.

Chinese Holly

The glossy, dark-green, stiff-spined leaves, often illustrated in books and magazines to depict hollies, are leaves of the Chinese holly (*Ilex cornuta*) group, which includes the well-known Burford holly. Chinese holly, which is native to China, prefers rich, moist, well-drained soils but will grow in most soil types. In spring, Chinese holly blooms with clusters of showy white flowers which are followed by ½-inch red berries in fall and winter.

The spiny, stiff, 2- to 3-inch-long quadrangular leaf and dense growth habit make Chinese holly an excellent plant for hedges, screening, or directing traffic flow around an area. Because of its bold, coarse texture and large size, Chinese holly should be given plenty of room to grow. The plant will grow about 20 feet high and 10 feet wide into its natural, rounded block form. Chinese holly is too massive and its foliage too shapely to force the plant into a 3-foot clipped hedge. For hedges, select one of the smaller dwarf selections which stay low without heavy pruning.

Dwarf horned (Rotunda), a nonfruiting, 3- to 4-foot-high Chinese holly selection, grows throughout the South except in the colder sections of the Upper South. It has a very globular form with 5-spined, dark-green foliage like its Chinese holly parent. Rotunda is an extremely tough, low-maintenance plant that grows in most soils; it is heat tolerant, drought resistant, and less susceptible to the scale problems affecting the other Chinese hollies.

Burford is the widely planted, large, broadly rounded holly which is the popular mental picture of a holly. Massive, coarse-textured, fast-growing, Burford reaches a height of about 15 feet in 20 years. Like Chinese holly it should be used as a screen, large hedge, small tree, or accent plant and given plenty of space to grow. Burford is easily identified by its dark-green, high gloss, 1½-to 3-inch-long recurved leaves that have only one stiff terminal spine. One of the heaviest fruiting hollies, Burford is self-fertile and will fruit even if planted alone. The clusters of ¼-inch berries turn bright orange red in fall and remain on the plant all winter until the birds eat them.

Dazzler is a selection exactly like Burford which has sparkling, bright-red berries; they are the largest fruit of any holly planted in the South. D'or is a Burford selection with yellow berries. O'Spring has a variegated cream leaf margin and new growth which has a purple tinge.

Dwarf Burford is a smaller, slower-growing selection which is only 6 to 10 feet tall. It is also more compact and has smaller, narrower foliage than Burford. Dwarf Burford is an excellent border or hedge plant for limited spaces.

Japanese Holly

The Japanese group (*Ilex crenata*) of hollies can be found in nurseries and garden shops throughout the South. Japanese holly, growing 10 to 15 feet high, has a dense, upright or spreading form, which makes it a good backdrop plant for shrubs and plants of seasonal interest. Japanese holly selections such as Convexa, Heller, and Hetz, produce black berries in late summer and fall. In general, the Japanese hollies prefer fertile, moist, well-drained soils in sunny or partially shady locations. Following are the selections which are generally available.

Compacta is a dark-green selection that is similar to Convexa, but it has a slightly looser branching habit which may be successfully sheared for use as a boxwood substitute. The foliage is about 1 inch long, elliptic, with a slightly crenate margin.

Convexa is a stiff, densely branching selection that grows 3 to 6 feet tall and 3 to 6 feet wide in an inverted wedge form. Due to this wedge form, it makes a poor hedge. However, because of its stiff branching habit, it should not be considered a substitute for the loosely formed boxwood.

Hetz is a fast-growing, densely branching selection that reaches 4 to 6 feet (or more) high. Its loose, almost horizontal form gives it value as an economical boxwood substitute or a low hedge. The foliage is cupped, about ¾ inch long, and dark green.

Some of the small selections such as Heller, Kingsville Green Cushion, and Stokes may be used in borders as ground covers. Heller is a slow-growing selection with very small foliage and a dense, compact spreading habit. Growing about 2 feet high and 3 to 4 feet wide, it is used as a ground cover or as a substitute for dwarf boxwood.

Kingsville Green Cushion is a smaller selection than Heller that has a more flattened form, and it is somewhat more tolerant of drought.

Stokes is another dwarf selection that is comparable to Heller but less globular in form. It is slow growing, 1 to 3 feet high, 3 to 4 feet wide with foliage ½ to ¼ inch long.

Native Holly

The native hollies are adaptable to all conditions in the South and basically have no insect or disease problems. Dahoon holly (*Ilex cassine*), native to the moist woods of the Coastal Plains region from Virginia to Louisiana. Often found as either a shrub or small tree form in garden shops and nurseries, this medium-textured holly can be used as a small, tree-form accent or framing plant in moist soils in sun or partial shade. Its ultimate size is about 20 feet high and 8 feet wide.

Dwarf horned holly is a 3- to 4-foot-high globular Chinese selection.

The deciduous hollies (above) are a tangle of gray stems and red berries in winter.

Yaupon (left) is the only holly with translucent berries.

Shrubs

Hetz holly, a Japanese selection, will take on a dense globose habit of growth when left unpruned.

Yaupon may be limbed up to form a multitrunked small tree.

Dahoon holly has flat, leathery, pale-green leaves, which are elliptic to lanceolate and range from 1¼ to 4 inches long. The foliage is relatively soft compared to American holly and may have a few spines toward the tips of the leaf. Dahoon has many nonshowy, small, white blooms in spring and fruits heavily, producing many red orange, ¼-inch berries in the fall.

Inkberry holly (*Ilex glabra*), native to swamps and lowlands of the eastern United States, will tolerate wet garden soils unlike many other landscape plants. Inkberry is a stoloniferous shrub that forms upright, branching clumps about 8 feet high and 5 feet wide if grown under cultural conditions like its natural, partially shady, fertile, moist habitat. Female plants bloom in spring with nonshowy white, solitary flowers and produce black berries in the fall. Inkberry does not have a distinctive landscape form or winter color as do many of the other hollies, but it is an excellent shrub for use as a backdrop plant for other low-flowering shrubs, annuals, and perennials of seasonal interest.

Another native holly shrub is the yaupon (*Ilex vomitoria*). This durable shrub form and its several selections have emerged as a group which includes the 15- to 25-foot native shrub and several dwarf and weeping forms. The yaupon holly is often found in shady soils and along the coast in the Upper, Middle, and Lower South. Yaupon is a fine-textured holly that grows well in sun or partial shade and also on the beach where its foliage is unaffected by salt spray.

Yaupon has an oval, upright, irregular, sculptural form. Large plants (up to 25 feet tall and 10 feet wide) may be limbed up to form multitrunked or single-trunked trees. Its dense growth habit makes yaupon a very effective plant for a screen or hedge. Yaupon is the only holly with translucent berries; and, in the sunlight, you can see the seeds inside the red, ¼-inch-wide berry.

A dwarf selection, Nana, grows only 2 to 4 feet tall and 2 to 4 feet wide. This selection does not fruit but, otherwise, has all the characteristics of the large plant. Stokes Dwarf is another dwarf selection that is slightly more compact and smaller than Nana. Shillings Dwarf is a small, stemmy dwarf similar to Stokes with tiny leaves that have a reddish cast.

Grey's Weeping is an upright, single-trunked selection which may grow to 25 feet tall. Its sparse, thin, pendulous branches give the plant a very airy look.

Two of the most popular deciduous landscape hollies are native to the Southern region. Common winterberry holly (*Ilex verticillata*) has strong merits as a plant that grows well in wet areas and limestone soils. Winterberry is an upright, broadly arching, deciduous holly that will grow to about 20 feet high. The foliage is a medium-green color and elliptic. In the fall, the foliage turns a dark, almost black color before dropping. Its red berries remain on the gray stems of the female plants for a short while after the foliage drops.

Possum haw (*Ilex decidua*), a second native deciduous holly, may reach 30 feet high in its slender, upright form. It is slightly larger and less arching than winterberry and has similar, slightly smaller, thinner foliage that is 1½ to 3 inches long, oblanceolate, serrate and turns reddish brown in fall. The female possum haw keeps its bright-red berries on bare gray stems all winter or until the birds eat them.

Hydrangea
A summer full of color

Almost everyone is familiar with the hydrangeas, a collection of coarse-textured deciduous shrubs that seemingly explode with color throughout the summer. In much of the South, it would not seem like summer without the cheery white panicles waving gently in summer breezes. These are a group of plants that seem to have gone out of fashion; but for the gardener who does not mind a brief period of maintenance in the fall months, the plants are dependable, disease free, and matchless in their summer flowering show. Four plants are widely available and used frequently in the South: the native oakleaf; snowhill hydrangea, also derived from a native plant; French hydrangea; and peegee hydrangea.

French Hydrangea

The French hydrangea *(Hydrangea macrophylla)*, a favorite garden hydrangea, has suffered a decline in popularity for several years. But the plants may be on their way back and with good reason; these sturdy, deciduous shrubs thrive in the heat of summer and provide weeks of garden color.

A woody shrub, French hydrangea is more successfully treated as a large perennial, since it requires specific care to look its best (perhaps the reason for its decline in popularity). The plant has an abundance of wide, slightly rough-textured foliage that is deep, dark green with good fertilization.

French hydrangeas, though, are celebrated for the massive flowers that decorate the summer landscape. These large panicles, composed of both fertile and sterile flowers, seem to explode from the ends of the plant's new growth and may last for almost 2 months. This profusion of bloom easily can be the highlight of shady and semishady gardens. French hydrangea provides beautiful summer color in the garden, either massed underneath shade trees or punctuating a garden border. While one plant makes a good accent in a border planting, a mass of the brightly colored flowers brings a surprising sweep of color to the landscape.

Plants generally look best when maintained at a height of between 4 to 6 feet and when they take on a rambling but upright appearance. Since the plant flowers on new growth, this requires some artful pruning. Thus, to keep the plant from getting too large, the woody stems must be cut back to a point just above a leaf bud where next year's growth will begin. The plant can be cut back almost to the ground; this will produce much larger flowers but will keep the plant around 3 to 4 feet in height. All pruning should be done immediately after the flowering and before winter sets in.

Oakleaf Hydrangea

Oakleaf hydrangea (*H. quercifolia*) is one of the finest of the South's native shrubs. It is a handsome plant with a loose, irregular form and mounding habit of growth. The foliage is large and coarse textured, resembling the leaves of red oak. It has a brilliant autumn color that may range from brownish red to scarlet; and when the leaves are gone, the oakleaf hydrangea reveals its twisting stems and attractive peeling bark.

AT A GLANCE
Light: partial to full shade
Water: moderate to moist
Soil: moist, well-drained, fertile soil
Growth Rate: rapid
Size: if unpruned, grows to 12 feet
Remarks: most potted specimens will transplant to garden

Snowhill hydrangea has large round panicles of white flowers which turn pale green as they mature during early summer.

French hydrangea looks its best when massed in a garden border.

Gumpo azalea, page 89.

Peegee hydrangea, page 124.

Vanhoutte spirea, page 153.

Sasanqua camellia, page 100.

Cluster mahonia, page 132.

Japanese andromeda, page 126.

Formosa firethorn, page 113.

Leatherleaf mahonia, page 133.

Dwarf pittosporum, page 142.

Winged euonymus, page 110.

Mountain laurel, page 134.

Shrubs

Peegee hydrangea is frequently trained as a tree-form specimen—a use which accents the flowers' pronounced weeping habit.

Oakleaf hydrangea, a native of the South, has long spikes of creamy white flowers which appear in early summer.

The most spectacular effect of oakleaf hydrangea, however, comes from its flowers. They appear in early summer and continue until fall, almost covering the plant with large, white blooms. A single cluster may be as much as 1 foot long. Snowflake (*H. quercifolia* Snowflake), a patented selection, has clusters up to 2½ feet long. During the hottest part of summer the flowers are creamy white; but as the weather starts to cool, they begin to take on a pinkish blush that eventually deepens into a glowing rose. In the latter part of autumn, the flowers turn a handsome parchment brown. This effect may last throughout the winter and into spring.

Native to the rolling hills of north Georgia and Alabama, oakleaf hydrangea can be grown in every region of the South except south Florida. It prefers a well-drained soil rich in organic matter, but will tolerate a heavier soil if it is supplemented with generous amounts of sand and peat moss or leaf mold. In the lower portions of the South, particularly in the Mississippi River Valley and the areas along the Gulf, the oakleaf hydrangea should be placed well above the ground, like azaleas and camellias, to protect the roots from too much water. The plant can be grown in sun or shade.

Peegee Hydrangea

The peegee hydrangea (*H. paniculata* Grandiflora) is another popular hydrangea in the cooler areas of the South. It is an upright grower with a coarse texture and is often trained to grow with a single trunk. White flowers are borne in conical clusters, measuring a foot or more in length. The flowers slowly fade to a pinkish bronze as they mature.

Peegee is the most cold hardy of the hydrangeas and, consequently, has widespread popularity in the Upper South. The growth is vigorous, and mature plants can easily reach 20 feet tall. Peegee is frequently trained as a tree-form specimen—a use which accents the flowers' pronounced weeping habit.

If planted in mass, peegee gives an unsurpassed summer show, but it is weak as a landscape element during the winter months and early spring. It can be very successful if provided with a low-growing evergreen underpinning, which will give some structure and form to the planting until it explodes into flowers.

Snowhill Hydrangea

The parent of this selection is the small and comparatively unnoticed *Hydrangea arborescens*, which is native to most woodlands throughout the South. Snowhill hydrangea (*H. arborescens* Grandiflora) gets its hardiness and rounded, slightly open form of growth from the parent.

Snowhill hydrangea has great, wide, rounded panicles of flowers that are carried upright on the stems in early summer. The individual panicles may be as wide as 10 inches across and are conspicuous from a distance—a good use of this hydrangea is to plant it as an accent where it may be viewed from a distance. The foliage is large and coarsely textured, closely resembling that of French hydrangea. The plant matures to approximately 8 feet in its largest form, but it generally does not exceed 5 feet. It may be successfully used either in mass or as an accent in the same way that the oakleaf and the French hydrangea are used.

Indian Hawthorn
Evergreen and tidy

Gardeners often overlook dwarf plants in favor of larger, more spectacular shrubs and trees that will reach maturity in three or four years. But low-growing evergreen shrubs can eliminate a lot of maintenance, particularly pruning, when used wisely in the garden. A good example is the Indian hawthorn (*Raphiolepis indica*). Native to southern China, Indian hawthorn is hardy throughout the South except in West Virginia, Maryland, and northernmost Kentucky, Arkansas, and Oklahoma. Also, performance may be less than satisfactory west of Dallas and Houston.

Indian hawthorn works well with other low-growing plants in a border or in a foundation planting. Situated atop a wall, the lower branches may cascade slightly. Use Indian hawthorn to edge a border of tall shrubs or as a background in the flower border. In Florida, where plants may reach 6 feet in height, Indian hawthorn may be used for screening. In massed plantings, space the plants about 4 feet apart on center in order to create a gently mounding drift.

Although not as well known as some of the plants it resembles (such as Wheeler's dwarf pittosporum or dwarf yaupon), Indian hawthorn has slowly gained recognition in seashore gardens of the Lower South, where it is appreciated for its salt tolerance. Leaves are dark, glossy green, and ovate to slightly rounded at the tips. The flowers, appearing in late spring, are white to deep pink depending on the selection. The flowers are followed in late summer by dull-blue berries.

Several selections of Indian hawthorn are available at nurseries throughout the South. Among the best are Enchantress, a dwarf plant that blooms profusely from late winter until early spring; Snow White, another dwarf selection that grows in a spreading habit and blooms from early spring well into the summer; Fascination, a densely branched, compact plant with star-shaped flowers that appear in late spring; and Springtime, a faster-growing selection with dense, leathery, bronze green foliage and whose flowers last from late winter to mid-spring.

The form of the plant may vary with geographic location and the type selected. Generally, Indian hawthorn grows slowly in a low, compact mound, reaching about 4½ feet in height with a nearly equal spread. When grown in an excessively shady location, however, plants tend to become leggy and sparse. Although Indian hawthorn shows moderate drought tolerance, it grows best in fertile, well-drained soil where it can be watered during dry spells.

AT A GLANCE
Light: full sun or partial shade
Water: partially drought resistant
Soil: fertile, well-drained soil; tolerates sandy soil
Growth Rate: slow to moderate
Size: 3 to 4 feet; taller in Florida

Because of its low, compact form, Indian hawthorn can be planted near buildings and other structures without needing constant pruning.

Planted where it can reach its natural form and size, Indian hawthorn forms neat, compact mounds of evergreen foliage.

AT A GLANCE

Light: partial sun in Upper South or cooler elevations
Water: moderate amount, does not tolerate drought
Soil: moist, well-drained acid soil, similar to that required by azaleas
Growth Rate: slow to moderate
Size: eventually 6 to 8 feet

Japanese Andromeda
A delicate and noble Heath

From late summer to early fall and throughout the entire winter season, Japanese andromeda (*Pieris japonica*) seems to be draped with delicate, pale-green chains. The ornamentation which emerges from the ends of the branches is actually the terminal flower panicles laden with the coming spring's flower buds, and they drape in exquisite contrast to the whorls of deep-green leaves so characteristic of the *Ericaceae* or Heath family. The white, open flowers make the shrub appear as though it were showered with pearls and are reminiscent of the flowers of the perennial lily-of-the-valley with which it shares one of its common names.

Japanese andromeda does not end its landscape effectiveness with the emergence of the flowers. In fact, it is one of the finest members of the Heath family, boasting splendid evergreen foliage and a wandering, slightly irregular habit of growth. Japanese andromeda generally grows upright, but the plant tends to wander and twist—it is never without an individual character that defies matching or pairing it with another plant. The foliage is deep, glossy green and covers the branches in handsome whorls. When the new growth emerges, shortly after the flowers appear, it is light olive green tinged red and appears in marked contrast to the deep green of the previous year's growth.

Because of its intriguing form and attractive flowering habits, Japanese andromeda is adaptable to almost any style garden, whether naturalized in a border, used as a naturalistic planting, or placed as a specimen in a more formal planting.

Like all Heaths, Japanese andromeda prefers moist, well-drained acid soil. It adapts with almost any other member of this family; and because of its hardiness, Japanese andromeda can be planted with either rhododendrons or with the more widely distributed evergreen azaleas. The Japanese andromeda bush is hardy in the higher elevations of the Upper South, where it may be grown in partial sun, and throughout the Piedmont South, where it must be planted in shady settings for best growth. It is possible to grow Japanese andromeda in shady locations in the Coastal and Gulf South, but the heat of the climate will greatly restrict the performance of the shrub.

Since it is a handsome evergreen shrub year-round, Japanese andromeda is a popular plant in many gardens.

The panicles of white flowers appear in early spring and resemble the perennial lily-of-the-valley.

Japan Cleyera
The colorful evergreen

Japan cleyera (*Ternstroemia gymnanthera*) has a dignified appearance, and this handsome evergreen of upright, rounded form and shining foliage can be used in a multitude of ways in the Southern garden. It offers a remarkable diversity of seasonal effects as well.

Although Japan cleyera is an evergreen, the color of its foliage changes with the seasons. The fresh new growth of spring is brilliant copper; this slowly darkens to a glowing bronze, and finally, to deepest midnight green. In winter, Japan cleyera takes on a rich burgundy blush which may, during prolonged periods of cold, become a vivid wine.

Creamy white flowers in late spring are another feature of Japan cleyera. Delicately scented with the fragrance of citrus blossoms, these flowers, which may be as much as ¾ inch in diameter, are followed by dark-red berrylike fruit in early summer. Ripening in autumn, the fruit gradually opens to reveal a cluster of orange red berries which remain attached throughout the winter.

A dependable plant for gardens in the Middle and Lower South, Japan cleyera will need some protection in the colder regions of the Upper South. It can be grown in either sun or shade and in a variety of soils. Very heavy clays, however, should be amended with peat moss, compost, or shredded pine bark mulch to improve the soil texture. Poorly drained locations should also be avoided to reduce the risk of leaf spot—the only real disease problem of Japan cleyera. See insect and control on page 250.

Frequently used for screens and hedges, the handsome form and foliage of Japan cleyera makes it useful as an accent plant as well. Set into a bed of ground cover or against an architectural backdrop like a fence or wall, the special qualities of Japan cleyera are well displayed. The dense, upright form of Japan cleyera makes it a good choice for locations where space is limited, like courtyards and city gardens. A tolerance of dry soils and of root competition from surrounding plants are additional advantages of the cleyera in restricted areas.

Note: The scientific name is often given as *Cleyera japonica*, which is incorrect.

AT A GLANCE
Light: full sun to shade
Water: moist to dry; drought resistant
Soil: adaptable; intolerant of heavy clay and wet feet
Growth Rate: moderate
Size: medium shrub; to 10 feet high and 5 feet wide

Japan cleyera takes on a globose, layering form at maturity.

The fruit (above) hangs like a cat's paw and is brilliant red.

Generally purchased in the 2- to 3-foot size, Japan cleyera (left) easily attains a height of 10 feet in 10 to 12 years.

Shrubs

Jasmine
Tumbling with flowers

As the name implies, winter jasmine becomes a mass of yellow blooms during late winter and resembles border forsythia from a distance.

If you are looking for a shrub with a mounding habit of growth as an out-of-the-ordinary planting for a foundation on a steep bank, then plant jasmine (*Jasminum sp.*). Not only do they have a light and airy texture, but they sparkle with bright-yellow flowers. Jasmine is one of the best casual plants for the garden. The plant sends out long runners, like thorny elaeagnus, that layer over themselves to create the soft-looking green mound of foliage that is the plant's hallmark.

Relatively inexpensive, jasmine is a good plant to use where a large expanse of ground must be covered with a single plant. It usually grows to a mature height of around 4 feet. The delicate foliage and soft appearance of the plant make it a good choice for cascading over a retaining wall, where the flowers can be appreciated for their form and fragrance.

The plant prefers a well-drained soil and is moderately tolerant of drought, but long periods without water will result in foliage dieback. The plant will rarely die, however, and will rapidly replace the damaged growth with new foliage the following season. While jasmine is tolerant of most soils, it will grow best if the soil is loose and friable. Heavy clay, for instance, must be loosened with peat moss, ground bark, or a suitable substitute; but, once established, jasmine is dependable.

Primrose Jasmine

Primrose jasmine (*J. mesnyi*) is the largest of all the jasmines. Growing to 5 to 6 feet in the Lower South, this evergreen makes a handsome specimen or unusual mounding hedge. It has single (occasionally double) yellow flowers, which cover the plant in early spring and continue lightly blooming through midsummer. This plant is not cold tolerant below 15 degrees and should be grown only in the Lower South.

Showy Jasmine

Showy jasmine (*J. floridum*) is the most popular of the jasmine types. The leaves are compound, usually in 3 to 5 leaflets. The foliage is evergreen in most of the South; but during severe winters, the plant may become deciduous in the Upper South. The yellow, star-shaped flowers are borne on long pedicels, beginning in May. The peak flowering period is from mid-May to late June, although the flowers will appear sporadically into August and sometimes September.

Winter Jasmine

Winter jasmine (*J. nudiflorum*) derives its name from the flowers appearing on the bare winter branches. This deciduous plant has tiny yellow flowers which literally cover the green bare branches in late winter and early spring. It is one of the few plants that will burst into flower with several days of warm weather. Always treat this plant as a winter accent. It is the most desirable species for the Upper South.

Primrose jasmine is the largest of the selections.

Showy jasmine is a mounding shrub that flowers profusely in spring and then sporadically all summer.

Laurel
Lustrous broad-leaved evergreen

Gardeners looking for broad-leaved evergreens should look at the versatile laurels. These evergreen members of the cherry or plum genus (*Prunus sp.*) offer an unusual array of form and foliage for gardeners from parts of the Upper South to the coastal and gulf locations. Some special selections are even hardier than their parents and, therefore, are suitable for limited areas in the severely cold regions of the Upper South. The common name, laurel, is confusing since it is also associated with many other species of plants; but it does call attention to the group's dominant landscape characteristic—handsome, glossy, almost leatherlike foliage.

There are two divisions of the laurel—the native species, or Southern cherry laurel (*Prunus caroliniana*), and the imported English cherry laurel (*Prunus laurocerasus*) and its selections. Both groups are tolerant of a wide range of horticultural conditions. For example, usually the plants will retain their foliage if planted in full sun or complete shade; some selections even grow dependably in deep shade. In addition, the plants are not particular about soil, preferring only that the planting medium not be heavy and poorly drained clay. This horticultural diversity makes them a very useful evergreen group, especially since they tend to be long-lived and comparatively disease free. Landscape use varies with the different groups since their form and growth habits dictate how they can be effectively developed in the garden.

English Cherry Laurel

English cherry laurel (*Prunus laurocerasus*) and its selections are being rediscovered among gardeners. These large-leaved evergreens are exceptionally attractive and have many applications in the home garden. Ironically, some of the selections of this species are more popular than the parent. In its mature form, English cherry laurel is a large, rounded shrub covered with an impenetrable layer of thick 4- to 5-inch-long evergreen leaves. English cherry laurel makes an excellent screen or hedge plant. It is durable and relatively disease free, and it will grow extremely well in full or partial sun. The plant must have room to grow; mature plants may reach at least 20 feet in height and equal breadth. Other

AT A GLANCE

Light: full sun to complete shade
Water: moderate amount; signals need by dropping foliage
Soil: moist, well-drained soil
Growth Rate: moderate to rapid, depending on species
Size: varies with selection
Remarks: cannot withstand drought during establishment; well-drained soil a must

Southern cherry laurel adapts well to pruning into tree form and also makes an excellent hedge.

Schipka cherry laurel is a handsome evergreen background plant with lustrous, dark-green foliage. Its form is upright and spreading.

English cherry laurel is a massive coarse-textured shrub which performs better in the Middle to Upper South.

Southern cherry laurel makes a good tall screen when it has an arched underpinning or low shrubs planted with it.

types of English laurel with similar growth habits are: Zabel cherry laurel (*P. laurocerasus* Zabeliana), which has long, narrow, light-green leaves and a spreading habit of growth; and Otto Luykens cherry laurel (*P. laurocerasus* Otto Luykens), a dwarf type that reaches less than 3 feet in height at maturity. Of the many and varied selections, the low-growing types are more often grown and are more widely distributed. Each has characteristics of the parent but with handsome features that make them desirable plants.

Schipka Cherry Laurel

The spreading-branching habit of Schipka cherry laurel (*Prunus laurocerasus* Schipkaensis) creates a layering of dark-green, oval leaves to form a plant almost 6 feet tall and 6 to 8 feet wide at maturity. Although dense, it retains an informal character. Massed plantings of Schipka cherry laurel make a beautiful green background for a display of annual color, without the formal feeling of a hedge or wall. Schipka cherry laurel flowers in late spring or early summer. Small, white flowers with a slightly pungent fragrance cover the plant on ascending racemes that resemble upright plumes. After flowering, small black fruit appears and lasts all winter.

With proper care, Schipka cherry laurel can adapt to a wide range of planting locations. Since it will grow in full sun or deep shade, it is a good companion plant for flowering ornamentals as different in form as rhododendron and Florida jasmine. Schipka cherry laurel is intolerant of moisture variations. The plant will signal water deficiency by dropping leaves. If you notice this condition, water quickly and thoroughly. Once established (about two years after planting), Schipka cherry laurel is less demanding and requires only annual mulching and seasonal fertilization.

Southern Cherry Laurel

Southern cherry laurel (*Prunus carolininana*) is native to every Southern state and has, since early colonial times, been collected from the wild for garden use. The plant's hallmarks are the deep, charcoal black bark; glossy light-green, 2- to 3-inch leaves; and a dense, upright habit of growth. In addition, Southern cherry laurel flowers in March or April with small racemes of white flowers that appear in the axils of the previous year's growth. The fruit that follows these flowers is blue black and can be littersome.

Southern cherry laurel may be used in the landscape as either a small tree or a very large shrub. The plant grows rapidly and can easily reach 25 feet or more in height in a short time if planted in the rich, well-drained soil it prefers. The form is rounded; and, in fact, given sufficient time and if the lower branches are carefully pruned, Southern cherry laurel will make a suitable visual substitute for live oak in locations where the latter would be too large. In addition, the plant makes an excellent clipped hedge. This use was popularized at Williamsburg by early colonists who quickly learned the versatility of this native plant. Unless you are planning to spend sufficient time to keep this plant in bounds, it is best planted away from the house where it will have room to mature. Southern cherry laurel is a good evergreen for border plantings. A more compact selection is Bright 'n Tight.

Leucothöe
Glossy, graceful form

The leucothöes make a fine addition to the Southern garden. This genus offers two species that can be relied on for dependable, steady growth and unsurpassed garden grace. Both plants, Florida leucothöe (*Leucothöe populifolia*) and drooping leucothöe (*L. fontanesiana*), are superb in mass plantings in a shady landscape. But because of their size and region or origin, each has its own particular landscape expression.

A member of the *Ericaceae* or Heath family, these native leucothöes prefer moist, well-drained, acid soil rich in organic matter. In fact, the drooping leucothöes are only found in areas where the natural leaf fall has been undisturbed and the soil is a rich composite of humis and organic material—a valuable key to a successful planting. In addition, both plants need some protection from too much full sun, particularly the hot afternoon sun of summer. The high-filtered shade of pine trees is almost perfect for the leucothöes, although they will thrive in the deep, dark shade of a deciduous forest also.

Drooping Leucothöe

Drooping leucothöe is matchless in the beauty that it brings to shady plantings. Perhaps the only comparable plants that have a similar form—a slightly weeping, mounding habit of growth—are ferns; and they lack the deep, glossy-green foliage that makes this mountain plant so desirable.

The plant has several broadly arching stems that emerge fountainlike from a central base. While these main shoots (which grow to a height of 4 feet or more) may have side branches that expand the weeping effect, the overall appearance of the plant is a slightly irregular mass of foliage that layers casually over the ground. The broad, deep, glossy-green leaves, which can be 5 inches long, are arranged alternately along the stems and project horizontally from the branch.

In spring, drooping leucothöe offers a superb flower show. Racemes of white flowers up to 3 inches in length emerge from the auxiliary buds (located in the angle between the leaves and stem) to droop like clusters of tiny bells.

Florida Leucothöe

The Florida leucothöe is a lovely, low-maintenance evergreen shrub which is native to the upland forest from Virginia to Georgia and northern Alabama. It has an elegant weeping form and rich-green leaves, and Florida leucothöe makes a fine addition to the Southern gardener's collection. Its upright, arching habit of growth makes this leucothöe a good choice for an informal screen. It is also an interesting understory plant for naturalized areas.

Keep leucothöe unpruned; the natural form shows it off to best advantage. The leucothöe is relatively slow growing, but a 10-year-old plant may be as much as 12 feet high and wide. When the plant is allowed to go unpruned, individual stems get to be as much as 10 feet in length, growing straight up for about 6 feet and then arching dramatically out and downward. New growth is tinted red.

Florida leucothöe also flowers profusely; the white flowers appear in spring on long racemes. Florida leucothöe is less cold hardy than is drooping leucothöe, but it should perform well in the Piedmont and in the Coastal South.

AT A GLANCE
Light: partial to deep shade
Water: high; drought will damage severely
Soil: moist, well-drained, acid soil; similar to soil required by rhododendron or azalea
Growth Rate: moderate
Size: drooping leucothöe—to 4 feet; Florida leucothöe—to 12 feet

Unlike Florida leucothöe, drooping leucothöe (above) is low growing and rarely reaches a mature height in excess of 4 feet. It is also noted for its spring flower show.

Florida leucothöe (left) may attain a height of 10 to 12 feet and produce long, upright, arching stems which contribute to the plant's weeping form.

Shrubs

Mahonia
Striking form with flowers and fruit

AT A GLANCE
Light: partial shade is best;
3 to 4 hours of direct sun
will enhance flowers
Water: moderate amount
Soil: well-drained, sandy
soil, either slightly acid or
alkaline
Growth Rate: rapid except
for Oregon grape
Size: varies from 5 to 10
feet

Leatherleaf mahonia becomes a living sculpture after careful pruning.

Gardeners who are intrigued with the upright form and leathery evergreen foliage of mahonias have an array from which to choose. And although each species offers a slightly different landscape look, the genus is striking and will attract attention to any corner of the garden. As a rule, mahonias are plants for accents in the landscape. Each species has an irregular, upright habit of growth that is topped with fountainlike sprays of varied textured foliage. Even the Oregon grape is resplendent with the spiny foliage that is the hallmark of the plant.

As a group, the mahonias will grow best in a light, moderately sandy, garden soil with a generous amount of organic matter. In addition, the plants prefer high-filtered shade. Quite often the plants are located in full sun, but the direct rays of the sun will sear and burn the foliage. However, three to four hours of sun will encourage flowering and the sculptural qualities of the plant.

The hardiness of the separate species varies as do their landscape uses and other qualities. But the mahonias have several common characteristics—their attractive spiny foliage, the bright-yellow flowers that appear in racemes at varying times of the year, the attractive fruit that is quickly consumed by birds, and the unpredictable, upright habit of growth.

Chinese Mahonia

One of the best mahonias for the Lower South is Chinese mahonia (*Mahonia fortunei*), a narrow-leaved plant that loves the heat of the Coastal Plains. Chinese mahonia has a smaller, longer leaf that lacks the sharp spines of leatherleaf mahonia. In fact, the plant strongly resembles nandina when used in a mass planting. While most mahonias are better used as accent plants, Chinese mahonias can be used as a mass planting to fill in narrow planting beds. Mature plants will eventually reach 5 feet but still retain the lower foliage, appearing almost like they have been clipped into a hedge. Since Chinese mahonia does not have long spines, the plant may be used near seating areas or close to walkways without the nuisance of snagging the clothes of passers-by. The foliage is a deep, dull green that varies little throughout the year, and so the plant should be used in a location that will allow the texture to be displayed. Flowers and fruit are borne on 2-inch racemes and can be striking. Chinese mahonia can endure an amazing amount of heat, making it a good landscape plant in the hottest climates. However, if beds are planted in full sun, the plant will burn. It requires a minimum amount of moisture and prefers a well-drained soil that is slightly acid. Remember, this plant is recommended for the Lower South.

Cluster Mahonia

Cluster mahonia (*Mahonia pinnata*) can tolerate more sun than the other mahonias but still requires shade from intense summer sun. Cluster mahonia is hardy through the Middle or Piedmont South and is rarely used in either the Upper South or the extremely hot areas of the coastal and western regions of the South. The plant is aptly named, since it clumps together to form tall, stemmy plants that may reach 6 or 7 feet. In fact, cluster mahonia is more suited to a mass planting in the landscape because, once installed, it spreads rapidly and fills a large area. The foliage bears the characteristic spiny leaf of the mahonias, yet it has a blue gray color that turns to a deep purple in winter. In the landscape the plant appears as a coarse gray blue mass. The flowers are yellow and are borne on racemes that occur at the tips of the stem. The fruit is bluish black and contributes to the plant's landscape interest.

Leatherleaf Mahonia

The form, foliage, and seasonal interest of the leatherleaf mahonia (*Mahonia bealei*) make it a natural choice for use as a piece of living sculpture in the landscape. Dark, glossy-green leaves give it a spiny, almost hollylike appearance; but the multistemmed character keeps the mahonia from looking quite as heavy as the hollies. Spikes of bright-yellow flowers form on the tips of the branches in the late winter or early spring. They have a delicate fragrance similar to a citrus blossom. The flowers are followed by large clusters of purplish blue berries that remain on the plant throughout the summer—if they last that long. Birds love the fruit, and a mature plant will attract them in large numbers. A full-grown specimen may be as much as 10 feet in height and 6 to 8 feet (after 25 years) in width. Its size and appearance make it an eye-catching accent plant. In fact, it is probably one of the best plants for capturing a viewer's attention.

Oregon Grape

While Oregon grape (*Mahonia aquifolium*) is the smallest of the mahonias, it is also one of the most appealing for the Piedmont and the Upper South. The shrub reaches a height of 6 feet eventually, although it is a slower grower than the rest of the genus. The yellow flowers are borne in early spring, appearing in racemes that fit snuggly against the stems of the plant. The fruit is blue black and, compared to the flowers, is not conspicuous. One of the most attractive features of Oregon grape is that in winter the foliage will turn bright ruby red. The plant is stoloniferous and will spread underground into a mass of stems and foliage about six feet in breadth. As a landscape plant, it can be used either as a specimen for moderate impact or as a mass planting in a smaller planting area.

Chinese mahonia, which is limited to the Lower South, resembles nandina when used in a mass planting.

Cluster mahonia, because of its upright habit of growth, combines with these dwarf horned hollies in this foundation planting.

Leatherleaf mahonia produces spikes of yellow flowers in the winter which are followed by purplish blue fruit.

Mountain Laurel
For late-spring color

AT A GLANCE

Light: partial shade
Water: needs regular moisture
Soil: well-drained, sandy, or peaty loam; acid soil
Growth Rate: slow to moderate
Size: 10 to 30 feet

Mountain laurel may reach 20 feet or more, so it is wise to plant it away from buildings where it will not require pruning to control size.

The gardener who thinks spring ends in April has never seen the late-spring show of mountain laurel (*Kalmia latifolia*). Fortunately, despite its name, this native evergreen is not confined to the mountain regions of the South; it can be grown anywhere rhododendrons thrive. Mountain laurel is native throughout the Upper and Middle South, in some areas of the Florida Panhandle, and west to Baton Rouge. Even in Texas and Oklahoma, where the soil may be too alkaline for mountain laurel, it can be easily grown in a container for use on a deck or terrace.

If you have recently acquired property on an undisturbed site, you may already have mountain laurel growing there; so be sure to inventory the plants you have before construction begins, and make provisions to move or protect mountain laurel. Seedlings are easy to transplant, but mature plants are best left undisturbed.

Mountain laurel is readily available from local and mail-order nurseries and can be grown as either a large shrub or small tree. In its first few years, mountain laurel may be bushy and somewhat compact; then it becomes increasingly treelike. Though most prized for its spectacular clusters of white-to-blush blossoms that densely cover the plant in late May and June, mountain laurel is handsome throughout the year. Its trunks curl and twist with age, giving mature plants an almost Oriental character. And on older specimens, the gray bark becomes deeply fissured and often takes on a reddish tinge, adding to the plant's year-round interest.

The best key to the culture and landscape uses of mountain laurel is its natural habitat—along banks of creeks and rivers, on mountainsides, or any location protected from the summer sun where the soil is moist, well drained, and acid. Besides supplying these conditions in the home landscape, you should mulch mountain laurel heavily with pine straw or wood chips to conserve moisture and help the plant survive periods of drought.

Because mountain laurel is a woodland plant, it is at its best when planted among hardwoods like oak and hickory. Given proper growing conditions, it can also be massed to create a screen, used as an accent in a shady shrub border, or displayed as a specimen on the north or east side of a home where the garden is protected by a canopy of large trees. It is most at home in partial shade but seldom blooms satisfactorily in deep shade.

Mountain laurel is an ideal plant for the low-maintenance garden where shrubs are allowed to grow to their natural form and size, unhampered by pruning. In fact, it is best not to prune mountain laurel except to remove dead or damaged wood. Pruning to reduce size or to shape plants into a hedge will inevitably mar mountain laurel's naturally pleasing form. It is important, however, to remove spent flower heads if plants are to bloom consistently from year to year.

Mountain laurel has few disease problems, but the most obvious is a leaf-spot disease that scars leaves with gray to silvery spots edged in red or purple. See page 251 for controls.

Nandina
Prized for its foliage

Nandina (*Nandina domestica*) is one of the most misrepresented Southern landscape plants. It is too often unshapely pruned into a flattop or planted against a background, such as red brick, that clashes with the red foliage and berries. Let it grow into its upright, stalky, bamboolike form; move it away from a red background; and plain clumping Nandina metamorphoses into a spectacular plant.

Spreading from underground rhizomes (stems) and eventually reaching 8 feet high and 4 feet wide, the finely textured evergreen plant can be used in shrubbery borders or planted in mass as a lightweight hedge or screen. It can also be planted in a dark corner as an accent. Nandina is one of the few landscape plants that will produce flowers and berries in the shade. Nandina's fine texture provides a good contrast against many coarsely textured evergreens, such as leatherleaf viburnum, holly, camellia, and sweet olive.

In spring, Nandina, commonly know as heavenly bamboo, blooms with a large panicle of small white flowers held on top of the foliage-covered canes. Later, green ¼-inch fruit forms on the panicle to produce an 8-inch cluster of green berries, which turn brilliant red by early fall and hang like bunch grapes from the top of the canes all winter. The selection Alba produces white berries.

The foliage varies in color with age, location, and season. The young foliage is always coppery and becomes green as it matures. In the shade, the lacy, tri-pinnately compound adult foliage is a dark blue green; but in the sun, the foliage is tinged red. In winter, the 1- to 2-foot-long foliage is usually predominately red. Nandina is a low-maintenance plant. It requires no pruning other than thinning to control the density and plant height, if desired. To retain the plant's form as you prune, remove the longest canes in early spring by cutting them at various heights from the base of the plant. If you want to keep the plant below 3 feet high, plant the smaller selection Compacta, which has slightly smaller leaves, narrower canes, and does not grow over 3 feet.

Nandina is relatively pest free and is bothered only by general pests, such as mites and scale. Although nandina grows best in fertile, acid, well-drained soil, it will also grow in poor soils, including well-drained sand and clay. With good conditions nandina is a moderately fast grower after it is established. It is also relatively drought tolerant, but nandina should be well watered for the fastest growth and best condition.

AT A GLANCE
Light: sun or shade
Water: tolerates drought; best in moist soil
Soil: any well-drained soil
Growth Rate: moderate
Size: 8 feet high, 4 feet wide

Nandina's delicate foliage appears in whorls at the ends of each stem.

The layered foliage of this specimen is the result of several growing seasons after proper pruning.

AT A GLANCE

Light: full sun or filtered shade
Water: very drought resistant
Soil: sandy, clay, alkaline, wet, or dry soil
Growth Rate: rapid
Size: 8 to 12 feet

Oleander
Colorful and fragrant

When a plant is used as often as oleander (*Nerium oleander*), there must be a reason. Oleander is tough and thrives in heat, humidity, drought, and some of the poorest soils in the South. Oleanders are also noted for their tolerance of urban pollution and coastal conditions. In addition, oleander is immune to most common insect pests and diseases. See page 245 for insect problems. Remarkable for its long-bloom season and low-maintenance requirements, oleander is a highly valued landscape plant in the Middle and Lower South. This dense, upright evergreen usually grows to a height of 8 to 12 feet with a nearly equal spread. Under optimum conditions, however, oleander may grow to 20 feet. Native to the Mediterranean area where they are often grown as single-stemmed trees, oleander needs little or no attention once it becomes established. Among the best-known selections are Calypso (pink flowers), Cherry Ripe (red), Sister Agnes (white), and Isle of Capri (yellow); many selections are commercially available.

The fragrant flowers are red, pink, white, or yellow and about 3 inches across; they bloom from April until mid-fall. If the plant fails to flower, it is usually the result of suckers that arise at the base of flower trusses and sap energy from flower production. Remove suckers whenever you notice them. The leaves, which are evergreen, are lanceolate in shape, 6 to 8 inches long, and nearly 1 inch wide.

Oleander makes a showy specimen or accent plant, particularly when trained as a single-stemmed tree. Planted away from buildings and other structures, oleanders may be massed to create a screen or to accent dense screening plants. One caution: all parts of the oleander are poisonous. Contact with the leaves may cause skin irritation; do not plant oleander too near terraces or other outdoor living spaces. Locate oleander in full sun or filtered shade. Tolerant of poor soil, salty seaside locations, marshy soil, or dry, heavy soil, oleander is most highly valued for its ability to grow where little else will. A single application of 5-10-10 each spring satisfies the fertilizer requirements of oleander.

Pruning needs vary with the region in which oleander is grown. In the lower extremities of the growth range, oleander grows vigorously and annual pruning in late winter will be necessary to control the size of the plant. Prune the new growth by two-thirds or more. In the upper reaches of the growth range, by contrast, growth is considerably slower and winter-kill of tender twigs results in a natural pruning.

Popular throughout the Middle and Lower South, oleander makes an attractive hedge when correctly pruned.

Because of its prolific flowering, oleander makes a showy large shrub in the Lower South.

Osmanthus
Fall fragrance in a big way

The osmanthus are large evergreen shrubs; and, depending on the type, they grow from about 6 to 20 feet tall. Three species are commonly available in the nursery trade: Fragrant sweet olive (*Osmanthus fragrans*), holly olive (*O. heterophyllus*), and Fortunes osmanthus (*O. x fortunei*), which is a hybrid of the first two. Devilwood (*O. americanus*) is native to much of the South and is hard to locate in the nursery trade. Sometimes called false hollies, the sweet olives are considered holly substitutes in many landscape situations. Although their fruit is less spectacular than that of the hollies, the sweet olives are noted for their small but extremely fragrant early fall flowers. Another outstanding feature of osmanthus is its lustrous foliage. Medium to coarse in texture, sweet olives are good background plants that can be successfully combined with plants of a coarser or finer texture.

AT A GLANCE
Light: partial shade; full sun in Upper South
Water: moderate amount
Soil: almost any fertile soil
Growth Rate: moderate to rapid
Size: 6 to 20 feet; devilwood to 40 to 50 feet

Devilwood

Although most species of osmanthus were imported from the Far East, one devilwood (*Osmanthus americanus*) is native to the Southeast. This large shrub or small tree often goes unnoticed since it strongly resembles another native, wax myrtle. Devilwood reaches a height of forty to fifty feet. The loosely rounded crown has a spread of about two-thirds the height of the plant. In late spring (the exception to fall flowering), devilwood produces small clusters of white auxiliary flowers which become dark-blue fruit in early fall. Leaves differ from other types of osmanthus in that they are smooth along the margins. Hardy throughout the South, this tree is not as widely planted as it should be.

Devilwood osmanthus is a loose, open-form native species.

Fortunes osmanthus is a massive shrub which grows rapidly up to 20 feet high with an equal spread.

There are numerous selections of Fortunes and holly osmanthus that take on an upright, rounded form.

The foliage of holly osmanthus resembles that of American hollies, hence the name.

As a specimen or accent tree, devilwood can be used in most situations except where the falling fruit may be untidy. At the edge of a woodland planting, devilwood provides an informal crown of evergreen foliage. Because it is native, it is more resistant to the extremes of weather so often experienced in the South.

Fortunes Osmanthus

Fortunes osmanthus (*O.* x *fortunei*) is a hybrid of holly osmanthus and fragrant sweet olive. Fortunes osmanthus usually grows to a 15- to 20-foot oval shrub. Leaves are more sharply dentate (having teeth) than those of *O. fragrans* but not as toothed as the leaves of holly osmanthus. This species, too, produces small, fragrant flowers in fall. Because of its size, Fortunes osmanthus is the most limited of the osmanthus group in landscape uses. It may be used as a lawn specimen, but there are many more spectacular specimen shrubs than Fortunes osmanthus. However, Fortunes osmanthus is a good choice for a large garden, where a partially shaded area may need a large shrub. Ideally, Fortunes osmanthus should be used where you need a large screen but have room for only one plant.

Fragrant Sweet Olive

Fragrant sweet olive (*O. fragrans*), also called tea olive, is a large shrub, often reaching 20 feet or more when grown under optimum conditions in the Lower South. Further north, plants are smaller, reaching 10 to 12 feet and attaining an upright form. Leaves are 4 inches long, about 1½ inches wide, and finely toothed along the margins. This plant suffers from cold damage in the Upper South.

If you have adequate space in your garden, fragrant sweet olive makes an imposing specimen, a dense hedge, or an impenetrable screen. Used as a specimen, fragrant sweet olive may need an underplanting if limbed up to form small trees. As either formal or informal hedges, the sweet olives are hard to beat. One of the best uses of these plants is for screening. A single plant can provide a good screen, but in combination with American holly or similar large, broadleaf evergreens, fragrant sweet olive screens out undesired views and presents itself as a serene, timeless mass of greenery. However, if you intend to use fragrant sweet olive, give it adequate room to grow. Fragrant sweet olive also makes a superb tub plant for the deck or terrace. Depending on the container size, plants may grow 5 to 6 feet tall.

Holly Osmanthus

Holly osmanthus (*O. heterophyllus*), the most familiar of the sweet olives and the hardiest of the imported species, attains a form that is at once more rounded and more irregular than fragrant sweet olive. Plants may reach 18 to 20 feet in height with a nearly equal spread. The leaves, much smaller than those of the sweet olive, are deeply toothed and resemble the leaves of American holly. The small, white aromatic flowers appear in fall. Holly osmanthus is the best species for the Upper South but performs well in all regions. Like the other species, holly osmanthus is a valuable screening or hedge plant, particularly when it is used in combination with hollies, ligustrums, or similar broadleaf evergreens. Planted densely, such a screen can reduce street noise, highway pollution, and wind. There is also a variegated selection.

Pfitzer Juniper
Spiny foliage for sun and sea

Pfitzer juniper (*Juniperus* x *media* Pfitzerana) is probably one of the most overplanted and least understood of the junipers available to gardeners: overplanted because of its availability and ease of propagation; and misunderstood because it is not the typical 2-foot, spreading, low-growing juniper. It usually grows to a spread of 10 to 12 feet and a height of 5 or 6 feet.

Because of its size, Pfitzer juniper should not be used as a foundation plant for most homes. Yet it offers the homeowner an excellent low screen (5 to 6 feet) that is durable but informal. Even used as a screen, though, Pfitzer juniper needs room to grow. Since the branches arch and angle from the central stem, the habit of growth takes on a horizontal character. This gives the plant a great measure of dignity. One of the best attributes of the plant is that it will tolerate oceanside conditions in a properly prepared planting bed. Several selections are available—Nicks Compact, winter color is reddish, 2½ feet tall; Glauca, bluish foliage; Nana, to 4 feet with dense growth habit; and Aurea-Pfitzerana, leaves and twigs of new growth are bright yellow.

AT A GLANCE
Light: full sun to light shade
Water: moderate amount; drought hardy when established
Soil: any well-drained soil, either acid or alkaline
Growth Rate: rapid
Size: to 6 feet, spreading to 12

Pfitzer juniper has a fine, delicate, airy texture that is a beautiful contrast to most other plants.

Although fine in texture, Pfitzer juniper may be massive in size, generally spreading 10 to 12 feet; always allow plenty of room for growth.

Photinia
Needs more space than you might think

AT A GLANCE
Light: full sun
Water: moderate amount
Soil: fertile, well-drained soil
Growth Rate: rapid
Size: 10 to 30 feet

Fraser photinia is used here to visually scale down this home.

The key to using photinia successfully in the landscape is to plant it in the right place. One of the qualities that sets this group of medium- to coarse-textured shrubs apart from other large shrubs is their rapid rate of growth. The other is the brilliant red color of the new growth of Fraser photinia (*Photinia* x *fraseri*) and Japanese photinia (*Photinia glabra*). The bright-red new growth and vigorous growth habit require the plant to be planted in full sun and given enough space with respect to its bold texture and color.

Throughout the Lower, Middle, and parts of the Upper South, this group of evergreen shrubs is often overused as hedges and screens because they are inexpensive and fast growing. When planted in full sun and lightly pruned to encourage branching, Japanese photinia and Fraser photinia grow into dense, upright shrubs which form effective hedges or screens. Chinese photinia (*P. serrulata*), which is a much larger, coarser shrub that is native to China, may also be used this way in wide-open spaces, only because it will eventually grow to small tree size.

Chinese Photinia

All photinias have conspicuous blooms, but Chinese photinia produces a large, 6-inch cluster of small, white flowers in spring. Most people find the odor objectionable. Red berrylike fruit clusters hang from the tree from late summer through winter. Chinese photinia is a bold, coarse-textured, broadly oval, dense shrub which grows 20 to 30 feet tall and 10 to 15 feet wide and may become treelike with age. Large older shrubs are sometimes limbed up to form small trees. The thick, leathery, deep-green leaves of Chinese photinia are about 8 inches long and 2 inches wide with finely toothed edges.

Fraser Photinia

Fraser photinia, a cross between Japanese and Chinese photinia, has the best characteristics of both plants. Sometimes multitrunked, the upright, medium-textured shrub will grow to about 20 feet tall and 10 feet wide with glossy-green, toothed leaves about 4 to 5 inches long. Most people consider Fraser photinia the most desirable of all the types.

Japanese Photinia

Japanese photinia, native to Japan, is the smallest of the photinias, growing only 10 to 12 feet high. It is often used in sunny locations in the Lower and Middle South as a clipped hedge or screen. The smooth-edged foliage is brilliant red when young, eventually growing into a 3-inch-long glossy leaf. This upright, single or multitrunked shrub, with a strong vertical branching habit requires full sun and careful pruning to keep it compact. Prune branch tips in the spring and summer to stimulate new growth from the lower branches.

The pale-red, berrylike fruit of Chinese photinia (far left) is produced in winter.

The flowers of Japanese photinia (left), while showy, have an objectionable odor.

Pineapple Guava
Ornamental and edible

Pineapple guava (*Feijoa sellowiana*) can bring an exotic, almost tropical look to gardens of the Lower South. Perhaps the most versatile landscape plant for Florida, this durable, adaptable shrub provides a bonus—a delicious fruit that ripens in late summer and early fall.

Pineapple guava has a relaxed, carefree appearance that makes it a good evergreen choice for an informal screen planting or for use in mixed evergreen borders. Reaching a mature height of 10 to 15 feet, pineapple guava's texture and landscape appearance are somewhat similar to young wax myrtle, and it can be used similarly in the landscape. Accordingly, pineapple guava may be drifted through existing trees as an informal backdrop planting for lower-growing, more profusely flowering shrubs, or it may even be planted along the property line to provide enclosure. Single specimens may be used to anchor the corner of a building or to provide height in other plantings. Pineapple guava is a valuable landscape plant in gardens of the Coastal South. It is somewhat tolerant of salt spray.

The branches of the plant grow upright in an ascending habit that is similar to flowering pomegranite. This gives the plant a wide-spreading crown that, if allowed to grow unpruned, will eventually become slightly weeping in form. In the northernmost areas of the pineapple guava's hardiness range, shrubs are more dense and rounded because the stem tips are sometimes killed by cold.

One of the most attractive features is the elliptic foliage. Light green on the tops of the leaves, the undersides of the foliage are pubescent with a beautiful silver color. The slightest breeze shows the backs of the leaves and the plant shimmers in the garden. The flowers are pendulous and fragrant, appearing in late spring. The outside of the four-petaled inflorescence (flower) is white, while the inside is a contrasting purplish brown, giving the overall flower a reddish appearance. In addition, the stems are a brilliant crimson.

Edible fruit ripens in late summer and early fall, depending on the location. The further south they are grown, the earlier they ripen. In south Florida, fruit may drop before it ripens. At maturity the oval fruit is 2 to 3 inches long, and the deep-green skin turns yellow green. Locate pineapple guava in full sun for the best fruit. To set fruit, many selections of pineapple guavas must be cross-pollinated; that is, two different selections should be planted together so that pollen from one may be transferred to pollen of the other. Two new selections, Coolidge and Pineapple Gem, are self-fruiting, which means that a single plant may be expected to bear fruit.

Used only as an ornamental, pineapple guava tolerates partial shade. Soil should be a well-drained, sandy loam that has been supplemented with compost or peat moss. Only minimum pruning is necessary. Remove elongated or dead branches at their point of origin. Wait until late spring to prune, after the plants have flowered.

The pineapple guava usually grows to about 10 feet in height with an equal spread.

AT A GLANCE

Light: full sun for fruiting plants; partial shade for plants used as ornamentals
Water: needs regular water for fruit set
Soil: best in fertile, rich sandy loam
Growth Rate: moderate to rapid
Size: to 15 feet

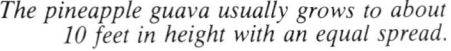

Fruit of the pineapple guava (left) has a pineapplelike flavor.

Pittosporum
Neat, clean, and compact

AT A GLANCE
Light: full sun or partial shade
Water: tolerates moderate drought
Soil: nearly any well-drained soil
Growth Rate: moderate to rapid
Size: 10 to 12 feet, standard; 3 to 4 feet, dwarf
Remarks: extremely tolerant of seaside locations

White-spot Japanese pittosporum has the same habit of growth as Japanese pittosporum, and it is best used as a garden accent.

Wheeler's dwarf pittosporum is a very compact, low, mounding shrub. It is particularly effective when used as a border plant or low hedge.

Finding shrubbery that withstands heat and drought is one of the challenges of the Southern gardener, particularly those in Texas. The welcome news is Japanese pittosporum (*Pittosporum tobira*). Available in both standard and dwarf forms, pittosporum can be used in nearly any planting area, large or small, if the soil is well drained and plants are protected from excessive cold.

All pittosporum selections share several landscape features in common: they are unbelievably crisp and clean in appearance. The dense habit of growth, combined with even rosettes of leaves carried at the ends of the branches, makes the plants appear soft and inviting. At its healthiest, pittosporum forms a gentle mound of foliage that looks good when plants are either massed or used singly.

Three types of pittosporum are available commercially and they differ in use as well as in appearance. The Japanese pittosporum (*Pittosporum tobira*), with its deep-green leaves, is a subtle and versatile landscape plant and can be massed to create a screen or informal hedge. In most Southern gardens, standard pittosporum grows to a 10- to 12-foot evergreen shrub and spreads to nearly twice its height. The leaves are borne in clusters at the ends of branches. These leaves are fragrant, leathery, about 3 inches long, oblong, rounded at the tips and tend to curl under along the sides. The tiny, white to pale-yellow flowers are inconspicuous but very fragrant in late spring. Native to the Far East, pittosporum grows well in the Middle and Lower South. During severe winters, some of the plants may be partially injured; but light pruning will restore plants to good form and vigor. Pittosporum grows in either full sun or partial shade.

The variegated type, whitespot Japanese pittosporum (*P. tobira* Variegata), with creamy, white leaf markings, makes a bright accent, particularly in a lightly shaded location. At an entry or near a terrace, variegated pittosporum provides a bright spot in the garden without being gaudy or overpowering. Variegated pittosporum can be the year-round highlight of the garden when it is used in combination with the deep-green shrubbery of a similar texture, such as hollies, viburnums, or standard pittosporums. The effect is also heightened when variegated pittosporum is planted in a bed of evergreen ground cover, such as Japanese pachysandra or Japanese star jasmine. However you use variegated pittosporum, be careful not to dilute its impact by using too many of them.

Dwarf pittosporum (*Pittosporum tobira* Wheeler's Dwarf), a smaller, more compact version of the solid green pittosporum, is not as cold hardy as its parent. At maturity, in the Lower South, Wheeler's dwarf reaches a height of about 3 feet and may spread 3 to 4 feet. It is a good foundation plant, since it requires no pruning to control size and yet adds enough dimension and texture to fill empty places in the garden. Wheeler's dwarf pittosporum makes a good background plant for low-growing annuals, such as French marigold or dwarf ageratum. Another pleasing use of dwarf pittosporum is to underplant it with mondo grass. The textural contrast makes both plants distinctive, and the mondo grass acts as a living mulch, keeping the bed free of weeds. Wheeler's dwarf pittosporum also makes a splendid potted plant, used either indoors or out, and is at its best when pruned to miniature tree form.

Podocarpus
Form and texture with no substitute

AT A GLANCE
Light: full sun to partial shade
Water: moderate to drought tolerant
Soil: well-drained soil
Growth Rate: moderately slow
Size: 15 to 40 feet

No other family of shrubs grown in the South provides the same combination of plant form and leaf texture than do the podocarpus. Each podocarpus species grown in the South offers a unique combination of leaf shape, plant form, and growth habit.

The combination of an upright, loosely columnar form, which branches to the ground, and linear, evergreen foliage is unique to Japanese yew (*Podocarpus macrophyllus*). The linear leaves, about 4 inches long and ½ inch wide, create the fine texture of the tall, dense shrub. A moderately slow grower, Japanese yew will easily grow to about 15 feet high and 5 feet wide in about 15 years. The largest, oldest plants are about 40 feet tall and 15 feet wide and are often limbed up as tree forms at this large size.

Japanese yew makes an excellent clipped hedge or screen in full sun because of its density and adaptability to close clipping. It can also be used in a container, as an accent plant, in plant groupings, as a backdrop for other low-growing shrubs, or for framing large structures. When grown in partial shade, podocarpus will survive well but its growth habit will be more open. The plant grows fast in full sun and is more compact. Indoors, its height is restricted by light, container size, and other cultural factors. Podocarpus will also grow in moist soils, including sand or light clay. However, it is susceptible to root rot if planted in a poorly drained soil. Podocarpus grows best in fertile, well-drained soil. Podocarpus is also tolerant of salt spray and can be planted along coastal areas other than directly on the beach. Because of its moderately slow growth rate, podocarpus does not need heavy fertilization—once a year is adequate for most areas.

Broadleaf podocarpus (*Podocarpus nagi*), with its broader, very dark, glossy green, elliptic leaves (about 3 inches long and 1 inch wide), is more open and treelike than Japanese yew. Broadleaf podocarpus can be considered loosely pyramidal as a mature tree form, but it has a more sprawling shape than the strictly pyramidal American holly. It also branches all the way to the ground with softly hanging branches from one or more leaders. Broadleaf podocarpus requires acid soils, like azaleas or camellias; it is often utilized as an accent plant, container plant, or free-standing tree form in Florida and along the Gulf Coast in full sun or shady locations. Like Japanese yew, broadleaf podocarpus will grow about 1 foot per year and reach an ultimate height of 30 to 40 feet in the warmer locations.

African fern pine (*Podocarpus gracilior*) is less hardy than the other two species but is a good plant for outdoor use in central and south Florida and extreme south Texas. Outside of its hardiness area, the treelike shrub is used very successfully as an indoor landscape or container plant. Its weeping form and thin linear leaves, about 3 inches long and ¼ inch wide, give the plant a very graceful, soft appearance. Even the central leader of this plant arches over at the top to give a drooping effect. African fern pine is slower growing than Japanese yew and broadleaf podocarpus, and it will reach an ultimate height of about 30 feet in warmer regions outdoors.

Although its outdoor use is limited only to lower parts of Florida and Texas, African fern pine makes a handsome treelike shrub.

Japanese yew is an excellent plant for hedges or espaliers, as it is easy to contain and responds well to pruning.

AT A GLANCE
Light: full sun to shade; yellow-edge California privet requires full sun to maintain variegation
Water: moist to dry; drought resistant
Soil: extremely adaptable; sand to heavy clay
Growth Rate: moderate to fast; roundleaf Japanese privet is slow growing
Size: generally large shrubs or small trees; size varies with selection

As waxleaf privet matures, its sculptural qualities will become more evident when pruned.

Privet
Vigorous, dependable, and varied

The privets (*Ligustrum sp.*) have provided the Southern garden with the best and the worst of landscape shrubs. The very mention of the word privet sends some people running for the herbicide, while others offer only words of praise. Both reactions are valid—as long as you know which privet you are discussing.

Like many groups of plants, the privets have a few undesirable species. In certain regions of the South, Amur privet (*L. amurense*), Chinese privet (*L. sinense*), and common privet (*L. vulgare*) have totally escaped cultivation; along with honeysuckle and kudzu, they have become major landscape pests. With these exceptions, however, the privets offer dependable and versatile landscape plants.

Roundleaf Japanese privet
The roundleaf Japanese privet (*L. japonicum* Rotundifolium) is a real landscape curiosity. A slow-growing, upright plant with rounded, almost contorted, dark-green leaves, it has the unique appearance of a piece of living sculpture. Since it is so unusual, however, roundleaf Japanese privet is best reserved for special accent plantings.

Much smaller and slower growing than its parent, the waxleaf privet, this plant seldom grows to more than 4 feet high. It also differs in its dense, columnar form. But the most intriguing aspect of the roundleaf Japanese privet is its foliage. Arranged in compact whorls around each stem, the foliage has an interesting rosette appearance; the bright-green color of the young growth, which sprouts from the ends of the branches, emphasizes this flowerlike effect.

Waxleaf Privet
Waxleaf privet (*L. japonicum*) is one of the few plants you can truly call a landscape bargain. It is relatively fast growing and, therefore, it tends to be a good long-term garden investment. Waxleaf privet is extremely tolerant of growing conditions, performing equally well in heavy clay or lighter, sandy soils; it will also grow in either sun or shade.

But most importantly, waxleaf privet is valuable for its landscape versatility; it can be used in so many ways in the garden. It will quickly provide a landscape effect while creating a backdrop for future garden developments. Although it can be used for formal hedges, waxleaf privet makes an excellent informal hedge or naturalistic screen. When the lower branches are removed, waxleaf privet will develop into a handsome small evergreen tree. Since the waxleaf privet is fast growing, however, the ultimate size of the plant is an important consideration for its landscape use. A healthy plant can easily attain a height of 15 feet or more within the first 10 years; it is not unusual for older plants to be as much as 20 feet in height and 15 feet across.

Waxleaf privet also makes a durable container plant, especially when pruned into a tree-form specimen. Plants with single trunks create a distinctive, formal look when grown in containers, while multitrunked plants will have a more informal character.

Yellow-edge California Privet
The yellow-edge California privet (*L. ovalfolium* Aureo-marginatum) offers a dramatic contrast to the other privets. Its upright, arching form and fine texture give it a graceful, delicate appearance, but the color of the foliage is what really sets this plant

apart. Perhaps the most conspicuous of all the variegated plants, the light-green center of each leaf is completely surrounded with a brilliant yellow gold margin.

Although it tends to be slow growing for the first year or two, the growth rate of yellow-edge California privet accelerates considerably as the plant becomes established. It is not unusual for 3-year-old plants to be 6 feet high and wide; a mature specimen may be as much as 10 feet high and 10 to 15 feet across.

Yellow-edge California privet is sometimes used for informal hedges, but it really does not lend itself to formal applications. Frequent pruning will cause the plant to lose its brilliant variegation and will destroy the graceful, arching form. Best appreciated as an accent plant, yellow-edge California privet is especially effective when set against a dark background. A full-sun location is necessary, however, since the plant will lose its variegation in the shade.

Roundleaf Japanese privet has the unique appearance of a piece of living sculpture.

Yellow-edge California privet has delicate, variegated foliage.

Waxleaf privet accents this entry when limbed up into tree form.

Quince
A signal of early spring

AT A GLANCE
Light: full to partial sun
Water: moderate amount;
Soil: average soil
Growth Rate: moderate
Size: varies with species

Quince (*Chaenomeles sp.*) is a marvelous tangle of spines, twigs, and blossoms. It introduces spring—this champion early-blooming shrub opens the season with brilliant and soft pastel colors in late February. The sculptural flowers are simple and delicate, appearing both singly and in clusters along the spiny branches. Because of their gray brown color, the branches fade into the background. The flowers are extremely resistant to cold damage, emerging almost two weeks before the foliage and sometimes persisting for almost a month in sporadic displays. Colors range from pure white to reddish orange.

Quince spends the late spring and early summer quietly covered with deep-green foliage. It loses some leaves in July and August, revealing the large yellow fruit that can be harvested for making preserves. The leaves that remain will turn lemon yellow in the fall.

The growth habit of flowering quince is another clue to its landscape use. There are two species prevalent in the South, each with a different growth habit: Japanese quince (*Chaenomeles speciosa*) and lesser flowering quince (*C. japonica*).

Japanese quince is characteristically a large (6 to 8 feet tall), upright, rounded plant. Its shape can be put to good use in a narrow border garden between two houses; used in this manner, quince can be planted in a series of two or three with only a ground cover as a companion plant.

Lesser flowering quince displays a prostrate growth habit. Because of its dwarf size (3 to 5 feet) and random informal character, it is possible to have the profuse bloom and color diversity of quince in a wider variety of landscape locations. Lesser flowering quince makes a fine deciduous ground cover in front of an evergreen hedge or screen planting. For instance, use it to fill in underneath a waxleaf privet hedge or beneath a planting of Japanese black pine or spruce pine.

Quince grows best in average soil in full sun or partial shade; however, flower production is more profuse in a sunny location. It is heat tolerant and can take the reflected heat on the south side of a building. Although tolerant of hot, dry conditions, quince will signal water needs with a yellowing of foliage followed by leaf drop.

If planted with sufficient room to develop, quince needs little pruning. However, selected branches can be clipped and taken inside for forcing as early as January and will hold their blossoms indoors for as long as two weeks.

Plants are usually sold by color. Be sure to purchase according to types or in early spring while the plants are in bloom. Popular selections are: Texas Scarlet (*Chaenomeles japonica*), Nivalis (*C. speciosa*), Cameo (*C. speciosa*), and Toyo-Nishiki (*C. japonica*).

The dark background of pines silhouettes the delicate flowers of quince (left), while the trunk of a crepe myrtle provides a surprising accent.

The large yellow fruit of quince (right) is ornamental and edible.

Rhododendron
2 weeks of color, 52 weeks of beauty

AT A GLANCE
Light: light shade
Water: needs to be kept moist
Soil: acid, moist, well-drained soil
Growth Rate: moderately slow
Size: depends on selection
Remarks: needs heavy mulching

The stately landscape effects that are achieved with rhododendrons can be attributed to their handsome form and foliage. Whether it is the wandering, twisting limbs of the giant rosebay or the friendly, mounding growth of the smaller selections, the look is in the garden year-round—the blossoms are a two-week bonus in the spring.

But, oh, what a bonus. Few plants pop into color like rhododendrons. The magnificent collective flowers, with as many as 24 individual flowers in a single cluster, have the visual impact of a bouquet. In fact, the flowers are generally called trusses because they are so massive. In addition, rhododendron flowers occur in terminal displays—held out at the end of the stems and emerging from a characteristic rosette of leaves. The large, colorful trusses seem to be resting on a bed of foliage—bright flower color displayed against the green background of the foliage. There is a wide range of color—from white to yellow, to pinks and reds, to lavender and deep purple. There can be a color for any landscape where the plants will thrive; and for the two weeks out of the year that they are in bloom, it is one of the most majestic color shows available in a garden. Unlike their flamboyant cousins, the azaleas, rhododendrons bequeath a certain dignity to their display—a show that appears at once joyous, but reserved. This imparts a classic character to the rhododendron, and few plants are as enduring or as endearing. Yet too often rhododendrons are purchased solely for their flowers while the clean, regal look that a mass planting can bring to a shady home landscape remains neglected.

The characteristic growth habit of rhododendrons is a key to their landscape use. If the plant is healthy, the new growth reaches for the available light, giving the foliage an upturned, happy look; the lower leaves appear to rest on the ground (in fact, they can take root), giving the plant a graceful transition to a lawn or ground cover. For this reason, rhododendrons rarely require companion plants to layer them to the ground. Rhododendrons should be used boldly in the landscape: as a sweeping evergreen border, lining a woodland path, or filling in a shady planting area. Along a narrow pathway, the lustrous, deep-green foliage can be touched, and the subtly fragrant flowers of some selections can be appreciated. If you lack sufficient room for an enclosed garden walk, plant rhododendrons as a curving border. When planted in this manner, they will lean out from beneath the tree canopy and flow gracefully to the ground.

Rhododendrons work well when planted in a mass beneath the canopy of most trees, especially those trees with high branches. In this type of planting, they can be used to define space in the landscape and balance wide expanses of lawn. In a similar use, they make a handsome replacement for sun-loving understory plants that have been shaded out by trees. They are also a fine choice for enclosing private spaces, such as a terrace.

Most rhododendrons are too large at maturity to make a satisfactory foundation planting, but there are some low-growing selections (4 to 6 feet) that may be suited for this purpose. However, the burgeoning growth of rhododendrons can be turned to advantage. Rosebay (*Rhododendron maximum*) may be planted to eventually create a ceiling of flowers and foliage or a walkway through trunks and branches. The effect is spectacular, but it takes 10 to 15 years.

The flower clusters of hybrid rhododendrons may be as large as 1 to 2 feet in diameter.

Rhododendrons and azaleas are combined to create privacy around an outdoor sitting area.

The evergreen foliage of rhododendrons makes them a fine choice for border plantings under existing shade trees. Notice the characteristic upturned growth habit of the lower leaves.

While masses of rhododendrons work best, one or several plants make a splendid specimen planting. However, they should be considered estate-scale plants, demanding a great deal of room and prominence. In the mountains rhododendrons cover the hills in a great maze of evergreen mounds that one can walk in, through, around, and about. A specimen planting should allow similar space so the plant can develop its full form and mature size. In the small garden, one rhododendron may be enough to provide the effect desired without dominating the entire garden. Plant in a central location or to anchor an empty corner, but plan for it to fill in 4 or 5 feet of space.

If planted properly, rhododendrons require little annual care (see Planting Rhododendrons on page 150). In addition, the plant signals exactly what it needs. Rhododendrons require moist soil and excellent drainage; they will signal a lack of water by drooping their leaves. It is best to see that they are watered thoroughly every 10 to 14 days. Always be sure the bed is draining properly, as drowning kills many rhododendrons. Should the leaves turn brittle and brown from the edges to the middle during winter, it indicates the plant is suffering windburn. This is a signal to water, even if the ground is frozen. The water in the ground is not available to the plant, and its broad leaves make it susceptible to dehydration.

Not only is the initial mulch important, maintaining a heavy mulch can provide almost all the care these plants need. Mulching heavily keeps moisture around the roots; as the mulch decomposes, it helps maintain the proper pH of the soil. In addition, mulch will serve as insulation in the winter, protecting the roots from severe cold. Many mulches will work, but pine straw and pine bark are recommended.

Rhododendrons rarely need food. Most feeding is necessary only to correct the soil pH or to amend any slight iron deficiency. Regardless of the feeding, never hoe or work the

The open, branching habit of this specimen gives scale to an entrance wall.

Shrubs

fertilizer into the soil around the plant. The risk of destroying the root network of these surface feeders is too great. If you do fertilize, just sprinkle it lightly on the ground and water thoroughly.

For a general feeding, organic fertilizers such as cottonseed meal or soybean meal are recommended. But a commercial azalea-camellia food will provide nitrogen in an ammonium compound and also does a good job. Super-phosphate applied in late winter or early spring will ensure bud set and promote the intensity of color. Corrective feeding may be needed if the following conditions exist. *Improper pH*: Test the soil periodically. If the pH ranges above 5.5, add ferrous sulfate to raise the acidity. The soil test report will also help you determine how much material is needed to maintain pH at the correct level. Most organic mulches will aid in maintaining proper acidity. *Chlorosis or iron deficiency*: Yellow discoloration of the leaves indicates this condition. It can be corrected with iron chelate. Since this material can be toxic, carefully follow the manufacturer's instructions for application.

When purchasing young rhododendrons for planting, do not be fooled by their shape. Because they are nursery grown, they will be stiff and upright and may seem too rigid and ungainly. But as plants mature, they spread out and the foliage weeps slightly. Bear in mind that it will take a few years for the plantings to loosen up and achieve their

The foliage of rhododendrons may be as coarse and large as that of sweetbay magnolias.

When using rhododendrons in specimen plantings, allow ample room for the plants to reach mature size and form.

SELECTIONS FOR THE SOUTH

Color	Tall (12 to 18 feet*)	Medium (6 to 12 feet)	Low (4 to 6 feet)
Lavender	*Catawbiense Grandiflorum *Roseum Elegans	Blue Peter Caroline**	Sapphire
Pink	Anna Rose Whitney** Cecile Roseum Superbum	Holden Van Nes Sensation** Vernus·	*Pink Cameo Pioneer *P.J.M.
Purple		Purpureum Grandiflorum	
Red	*Cynthia Noyo Chief	*America *Nova Zembla** Vulcan	Elizabeth Jean Marie de Montague
Rose			Boule de Rose
Rose Red		Ignatius Sargent	
White	*Album Elegans County of York White Pearl	*Catawbiense Album *Gomer Waterer Mrs. Tom H. Lowinsky	Boule de Neige *Cunningham's White Snow Lady
Yellow		Butterfly Old Copper**	Unique**

* Size after 15 to 20 years under ideal conditions
** May grow in Lower South

Shrubs

Proper bed preparation is essential. Space plants a minimum of 4½ feet apart, and add finely ground bark to the shallow dish-shaped excavation that will receive each plant.

Set the plant so the top of the root ball is 3 to 5 inches above the level of the bed; then carefully mound the prepared soil up around the root ball.

characteristic growth habit. So when selecting rhododendrons, look for well-branched, full plants. Limbs should be close to the ground and the foliage bright and healthy looking. The leaves should be turned upward, not drooping.

While the Upper South can grow a wider range of sizes and species, there are selections that may do well in the Middle and Lower South. Refer to the chart for selections known to perform well throughout the South.

Planting Rhododendrons

Proper planting assures young rhododendrons of a good start and will drastically reduce the need for maintenance. Locate rhododendrons in a part of the garden that is partially shaded. While they can stand warm weather, direct searing sun will inhibit growth severely and can destroy the plants. Ideally, rhododendrons should be planted in rich, friable, loamy, acid soil (pH range of 4.5 to 5.5) that is high in organic matter. Good drainage is a must. Depending on the site, extensive soil preparation may be needed. But it is extremely important that beds be properly prepared. This means tilling a bed 4 or 5 feet wider than the size of the root ball or container. It is preferable to do this the season before you plant to allow time for the soil to weather and break up. Following are the basic steps on bed preparation and planting.

—Till the soil in the bed vigorously, a minimum of 12 inches deep. Break up all soil, leaving no clods. Check the quality of the soil by squeezing a handful. If it clumps together in a claylike mass, it needs extensive work, so bring in sand and finely shredded or ground bark, and till it in until the soil is loose and friable. But if the soil spills out of your hand like sand, a combination of equal parts topsoil and fine bark will need to be worked in to provide a good growing medium.

—In almost every instance (unless other rhododendrons grow naturally nearby), plan to work finely ground bark into the soil at the specific location of each plant. This is in addition to any bark tilled into the original bed. This will ensure a porous soil for good drainage, provide a highly organic growing medium that is naturally acid, and help keep sufficient moisture around the roots in order to keep them from drying out.

—When planting, do not dig a hole in the prepared bed. Instead, make a shallow dish-shaped excavation with your hands; then set the rhododendron in the center of the dish. The top of the root ball should be 3 to 5 inches above the level of the bed. Carefully mound the loose soil in the bed around the root ball, and press it gently into place. Planting in this fashion will facilitate drainage and allow the plant to spread its surface root system downward into the bed.

—After planting, mulch the plant with 4 to 5 inches of loose pine straw; then soak the bed thoroughly.

Note: Hybrid rhododendrons are not generally grown in the Lower South.

Spirea
Rugged, graceful, and flowering

With names like baby's breath and bridal wreath, spireas (*Spiraea sp.*) sound interesting. These hardy shrubs have been a part of gardening for many generations, but recently they seem to be thought of as too old-fashioned for contemporary gardens. However, considering their beauty, durability, and ease of maintenance, there is nothing out-of-date about spireas.

Among the hardiest of the Southern deciduous shrubs, the spireas require a minimum of attention to keep them in top condition. The fact that they are sometimes found in overgrown or even abandoned gardens, where they have survived for years with no maintenance, attests to their dependability. But spireas are more than simply rugged. Their graceful forms, delightful flowers, and attractive foliages provide varied effects throughout the seasons. Adaptable to almost any soil, including heavy clays, spireas perform best in lighter, well-drained soils that are rich in organic matter. Although they tolerate a fair amount of shade, full sun is necessary for optimum flower production.

Because spireas have such similar cultural requirements, selecting the right one for a garden is simply a matter of personal preference. Since they do vary in size, foliage texture, and time of bloom, however, a brief outline of the more familiar spireas follows.

AT A GLANCE
Light: full sun to partial shade
Water: moderate amount
Soil: fertile to poor soil
Growth Rate: rapid
Size: 2 to 12 feet

Anthony Waterer Bumalda Spirea

The selection of Anthony Waterer (*S.* x *bumalda* Anthony Waterer) is ideally suited for Southern gardens. It tolerates heat and drought remarkably well but can also take the heavy rainfall and humidity of Southern summers. A dense, compact plant with an irregular, spreading habit of growth, its deeply serrated, matte-green leaves give Anthony Waterer spirea a more delicate appearance than might be expected from such a rugged plant. Rarely growing to more than 2 feet high and 2 to 3 feet wide, this spirea is a good choice for sunny locations where space is limited, or it may be used as an accent plant for

Bridal wreath spirea is the most upright of all the spireas when it is left unpruned.

Vanhoutte spirea is a mass of white flowers in spring but blooms much earlier than a similar selection, Reeves spirea.

The delicate dark-green foliage of bridal wreath in summer gives way to a brilliant orange red fall color display.

Anthony Waterer bumalda spirea is a basic green in spring and produces deep-magenta flowers in summer.

entrances or other prominent locations. The deep magenta flowers of Anthony Waterer, which are arranged in flat-topped clusters, ornament this little plant throughout the heat of summer. Although they never completely cover the plant, as do the flowers of the spring-blooming spireas, there is hardly any time from June until September when you cannot find at least a few of the brightly-colored blossoms—plus a few stems with white to yellow foliage which adds an extra spark of interest.

Bridal Wreath Spirea

Bridal wreath spirea (*S. prunifolia*) is an upright-growing, vase-shaped plant with dark-green, glossy leaves. Although it may get to be as much as 6 feet high and 5 or 6 feet wide, bridal wreath is a relatively slow-growing plant, so a height and spread of 3 to 4 feet are more typical. Blooming several weeks after Thunberg spirea (see below), the ¼-inch, powder pufflike flowers of bridal wreath line the dark-brown branches with a pure white filigree. Since it flowers about the same time as most azaleas, the white blossoms of bridal wreath make it a good companion for these plants; later in the season the dark-green, finely textured foliage of bridal wreath makes a handsome background for summer annuals as well. Bridal wreath is also the best of the spireas for autumn color. Starting in late summer, the foliage gradually changes from yellow green to orange and finally to brilliant red. During the winter, the dark-brown, arching branches of the bridal wreath offer an attractive wandlike effect.

Garland Spirea

Garland spirea (*S. x arguta*) is almost identical to Thunberg spirea; the two are sometimes confused in the retail trade. However, there is one big difference: Garland spirea blooms in mid-May—substantially later than the baby's breath spirea. So if the early flowers are desired, plants should be selected while they are in bloom. Otherwise, they may be disappointing.

Reeves Spirea

Reeves spirea (*S. cantoniensis*) is, perhaps, the most elegant of the spireas. It has a graceful, arching form, medium-fine texture, and blue green, deeply serrated foliage. Growing to a height and spread of 4 to 5 feet, the mounded, almost symmetrical growth habit of Reeves spirea also gives it a more formal appearance than the other spireas listed here. The flowers of Reeves spirea are carried in dense, bouquetlike clusters down the length of every stem; when the plant is in bloom, it has the appearance of a foaming white fountain. Reeves spirea comes into flower about the time the bridal wreath spirea starts to fade, so a combination of these plants provides a prolonged display of white throughout the spring. Although Reeves spirea does not take on significant autumn color, the blue green foliage is quite persistent, sometimes remaining on the plant into the early winter. Once the leaves are gone, the plant reveals the handsome, delicate quality of the dark-brown branches.

Thunberg Spirea

Thunberg spirea (*S. thunbergii*), or baby's breath spirea as it frequently is known, is the earliest blooming member of the group. Distinguished by its broadly rounded, arching form, dense twiggy structure, and delicate finely textured foliage, Thunberg spirea sometimes starts to bloom as early as January. The dainty, white, clustered flowers always precede the foliage. The leaves of Thunberg spirea are very small, less than ¼ inch wide, and rarely more than 1½ inches long with a light, fluffy look. Bright yellow green throughout the growing season, the foliage turns yellow gold or orange in the autumn and may persist until Thanksgiving. A somewhat slow-growing plant, Thunberg spirea may attain a height and spread of 6 feet after many years, but 4 to 5 feet high and wide is a more typical size. The plant can be kept below 3 feet by simply removing older branches at the ground line. Pruning should be done in spring, after the flowers have faded.

Vanhoutte Spirea

In many ways, Vanhoutte spirea (*S.* x *vanhouttei*) appears to be a larger version of Reeves spirea. Frequently growing to 6 feet high and spreading to as much as 5 or 6 feet wide, Vanhoutte is more upright than Reeves spirea, with a tendency to be more open at the base. Also, the flowerets are single rather than double. Since its form becomes somewhat ungainly with maturity, Vanhoutte spirea is better suited for background plantings than as a free-standing specimen. The many-flowering clusters of Vanhoutte spirea also resemble those of Reeves, but they appear as much as two weeks later in the season. For this reason, Reeves and Vanhoutte spireas are frequently planted together for a longer flowering effect.

Note: The use of spireas in Florida is limited to areas north of Gainesville and to the panhandle regions. Even in Gainesville, their blooming quality is somewhat sparse. On the other hand, in Tallahassee and areas further west, their blooming character is much improved.

Reeves spirea produces masses of white flowers against blue green foliage in early spring.

Double bridal wreath spirea may be pruned to the ground after flowering to produce a blooming stemlike mass the following spring.

Reeves spirea has an upright but arching form and a mounding habit of growth.

Shrubs

Viburnum
Undervalued, underused, and undiscovered

Sweet viburnum works well in courtyards where a confined root system is a must.

The viburnums are a widespread and incredibly diverse group of plants that will fit any landscape or garden location, whether sunny or shady, wet or dry. And remarkably, it is possible to choose from at least four or five species in every part of the South except Florida. Perhaps one of the puzzling features of this plant genus is its diversity. More than 200 types are known and most of them are available somewhere in the nursery trade. They are both evergreen and deciduous, fragrant and nonfragrant; and they vary widely in form, flowering habits, and landscape appearance. However, they share several characteristics that make them readily identifiable as a group. All viburnums have oppositely arranged, simple leaves and bear flowers in terminal (end of the branches) panicles or umbrellalike cymes (a flower cluster where the central flower usually opens first).

Selecting viburnums is a delightful dilemma—the group is so diverse that there can be a featured viburnum in every garden, perhaps with a viburnum planting used as a backdrop. But, as with any group of plants, the exact effect that is needed in your garden should determine the species. If you want to use the plant as a screen or to create privacy, then one of the evergreen plants would be best. Gardeners who want a fragrant garden can plant Judd viburnum, Korean spice viburnum, Burkwood viburnum, or the old-fashioned favorite sweet viburnum. If showy flowers are what is needed in the landscape, then Southern black haw, Chinese snowball, or doublefile viburnum would be an excellent choice. For late summer and autumn display, cranberry viburnum, Wright viburnum, or hobblebush make superb landscape plants because of their fall color and heavy crop of berries. Keep the season in mind; plant one of these fine and underused shrubs.

The landscape uses of viburnums usually depend on the individual species or selection. And the entire group is more easily discussed when the individual plants are grouped into two categories: deciduous and evergreen viburnums. The deciduous viburnums are more varied than the evergreen selections. In particular, the flowering characteristics of the deciduous species exhibit greater diversity than their evergreen counterparts.

Deciduous Viburnums

Burkwood viburnum (*Viburnum* x *burkwoodii*) is an upright, irregularly branched plant with an informal, vase-shaped habit of growth. The plant is open and light, and not heavily foliated. The foliage is fuzzy, deeply furrowed or grooved, and attractive. The heavily fragrant, pinkish-to-white flower clusters are borne in early May and are followed by black fruit that is of little ornamental value. The plant is a good free-form border plant, reaching an eventual height of about 10 to 12 feet. Since the foliage is sparse, it is not an adequate screening plant and is best displayed against either a neutral backdrop, such as a wall or fence, or against the foliage of an evergreen planting. Burkwood viburnum is a vigorous grower in either full sun or partial shade and is not particular about soil.

A tall, upright, and spreading deciduous shrub, Chinese snowball (*V. macrocephalum* Sterile) reaches a height of 12 feet or more at maturity and attains a nearly equal spread. Chinese snowball makes a stunning accent plant, especially in mid-spring when the plant bursts into bloom and is laden with white, globular flower clusters measuring 6 inches or more across. Because of its massive, upright form, Chinese snowball should be located out in the landscape instead of being used as a foundation plant. In small gardens, it is large enough to be totally overwhelming. In larger landscapes, Chinese snowball is the perfect form to strongly accent pyramidal evergreens, such as Southern magnolia, American holly, or, in the Upper South, white pine or hemlock. Locate Chinese snowball in either full sun or partial shade. The plant is not particular about soil, provided the planting site is well drained and not so heavy in clay content that the surface is prone to crust and crack during dry weather.

Cranberry bush viburnum (*V. opulus*) is one of the most decorative of the deciduous viburnums. The plant is a bushy, upright grower with dense, maplelike foliage. In spring, the white flowers appear in broad, flat-topped cymes; the marginal flowers of these cymes are showy and infertile. In late summer, the fruit from the fertile flowers matures into a vivid cranberry red cluster that contrasts brightly with the dark, rough, green foliage. In fall, the entire plant turns vivid red and, when the leaves fall, the fruit remains as ornamentation. Several selections are available including Compactum, which is a dense dwarf reaching only 5 or 6 feet, and Roseum, the common snowball of old gardens, which has larger, sterile flowers. Cranberry bush viburnum is an excellent plant for naturalizing or for use in border plantings. It is dense enough to be used as a free-form screen or hedge but will look better in the landscape if it is silhouetted against a neutral or evergreen backdrop. Mature plants will reach about 12 feet. It tolerates many kinds of soil and will flower and produce more berries if planted in a full-sun location.

Doublefile viburnum (*V. plicatum* Tomentosum) is a striking contrast to the form and flowering habits of other viburnums. A selection or type of Japanese snowball (*V. plicatum*), doublefile is a small tree that will reach 15 to 20 feet tall. The plant is horizontally branched; the foliage layers off the top of the branches and reinforces the branch structure of the plant. When in flower, in late April or early May, the tree is breathtakingly attractive; the cymes are carried on the top of the branches and layer along the limbs like epaulettes. In fall, the plant turns vivid scarlet.

Fragrant snowball (*V. x carlcephalum*) is one of the most desirable hybrid viburnums for the garden. A cross between Korean spice viburnum (*V. carlesii*) and Chinese snowball (*V. macrocephalum*), fragrant snowball is an upright, open shrub with 5-inch fragrant flowers. The flowers appear densely in April or May. The foliage is wide and coarse, and in the fall, the color is orange brown. The growth habit makes it more suited to use as a spring accent plant in a border or as an ornamental located near a terrace where the fragrance can be enjoyed. Fragrant snowball is exceptionally cold hardy. In the Upper and Piedmont South, it may be planted in full sun, but fragrant snowball prefers light shade in the warmer regions of the Piedmont and Coastal Plains.

Hobblebush (*V. alnifolium*) is a well-known plant in the Upper and Piedmont South, particularly in the mountain areas. This native, which will reach 15 feet or more with wandering twisting limbs, brings an extraordinary amount of color into the understory in fall. The broad, wide leaves, which are light green throughout the spring and summer, gradually turn yellow and then ultimately flush to a deep claret. Hobblebush is a plant for

The flowers of doublefile viburnum layer much as those of dogwoods do—a contrast to the flowering habits of most viburnums.

Cranberry bush viburnum is noted for its outstanding fall fruit display.

Shrubs

Sweet viburnum (above) is popular as a loosely pruned hedge in many Florida landscapes.

The flowers of Korean spice viburnum (below) are among the most fragrant of the species.

most wooded locations and so it is an excellent plant for naturalizing in shaded plantings. The flowers are borne on flat-topped cymes in early spring. The marginal flowers of the cymes are infertile and extremely showy. The fertile flowers, in the center of cyme, turn into black fruit that is gathered by mountain folk and used to make jellies.

Judd viburnum (*V.* x *juddii*) is a broad-spreading shrub that bears fragrant flowers in 3-inch clusters in April or May. The foliage covers the shrub in a dense, bushy manner that makes it suitable to use as a screening plant or deciduous hedge. At mature height, the hybrid rarely reaches over 8 feet tall. The flower clusters are followed by reddish black fruit which may be extremely ornamental. Judd viburnums adapt to many soil conditions but will flower best if planted in full to partial sun.

Korean spice viburnum (*V. carlesii*) is one of the standbys of its group. This shrub has been popular for many generations and with good reason. It is a dependable grower in sunny or shady locations and produces 3-inch, globe-shaped clusters of fragrant flowers. The flowers appear in early spring and are pinkish to white in color. They are followed by black fruit that becomes noticeable in midsummer. Korean spice viburnum is not by itself dense enough to create a screen but it mingles well in a mixed border and provides a striking fragrant accent in the spring landscape. Korean spice is an extremely hardy plant and will grow well throughout the Upper and Piedmont South and slightly protected locations in the Lower South.

Maple-leaf viburnum (*V. acerifolium*) is native to mixed hardwood forests throughout much of the South. This loose, irregularly growing shrub rarely reaches over 5 feet in height. Its habit of growth makes it an excellent shrub for naturalizing in mixed borders or in shady wooded settings. The plant grows in an upright clump and suckers heavily. Once established, it requires very little care. Maple-leaf viburnum will grow in any soil of medium fertility. It is shallow rooted and requires annual mulching to protect the root system. It grows in all but the warmer parts of the South. April and May bring clusters of flowers that project 2 or 3 inches above the leaves. The fruit is blue black. One of the most attractive features of this shrub is that it brings fall color into the woods beneath the understory trees—the dark-green, maple-shaped leaves turn a purple rose to red in autumn.

Southern black haw (*V. rufidulum*) is an old standby native small tree or large shrub, which eventually reaches 25 feet in height. Best used as a small accent or border tree, Southern black haw becomes covered with clusters of white flowers in late April and early May. The flower show will hold for 10 days to two weeks. The fertile flowers develop into blue black fruit that makes exceptionally good wildlife food and has a striking ornamental appearance. In fall, the tree turns a reddish orange color. Since the plant is native and has few, if any, diseases or pests, it is a superior ornamental that should be more widely planted. Southern black haw is an excellent understory tree or large shrub for the entire South.

Tea viburnum (*V. setigerum*) is one of the best of the upright forms of this genus. The plant is covered with long foliage that makes a dense and visually impenetrable plant.

Showy flowers are borne in late spring and are followed by clusters of bright-red fruit that dangle against the green foliage. In landscape use and hardiness, the plant is extremely close to cranberry bush and should be used similarly in borders or in the open as specimens.

Wright viburnum (*V. wrightii*) is a plant more noted for the fall fruiting show than for its springtime flowers; in fact, many people consider this plant to be the best of all viburnums. Resembling maple-leaf viburnum in growth habit, Wright viburnum is upright and stemmy in form, and thus is best used as a specimen in a border or before an evergreen planting. Because of the comparatively inconspicuous flower show, the plant has its best season beginning in August when the large (to 3 inches) clusters of cranberry-size fruit appear. Wright viburnum will tolerate full sun to partial shade and a wide variety of soil conditions. It will do best in the Piedmont and Upper South and is particularly tolerant of severely cold weather.

Evergreen Viburnums

Like any group of plants, the evergreen viburnums are subject to the climate conditions of the region where they are planted; for example, as some of the plants are taken out of their hardiness range or to the extreme northern edge of it, the foliage will not remain dense. For the most part, however, the foliage of the following selections is persistent and handsome year-round.

David viburnum (*V. davidii*) is an attractive, low-growing type that rarely reaches over 3 feet in height. The foliage is deep, dark green, leathery in texture and extremely rugose, which makes the plant an extraordinary specimen. The flowers are white and dense, sometimes as much as 3 inches across, followed by blue fruit that appears in late summer or early fall. The plant is basically stoleniferous, spreading underground to form a large clump. David viburnum has a loose and irregular form of growth that is informal in character. In fact, the plant has a texture that is reminiscent of drooping leucothöe. It can be used effectively either as a single specimen in a bed of ground cover, for example, or as a low mass planting in a border. David viburnum is adaptable to either sun or partial sun and will grow throughout the Lower and Middle South.

Japanese viburnum (*V. japonicum*) is widely used as screening planting and as an accent plant throughout the Piedmont and Lower South. It is an excellent plant for the Coastal Plains, since it will tolerate the heat and direct sun. Japanese viburnum is a strongly upright grower with thick, leathery evergreen foliage. The plant is leggy when young, with leaders reaching a height of about 7 to 8 feet and often higher under ideal growing conditions. When planted as a dense screen, Japanese viburnum should be spaced no more than 4 feet apart. The flowers are very fragrant and appear in showy white clusters in late spring and early summer. They are followed by a small amount of bright-red fruit. Both flowering and fruiting are attractive, but this plant is most in demand for its strongly pyramidal form of growth and handsome glossy foliage. The plant is not particular about soils and is hardy everywhere but the extreme Upper South.

Laurustinus viburnum (*V. tinus*) is considered an indispensable shrub for the Lower

Japanese viburnum has a very upright habit of growth, and its foliage is a lustrous green but may be as coarse as that of Southern magnolia.

A typical flower cluster of the deciduous viburnums may easily last for two weeks.

Shrubs

Leatherleaf viburnum (above) has a bronze brown to deep-green, leathery foliage. In a favorable location, it may grow 10 to 12 feet tall.

Leatherleaf viburnums (below) produce bright-red fruit which turns black in late fall.

South. Also, it is possible to plant it in sheltered locations of the Piedmont and Upper South. The foliage is dense, medium in texture, and slightly smaller than the leaves of sweet viburnum. The flowers are pinkish to white and emerge from buds that are formed in late summer. Laurustinus always seems ready to break into bloom, and it is not unusual for this shrub to bloom in the warm days of December in the Lower South. Since the flowers are so anxious to open, it can be forced inside for a cheery winter look at spring. The flowers are followed by ornamental blue black fruit. Laurustinus may be used either as a free-form specimen or a clipped hedge. It is a fine plant to feature in the landscape. The plant is upright and rounded in form and, in favorable locations, will reach 10 feet in height. It grows well in either full sun or shade and, in fact, is suited for use in poor soils.

Leatherleaf viburnum (*V. rhytidophyllum*) is a highly adaptable plant that will grow well in most regions of the South. It may not tolerate the extreme summer heat of the Gulf South, but it is one of the most cold hardy of the viburnums. The foliage appears droopy in the colder regions of the South in winter. The foliage of leatherleaf viburnum is its most striking attraction. The leaves are long and narrow, deeply furrowed, and fuzzy, looking wrinkled and worn. Yellowish white flowers, which are not particularly showy, appear in large clusters in mid-spring and are followed by bright-red fruit that turns black late in fall. The plant is attractive and may be used in shady locations as a substitute for rosebay rhododendron. In full sun, the plant is upright and rounded in a habit, sending vigorous leaders up 10 to 12 feet tall (the mature height in most circumstances). Leatherleaf viburnums are excellent free-form screening plants that should never be pruned. They are frequently planted as a mass and make a dense screen. The plants can be located in full sun, but will grow much better in partial sun or shade.

Sandankwa viburnum (*V. suspensum*) generally reaches about 6 feet in height and forms a rounded, evergreen mass in the landscape. The foliage is rounded and slightly toothed. Pinkish white fragrant flowers emerge in early summer and are followed by bright-red fruit. Basically a Lower South viburnum, Sandankwa is adapted to both informal plantings and more refined or formal landscape plantings. This shrub does not like direct sun and will grow best in partial shade in a soil that has a lot of organic matter.

Sweet viburnum (*V. awabuki*) is one of the most attractive and handsome of the evergreen viburnums. This Lower and Coastal South plant is widely available in the nursery trade under another botanical name (*V. odoratissimum*). As the former specific name implies, the plant is fragrant. The white, fertile flowers appear in early spring and completely cover the plant. The fruit that follows is initially red and then turns black. Due to the early flowering characteristics, fruit may not appear in years with late spring frosts. Sweet viburnum is a prized plant, although it is frequently used to perform many functional landscape tasks, such as screens or clipped hedges. The evergreen foliage can be 6 inches long, and it covers the plant to create a visually impenetrable specimen. The foliage is deep, dark, leathery green, attractive and is sufficient reason to use the plant. Sweet viburnum serves well as either a specimen, where it will become rounded and full and reach 10 feet or more in height and breadth, or as a free-form screen or clipped hedge.

Wax Myrtle
A shrub or a tree

Wax myrtle (*Myrica cerifera*) has been a popular native landscape plant in Southern gardens since the early colonies. Wax myrtle is mentioned frequently in the journals of colonial gardeners from Virginia and the Carolinas, and its use in Williamsburg dates back to 1699; it also was considered among the finest native garden shrubs in French Louisiana.

There are many reasons for wax myrtle's popularity. Because this evergreen is native to the South, it requires little maintenance. Wax myrtle tolerates a wide variety of soil types and even grows in the salt spray and sandy soil found along the coast. It will grow in sun or shade and has almost no problems with insects and diseases. This plant is completely cold hardy, and it also withstands heat and prolonged periods of drought without serious effect.

When the lower branches are removed to reveal the silver gray trunks, wax myrtle can be grown as a shrub or as a small tree in the landscape. Use it to add a sculptural accent to a small courtyard or entrance planting, or group several to create a shaded retreat around a patio or terrace. As a shrub, wax myrtle can be used as a dense, large-scale screen or naturalistic hedge. If it gets too large for the location, reduce its size by removing entire branches rather than pruning it. Shearing will destroy the form and cause the plant to become more open.

The soft, delicate texture of wax myrtle blends well with a variety of other landscape plants; but the combination of a wax myrtle hedge and tall, open pines is especially attractive. Along the margins of the garden, the evergreen foliage provides a good background for such deciduous plants as oakleaf hydrangea, sumac, and forsythia. Mixed with other evergreens, the grayish foliage creates interesting color contrast, making the darker greens of juniper, magnolia, and Florida anise tree seem even richer or darker. Because of its durability, wax myrtle has found its way from the home landscape into the landscape plantings of Southern cities. It makes an excellent street tree or container plant; and due to its ability to withstand temperature extremes, wax myrtle is a good choice for parking lots and other dry, exposed locations where other trees would fail.

AT A GLANCE
Light: full sun to shade
Water: moist to dry; drought resistant
Soil: very adaptable—sand to heavy clay; resists salt spray along coast
Growth Rate: moderate to rapid
Size: large shrub or small tree; to 10 feet tall and 8 feet wide

When the lower branches of wax myrtle are removed (right), this evergreen becomes a handsome small tree that creates an interesting sculptural effect in the landscape.

Planted along a property line, this row of tree-form wax myrtles (left) helps define the limits of the garden and provides enclosure without completely blocking views.

AT A GLANCE
Light: full to partial sun
Water: moderate amount
Soil: any soil but will thrive
in sandy loam
Growth Rate: rapid
Size: 15 feet in height

Winter Honeysuckle
The sweet smell of winter

If the temperature reaches above 60 degrees in winter months, you may get an early breath of spring from winter honeysuckle (*Lonicera fragrantissima*). From December into the coldest winter days, the plant is ready to burst into bloom; all it needs is a warm day. The flowers do not appear all at once, however, but rather as sporadic blooms all over the shrub. Thus, the fragrance is protracted throughout winter and can actually occur from December through April. The delicately sweet fragrance, which gave this deciduous shrub the widely used common name, breath-of-spring, is one of the garden's most delightful signs of the season to follow.

Sadly, winter honeysuckle is one of the forgotten deciduous plants; it is overlooked when gardeners select plants for the landscape. This is hard to understand since the plant is hardy, durable, and tolerant of almost any soil condition from the Coastal Plains to the mountains.

The individual, rounded leaves are arranged oppositely on the stem, coming to a point at the end. These eye-catching leaves are usually 1½ to 2 inches long and almost as wide. After the foliage emerges, winter honeysuckle becomes a plant in motion in the landscape. The upright, arching form can reach as much as 10 feet overall. The branches are long and willowy and move with the slightest stirring in the air. In fall, the foliage turns yellow. Winter finds the plant a tangle of light-colored branches that still makes a visually dense screen.

Often this freely branching and wonderfully informal plant is subject to merciless pruning, occasionally because it is planted in a location that is far too small for its mature size. This misdirected effort to confine the plant destroys the natural form. Should the plant have to be trimmed (to take a branch to force indoors, for example), thin it by selectively removing entire stems, thus retaining the free-form growth habit. Remember also to prune immediately after flowering, since the plant sets buds on the previous year's growth. Accordingly, winter honeysuckle should never be planted where it must be pruned. Instead, set the plant out in the landscape as a free-form border or as a backdrop plant for later-flowering plants.

The summer foliage of winter honeysuckle (left) presents a coarse medium in the landscape.

Winter honeysuckle (right) arches informally over this retaining wall; it is also popular as a screening plant in summer.

The springtime display of a single tree, the flowering dogwood, is one of the most anticipated events in the Southern landscape. And since it offers equally delightful qualities throughout the year, the dogwood is a testament to the magic that small ornamental trees can bring to gardens. If large trees create the majesty and grandeur of a garden, and shrubs establish the character of its spaces, then to the small trees falls the task of blending these two elements. Larger than most shrubs and yet diminuitive compared to major trees, the small trees form a vital link between a garden's ceiling and its floor.

While they are most often appreciated for their ornamental value, small trees can have a powerful design expression in the landscape, too. They can enhance the sense of scale within a garden, provide a wealth of seasonal effects, and bring a special intimacy to the landscape composition. This group of plants is so diverse in terms of cultural requirements, habits of growth, and overall appearances that there is no easy way to generalize the landscape applications of small trees. It is extremely difficult, for example, to offer a

Small Trees
Blending the large and the small elements of the garden

Star magnolia, page 194.

Redbud, page 179.

161

Crabapple, page 168.

Star magnolia and common boxwood, pages 194 and 96.

Bradford pear, page 165.

design recommendation that embraces both myrobalan plum and windmill palm; and yet these trees take on surprisingly similar roles in their respective regions. Since they each have a distinction that cannot be reproduced with any other plant, their placement in the garden must reflect this individuality. So, uniqueness is the key to using small trees in the landscape. They must be planted with deliberation, with a full appreciation for their particular merits, and with an eye for how they amplify, or contrast with, the other features in a garden.

Accepting this basic principle of design, it is not surprising that small trees are used primarily for their ornamental value. Given their distinctive forms, compact sizes, and seasonal displays of flowers, fruit, or foliages, it only seems appropriate that small trees be used as accent plants. Set against a neutral background such as an evergreen hedge, the flowers and foliage effects of Japanese maple, Chinese dogwood, star magnolia, and peach are displayed to excellent advantage. The delicate texture and interesting branching of trees like parsley hawthorn, Jerusalem thorn, and European fan palm, however, seem especially well suited to architectural backgrounds. But small trees are not limited to single, specimen uses. A grove of Chinese tallow trees, Yoshino cherries, yellowwoods, or redbuds can bring dramatic seasonal and spatial qualities to the landscape. Planted in a naturalistic manner, they create a pleasant woodland feeling for suburban or even city gardens.

Geometric plantings of small trees are also very interesting. A row of cabbage palms, Savannah hollies, crepe myrtles, or other upright trees creates dynamic line and rhythm in the landscape; when these trees are planted in a double row, the effect is more than doubled. Used to reinforce an entrance walk, or to link various portions of the garden, an allée planting adds a special dignity and focus to the total composition. Although they are not very common, a formal orchard of small trees like Bradford pear, Canary Island date palm, or loquat offers an enchanting variation of the kind of plantings frequently reserved for large estates.

Aside from their appearance, small trees are also valued for their relatively fast rate of growth. Unlike an oak or beech, which will not take on its full maturity for many years, a tree like Higan cherry, Chinese tallow tree, or goldenrain tree may grow 20 feet in five years or less. This quality can be particularly valuable for gardens where trees are completely absent. In addition, small, fast-growing trees can offer the necessary shade for shrubs and ground covers that need protection from the sun. Then, as the larger trees mature, the small trees will become an ornamental understory.

But the most important landscape value of small trees is their scale. They can be used to make a limited garden seem larger, or they can bring a quality of shade and foliage to a space too small for full-sized trees. In courtyards or city gardens, where space is at a premium, a small tree like hawthorn tree, star magnolia, saucer magnolia, or flowering peach will offer all the desirable qualities of a large tree without disrupting the proportions of the space. And since they require less area for root development, small trees may be the only way to enjoy the benefits of shade, privacy, and overhead enclosure in a very small garden or courtyard. Small trees can be especially useful in changing the apparent scale of garden spaces. Since objects in the distance appear much smaller than they really are, a small tree planted at the rear of a property will seem even smaller and farther away; as a result, the garden will appear much larger. This visual deception can be used to enhance the overall proportions of a small house, too. Instead of towering over the house—as would a sweet gum or tulip tree—a redbud, flowering dogwood, or loquat will merely frame the structure with a canopy of foliage at (or just above) the cornice line.

Since many small trees repeat the form or foliage character of larger trees, they can also help improve the sense of landscape continuity through repetition. Luster-leaf holly and Southern magnolia, for example, are remarkably similar both in their overall forms and the color, shape, and texture of their foliages. Japanese maple and red maple, or crepe myrtle and Japanese zelkova also offer unexpected similarities; when they are used in combination, the interplay of these trees can offer an exciting counterpoint to the more

Hume #2 holly, page 187.

White flowering peach, page 182.

163

Flowering dogwood, page 176.

Crepe myrtle, page 172.

Japanese maple, page 188.

traditional approaches to garden unity. Such combinations can also create an intriguing false perspective in the garden. If Southern magnolia, for example, is planted in the foreground and luster-leaf holly is placed in the distance, their striking similarity will create an illusion of distance and scale; this disception can be quite effective in the large garden, but in a small garden it can be dynamic.

Since the ultimate success of small trees is so directly linked to their individual qualities, careful consideration should be given to the desired effect before a small tree is selected. Flowering dogwood, for example, is remarkably diverse in its landscape applications, but it will not be desirable in every situation. Similarly, the strict formality of Bradford pear may not seem totally appropriate for naturalistic gardens. Also, regional considerations should not be overlooked when choosing a small tree. Even though windmill palms can be grown in certain portions of the Middle South, they look rather peculiar in an inland garden. There are, of course, no clear-cut rules governing the appropriateness of any plant; however, when they are selected with an appreciation for the general character of the landscape situation, the ultimate effect is sure to be more pleasant and enduring.

Bradford Pear
Formality in flowers and foliage

One of the earliest trees to bloom in spring, Bradford pear (*Pyrus calleryana* Bradford) has quickly proven itself as an important plant for the city garden. Bradford pear tolerates urban pollution, poor soil, drought, and most common pests.

Bradford pear is a small deciduous tree that generally reaches a mature height of 30 to 40 feet (sometimes larger in the Upper South) and grows in an upright, nearly oval habit. Leaves are nearly rounded but pointed at the tips, about 3 inches long, and turn orange to red in the late fall. Flowers are white and borne in clusters in early spring. The inedible fruit is small (less than ½ inch in diameter) and rust colored, usually eaten by birds before it falls off the tree. Although most Callery pears (the parent) have prominent spines, Bradford is spineless.

Part of the attractiveness of Bradford pear is the shiny foliage that appears almost evergreen, so lustrous is its appearance. It is a splendid shiny green and varies little until fall when the glossy green is transformed into a conflagration of fall colors. The tree's foliage is one of the most brilliant, deep reds of the season, rivaled only by the sumacs and perhaps black gum.

However, the form of the tree is more frequently noticed. Few plants are more rigid and upright in character than the Bradford pear—it never appears to relax and stands as though it were called to attention. It is excellent for landscape use, for unlike other ornamental trees that shed adolescent growth habits for a more relaxed form in their maturity, Bradford pear remains faithfully rigid. Therefore, it is perfectly suited for architectural uses or in locations where several specimens should be matched and visually have similar value. Such plantings are in formal beds or alongside a walk or a drive where the feeling of formalness must be reinforced by plantings. Under almost any circumstances, Bradford pear would look completely out of place naturalized in a border or planted as an open-lawn specimen. It is simply too unrelentingly rigid in form to be used successfully in this manner.

Although the parent tree is native to China, the Bradford pear was bred and released by the United States Department of Agriculture. It is adapted to all areas of the South except southern Florida and Texas. The Bradford pear is marginally adapted to western Texas and Oklahoma.

Tolerance to adverse conditions makes Bradford pear a highly valued street tree that is used increasingly in municipal plantings. It is also a good tree for the home garden and is noted, among pears, for its resistance to fire blight, a destructive bacterial disease. An ideal small shade tree, Bradford pear is compact enough to be planted near terraces and decks. For a flowering and fruiting deciduous tree, Bradford pear is not messy.

Plant Bradford pear in full sun and almost any soil. Roots develop well, even under the most restrictive and adverse conditions, including clay soils and drought-prone areas of the country. In addition, Bradford pear withstands exposure to winds and has no major insect problems.

Another commendable selection from the Callery pear is Aristocrat, which is more rounded than the conical Bradford.

AT A GLANCE
Light: full sun
Water: drought resistant
Soil: nearly any soil
Growth Rate: moderate
Size: 30 to 40 feet; may reach 50 feet in Upper South

The rigid form of Bradford pear makes it an excellent small tree for formal uses.

Small Trees

Chinese Tallow
Tough enough for summer

AT A GLANCE

Light: full sun
Water: drought resistant
Soil: nearly any, including wet and alkaline soils
Growth Rate: moderate to rapid
Size: to 30 feet

A stable, small green tree in the landscape during spring and summer, Chinese tallow tree has outstanding fall color.

In the plant world, toughness does not necessarily suggest a lack of grace; and Chinese tallow tree (*Sapium sebiferum*) is one of the best examples of an extremely durable tree that has an unmistakably airy landscape appearance. Even in the most severe heat and in the tough soils of problem locations in the Lower South, Chinese tallow tree can thrive, bringing a characteristic softness to its harsh environment. This small tree is light and open in habit, with a breezy feeling. In fact, it serves in the landscape of the Lower South with much the same effect that River Birch does in the Middle to Upper South, rapidly providing a dappled shade, with a vertical, upright form. Because of this effect, Chinese tallow tree makes a good shade or street tree, even though it is comparatively short-lived. Since it casts a filtered shade, you can plant Chinese tallow tree in a lawn without worrying about shade damage to lawn grasses.

Native to China and Japan, this 30-foot deciduous tree, with its rounded, stately crown, is reliably hardy only in the Lower South, although it may be grown in protected areas of the Middle South. In places such as south or west Texas, where the selection of plants you can grow is severely limited by climatic conditions, Chinese tallow tree may thrive for many years.

Chinese tallow tree is one of the few trees in the Lower South that provides good fall color. The leaves are nearly round with sharply pointed tips and turn yellow to orange red in fall. This is perhaps one of the most dependable trees for bold fall color in the Lower South and south Texas. This plant grows rapidly from seedling and thus may be a problem for some homeowners. In spring, tiny yellow catkin flowers appear, followed by brown capsules that eventually burst and fall off, leaving clean white, waxy berrylike seeds that persist into winter. For this reason, many residents of Charleston call this tree the "Popcorn Tree."

Plant in full sun. Chinese tallow tree tolerates most soils, including dry, wet, acid and alkaline. No significant pests attack the plant.

Here is a close view (above) of the white, popcornlike fruit of the Chinese tallow tree.

The tiny yellow catkin flowers of Chinese tallow tree (left) appear in spring.

Corkscrew Willow
A plant with a different twist

The corkscrew willow (*Salix matsudana* Tortuosa) is a real landscape curiosity. Instead of the fountainlike form usually associated with the weeping types of willows, the corkscrew willow seems to grow out in all directions, twisting and turning from its base to the very top of the tree.

The distinctive form makes corkscrew willow an excellent choice for creating sculptural effect in the landscape; for that reason, the plant is most effectively used as an isolated specimen. Planted against a dark architectural background or in a section of open lawn or ground cover, corkscrew willow is exhibited to its best advantage.

The corkscrew willow is a relatively fast-growing tree that may reach as much as 25 feet in height at maturity. Although the tree prefers a full-sun location, it will tolerate a certain amount of shade.

Willows require large amounts of water, particularly when young and in a vigorous state of growth. Since the root system of all willow trees is rather aggressive, root intrusion can be a serious problem if the tree is located near a waterline or sewer.

The soft, green leaves of the corkscrew willow give it an airy freshness throughout the summer. But the most desirable characteristic of the plant is best seen during winter, when the silhouette and shadow pattern created by the intricate network of stems and branches produce an effect that is unsurpassed in delicacy and grace. The branches are also useful when cut and taken indoors as an arrangement. This calls particular attention to their erratic, circular form.

AT A GLANCE
Light: full to partial sun
Water: moderate to wet
Soil: any soil
Growth Rate: rapid
Size: to 25 feet
Remarks: especially good in wet locations

The twisted, corkscrew-looking trunk gives corkscrew willow (left) its common name.

The sculptural effect of corkscrew willow (below) is an excellent accent for this small garden.

Crabapple
Two seasons of pleasure

AT A GLANCE

Light: full sun
Water: moderate amount—drought affects fruit color adversely
Soil: moist, well-drained, slightly acid soil
Growth Rate: moderate to rapid
Size: varies with selection

Shown here (right) is a properly pruned crabapple which displays the interesting rugged branch structure.

Sargent flowering crabapple is a dwarf crabapple that looks like a large, mounded shrub.

There are two seasons of pleasure from most crabapples, and they both fall at a time when the landscape is quiet and in need of a spark of rejuvenating color. The first season is in late spring in the quiet that starts before dogwoods open and can extend almost beyond the dogwoods' bloom. This is the season of the flowers, when this unbelievably diverse genus of plants washes the landscape in hues of purest white, soft and hot pinks, and deep reddish purples. And following the painting of the trees is the showering of the ground beneath with the delicate individual petals that have shattered from the wind, rain, or maturity.

The second season begins during the hottest weeks of summer, the end of July through August into the middle of October—the season of the fruit. Again these small-to-medium-sized ornamentals leap into prominence as the bright, waxy-covered pomes are displayed against the green backdrop of the foliage. The show is carnivallike—with fruit ranging in parti-colored and solid hues of yellow, orange red, and deep crimson. Its color can be an electrifying surprise in the garden—often overlooked, yet powerfully ornamental. Almost every flower of the previous spring seems to have matured into fruit, and the long bright stems that supported the flowers now droop with the weight of the vibrant-colored ornaments. The fruiting show may last as long as 4 months, and then the tree assumes its winter and fall silhouette of slate gray branches and its stemlike form.

Crabapples are among the most successfully grown and desirable ornamental plants for any home garden. Thanks to extensive variability and cross-fertilization there is an array from which to choose—literally almost a crabapple for every garden. If not primarily for their varying form and fruit, each garden should have one for its ability to attract birds into the garden.

Crabapples are special trees, and they need careful consideration when you plan the landscape. Foremost, they need room. Except for certain selections like Sargent, they will eventually mature into large round trees that are 25 feet tall and at least 20 to 30 feet across. Their mounding growth habit makes tucking them into the garden border almost physically impossible. If a crabapple is desired in the garden, then the space must be created for it, whether it be a specimen that anchors one corner of the garden or, in smaller areas, the dominant plant in an entire landscape. Unlike the cherries, which can maintain their grace and beauty in a shaded or crowded location that will cause the tree to wind and climb for light, crabapples persist in their natural form wherever they are planted. Generally, if insufficient room is allowed in the garden, the tree will look cramped and ungainly.

In addition, the beauty of crabapples lies in their dense mass of blossoms and fruit— they are (except for certain selections) a visually impenetrable concentration of color. Unlike trees that appear as lines of color or drifts of color in the garden (redbud and dogwood, respectively), crabapples are walls of flowers; even the softer colors have a slightly heavy feeling, as though the branches were going to shatter from the weight of the blossoms and fruit. This tendency to be visually "heavy" in the landscape is another key to design with crabapples—they look best either grouped in a drift, in the foreground of a composition of tree forms, or as a specimen, underplanted with a low ground cover. In fact, some of the most spectacular uses of crabapples can be as single specimens, planted in an open lawn.

However, crabapples need artful grooming. Vigorous growers by nature, they rapidly send up watershoots from the base and suckers from the spreading branches. Unless controlled, these suckers ascend rapidly and disrupt the form of the tree. Accordingly, crabapples must be cleaned of this growth each year, so that the tree develops the spreading form that is the hallmark of the genus.

In addition, when carefully pruned, the beautiful sculptural bark becomes a noteworthy landscape asset of the plant. The bark is characteristically a deep slate gray that may exfoliate in patches up the trunk and along the limbs with age. When crabapples are properly pruned, the network of branches that supports the rounded crown of the trees should be visible simultaneously with the foliage or the flowers and fruit. In winter, the tree should be a clean pattern of limbs that forms a rounded crown. The inner larger branches should appear as upward-reaching fingers—a statement of the strength and durability of these comparatively long-lived ornamentals.

When not in flower, or in full fruit, crabapples are a steady color in the landscape that ranges from light green to the deep purple red of some selections. Their foliage color is not eye-catching, but the thick covering of leaves accentuates the round spreading form of the tree. Up close, the foliage is thin and tapering and lightly toothed around the edges. Generally speaking, the fall color is not vivid but ranges in hue from soft yellow to orange.

One special feature that all the crabapples share is the change in color intensity from the young buds of the tree to the final color of the open blossoms. Most often the buds will appear as a darker or more intense color that changes or fades. For instance, the deep-pink buds of Japanese flowering crabapple *(Malus floribunda)* open to soft pink and eventually become almost white flowers. This characteristic persists throughout most of the widely available selections, except in some of the white selections that exhibit little color shift from bud to flower.

The previously mentioned variability of crabapples is their hallmark—extensive hybridization has been initiated to achieve improved blossom color, size, and form, as well as variability in fruiting color and size. In fact, some of the fruit is short-lived as ornamentation on the tree, because it is highly desired for jellymaking.

Crabapples are exceptionally cold hardy and will do well throughout the Piedmont and Upper South. They are not as suitable for plantings in the Gulf South due to the fact that the high temperature not only retards the growth but makes the plant more susceptible to fire blight.

Crabapples should be planted in full sun in well-drained soil. Pruning for shape and repair is best done in winter or after flowering in spring. Mature trees need only to be tipped at the branches to retain their form and to have periodic suckers removed.

Here is a look at some of the widely available selections for Southern gardens.

The second season begins during the hottest weeks of summer—the season of the fruit.

Flowers of the crabapple are generally grouped together in a dense mass.

Crabapples can be used as open-lawn specimens, and careful pruning will reveal the clean pattern of limbs that form a rounded crown.

Callaway Crabapple

Originating at Callaway Gardens, Callaway crabapple *(Malus prunifolia* Callaway) is a smaller, upright-growing selection suited for small garden spaces. The expanding buds are light pink and fade to white when open. The fruit is red and reaches just under an inch in diameter. It is a good selection for the warmer regions of the South.

Carmine Crabapple

Carmine *(Malus* x *atrosanguinea* Carmine) is noted for its profuse covering of large (1 to 1¼ inches across) carmine-colored flowers. The plant has a growth habit similar to floribunda crabapple with its arching branches. The fruit is not conspicuous but is dark red. Carmine is dependable and is not readily susceptible to apple scab.

Chinese Flowering Crabapple

Chinese flowering crabapple *(Malus spectabilis)* is an old-fashioned selection that has bright flowers up to 2 inches across, followed by yellow fruit of little ornamental value. Riversi has double pink flowers with 9 to 12 petals each that sport the same color. This tree is a durable and dependable flowering selection that has a broad-mounding, spreading growth habit.

Eleyi Crabapple

Eleyi crabapple *(Malus* x *purpurea* Eleyi) is another standby of the Southern garden. Following the single blooms of this deep purplish red, flowering selection is the slightly reddish foliage that gives it a deeper landscape foliage color than other selections. It flowers prolifically in alternate years and has bright-red fruit.

Japanese Flowering Crabapple

Japanese flowering crabapple *(Malus floribunda)* is one of the most prolific of the flowering crabapples. The deep pink to red buds open and fade to white single flowers with a slight pink blush. The flowers are very fragrant and are followed by red and yellow fruit that occurs in masses in late summer and persists until October. Floribunda flowers prolifically every year and has a rounded habit of growth, with a dense twiggy character. It is certainly one of the most dependable crabapples for almost the entire South.

Sargent Flowering Crabapple

Sargent flowering crabapple, *(Malus sargentii)* a dwarf crabapple, reaches over 6 to 8 feet tall with a wide-spreading growth habit and looks like a large mounded shrub. The single white flowers cover the zigzag habit of branches in a heavy display that is followed by bright-red fruit that persists until fall. One selection, Rosea, has bright-reddish pink flower buds that fade to white flowers and bloom much later than the species. Because of its low habit of growth, sargent crabapple is an ornamental that produces an unexpected show in the landscape.

Scheidecker Crabapple

Scheidecker crabapple *(Malus* x *scheideckeri)* is a double-flowering selection that bears pale-pink flowers with about 10 petals each. The small tree reaches just under 20 feet in height, and the flower is followed by reddish yellow fruit that is not of great value.

Siberian Crabapple

Siberian crabapple *(Malus baccata)* is one of the hardiest of the genus and also one of the most prolific bloomers of the species. Because of its durable character and variability, it has been used extensively in hybridization and from the species have come many popular and excellent selections.

The plant is slightly upright in habit and eventually becomes one of the larger-sized crabapples, reaching almost 40 feet in height. The species bears pure white, extremely fragrant flowers, followed by yellow fruit that is brightly flushed with red.

Selections believed to have been derived primarily from Siberian crabapple are:

Dolgo—This old favorite produces one of the finest types of apples for cooking that is available. The single flowers open pure white from pinkish buds and are almost 2 inches across. The fruit is bright crimson and extremely large; it is one of the earliest to show color and makes an exceptional show in late August. It flowers profusely in alternate years.

Dorothea—Dorothea is a comparatively recent selection, originating in 1943 at the Arnold Arboretum. The semidouble flowers have 10 to 16 petals that originate from carmine-colored buds and eventually fade to light pink. The yellow fruit is extremely ornamental.

Hopa—While only 50 years old, hopa crabapple is perhaps the most widely planted selection. The flowers are single, from expanding buds that are dark red to purplish red. They open rose pink with almost a white star in the center and may bloom only every other year. The fruit is bright red or crimson, usually yellowing on the shaded side of the fruit.

Katherine—Katherine may be one of the most striking of the crabapple selections. The expanding buds are rose red; they open pink, then fade to white. They are double, having generally 15 to 24 petals and spreading to well over 2 inches across. The fruit, by contrast, is tiny and yellow with a red blush.

Radiant—Radiant is noted for its bright-red fruit that retains its color well into fall. The expanding buds are deep red and open deep pink; the flowers are single. It is highly resistant to apple scab and fire blight.

Red Jade—Red Jade has a weeping growth habit which is very noticeable. In the spring, the flowers are a blush white, followed by a dramatic dark-green foliage. The fall display is the most spectacular feature of this crabapple, with the bright-red fruit hanging pendulously from branches that are secured by long stems in groups of 4 to 6 clusters.

Southern Crabapple

Southern crabapple *(Malus angustifolia)* is a wandering-limbed, vigorous-growing native tree. It has a twiggy appearance that gives it a character that is more naturalistic than the other species or selections. Accordingly, it naturalizes extremely easily. Flowers are fragrant and are born in April and May when the foliage is almost mature. The individual blossoms are wide and open, spreading to about ¾ to 1 inch across. The buds are pink; the flowers open pink, then quickly fade to white. The fruit is a small, hard, green apple, between 1 and 2 inches in diameter, and it is often used in jellymaking.

The beautiful sculptural bark is a noteworthy asset of the plant.

The flowers cluster profusely along the branches in late spring.

AT A GLANCE
Light: full sun
Water: moderate amount; drought tolerant when established
Soil: any well-drained soil
Growth Rate: moderate to rapid
Size: to 20 feet

Crepe Myrtle
For summer color

The long panicles of crepe myrtle (*Lagerstroemia indica*) crackle into bloom in the heat of summer and just never seem to stop. It is the premier small tree for this season in the South, adaptable to rugged conditions and offering unsurpassed color selections.

Crepe myrtle's plus as a landscape plant is its marvelous versatility. Horticulturally, it can be grown in a wide range of climatic conditions, thriving in either the hot broiling sun of the Southwest or in the cool highlands of the Upper South. More importantly, it is adaptable to any design use: used as an espalier on a bare wall, pruned into a standard (single-trunk tree form) for a planter, planted as a small street tree, or used as a screen.

But crepe myrtle reaches its zenith in its full-grown multitrunked form, planted as the dominant landscape feature. Rarely exceeding 20 feet in height when left unpruned, crepe myrtle gives a matchless show throughout the year.

Crepe myrtle's bark combines the sculptured sinewy smoothness of ironwood with the gentle exfoliating character of sycamore, and the hues vary from a light straw to a rich, deep brown. In winter, when the branches are bare of leaves, this sculptural form takes on striking dominance in the landscape.

Crepe myrtle provides light shade. Beneath mature plants there is a light, airy feeling of the sun being broken but not blotted out. This makes crepe myrtle an ideal small shade tree: it provides adequate cover to thwart searing sun, but is thin enough to permit breezes to penetrate.

Crepe myrtle is hardy, fast growing, and not particular about soil. But it will grow best in a heavy loam that is slightly acid (pH of 5 to 6.5). Most importantly, plant crepe myrtles in a sunny, well-drained location; set them slightly above the ground, much as you would plant an azalea or camellia. This serves two purposes: in full sun, the plant flowers abundantly (it will not flower well in shade); a well-drained location eliminates conditions conducive to mildew, which is the plant's greatest threat. Mildew is easily recognized by the presence of black spots on the leaves and a gray powder underneath the spotted area. For control, see page 246.

While pruning is not necessary, tip pruning (carefully removing the flower clusters after bloom) is the best type of pruning for crepe myrtle. This encourages bloom the following season without inhibiting the plant's natural form. Just nip the old clusters off with hand shears or lopping shears. Any additional pruning underneath the canopy to remove twiggy growth will keep the trunks clean and increase its sculptural character.

Stump pruning is a more drastic alternative to tip pruning. It should be done only in certain circumstances. Stump pruning involves cutting the plant back to a few main trunks at some arbitrary distance above the ground, and there are two variations. In one, the plant is cut back to eye level; the other involves cutting the plant almost all the way to the ground. This forces the plant to produce an abundance of twiggy growth that will bloom heavily, but it makes the plant lose its most desirable characteristic—its sculptural form.

Crepe myrtles are offered in a wide range of colors, from whites and pinks to reds and lavenders. In addition to color variations, selections based on maximum mature height are also available. These include dwarf types (less than 3 feet), semidwarf (3 to 6 feet),

Notice the exfoliating bark (above), which is one of crepe myrtle's outstanding features.

When massed and freestanding, crepe myrtle (left) creates the effect of a grove.

In full sun, crepe myrtle will flower abundantly.

medium (6 to 12 feet), and the more well-known tall selections that exceed 12 feet. These height groupings are approximate and will vary with local growing conditions and cultivation practices.

Obviously, there is a crepe myrtle type to suit almost any circumstance. Except for special landscape effects or locations that demand a dwarf selection (such as bonsai or a small planter), the tall and medium selections offer more for landscape use.

Select crepe myrtles for your garden when they are in bloom (there is no problem in planting then). This will eliminate any color surprises and the confusion of describing colors by selection name alone. Some of the more popular medium (M) and tall (T) selections include the following:

White: Glendora White (T), Ingleside White (T), and White Cloud (T)

Light Pink: Near East (M), Weeping Pink (T), and Yvonne (T)

Red: Carolina Beauty (M), Regal Red (T), Watermelon Red (T), and William Toovey (T)

Small Trees

The multitrunked effect of crepe myrtle silhouetted against a light-colored building enhances its sculptural qualities.

The summer flowers of crepe myrtle sparkle against the green landscape.

Lavender: Diane (T) and Majestic Orchid (T)
Purple: Kellog's Purple (T) and Parade Purple (T)

A decade of selecting at the National Arboretum has resulted in some new types that are highly mildew resistant and offer new colors and growth habits as well. The six new selections available are crosses of existing crepe myrtle types and have been named

Here are shown the pods of crepe myrtle from which the beautiful blossoms have emerged.

The winter landscape feature of the trunks of crepe myrtle is one of the plant's outstanding qualities.

after Indian tribes: Catawba, dark-purple flowers with a compact globose form; Cherokee, rich-red blooms and an open-spreading habit; Conestoga, lavender in an open-growth habit; Potomac, medium-pink flowers with recurrent bloom in early fall and strongly upright habit; Powhatan, light-lavender flowers in a dense compact growth habit; Seminole, medium-pink blooms in a clearly upright habit.

Additional experimentation has resulted in an outstanding new hybrid cross between common crepe myrtle (*Lagerstroemia indica*) and a rare white Japanese species (*L. fauriei*) that is more treelike than *L. indica* and has a rich, burgundy-colored underbark with a velvet texture.

The new hybrid combines all ranges of flower color, with bark color ranging from a pale cream to a dark, cinnamon brown. The hybrid vigor is demonstrated by 10-year-old trees being 35 feet tall and broad, with 18-inch trunks.

One such cross, a natural hybrid named Basham's Party Pink, has been planted extensively in Houston (where it occurred) and demonstrates the rapid strong growth and mildew resistance of the crosses. Other selections are currently being tested by the National Arboretum. Although not released commercially, they should become available soon.

Small Trees

AT A GLANCE

Light: partial sun best; Kousa tolerates more sun
Water: moderate amount
Soil: moist, well-drained, acid soil
Growth Rate: moderate to slow
Size: to 30 feet; Kousa to 20 feet
Remarks: see copy for cautions

Dogwood
There is nothing like it

The unfolding of the bracts of this native understory tree creates a magical effect in the landscape—airy drifts of white (and sometimes pink) that look like cloud banks nestled among the trunks of taller trees. No other tree can bring the woodlands alive like dogwood.

The magnificent display of flowering dogwood (*Cornus florida*) has generated both appreciation and folklore. The legends that surround the tree are efforts to explain its hallmarks: the erratic, even crooked, habit of growth and the twisting shape of the bracts that form the upturned floral display. It is to these bracts (modified leaves that open to expose the flowers) we owe the spring show.

The dogwood is expressive throughout the year. No two trees will ever look exactly alike. Unlike other ornamental trees whose mature form is predictable, the dogwood's shape is the product of the light conditions of its location. Dogwoods climb and reach for light, spreading higher and wider as they grow. If planted in partial sun, the tree will layer heavily with foliage to protect itself from the sun.

But wherever dogwoods are planted, they have an open-branching form, with the foliage appearing as horizontal layers. This is attributed to an unusual branching pattern: the new growth of the terminal bud of each branch is frequently exceeded in length by the new growth of the pair of branches immediately behind it.

The foliage is a soft, light green that contrasts with the deeper color of canopy trees; thus dogwoods seem to lighten the landscape. Characteristically, the shade created by the widely spreading branches of dogwood is light and airy.

Red glossy berries appear in late August in clusters at the ends of the branches, contrasting sharply with the still-green leaves. The berries, a favorite bird food, remain through the winter months or until consumed.

In September, dogwoods begin to blush slightly; then the color gradually deepens to a vivid crimson. With the foliage gone, the dogwood becomes a sculptured form of gray branches punctuated by silvery swollen flower buds that look like small ornaments at the ends of the twigs.

Dogwood looks best when used informally, as in nature. Planted in mass, they can provide a sweeping bank of bloom and foliage to enclose a corner of the garden. Or use several to visually soften the trunks of existing canopy trees and provide scale beneath their soaring crowns.

Its delicate foliage and coarse bark texture make dogwood an excellent choice for shading a terrace or patio. In the open lawn, several trees drifted informally will frame a space with their wandering trunks to create a natural seating area.

Although the native flowering dogwood is hard to surpass as a landscape plant, there are several selections that make outstanding additions to the garden. Among the most popular are Cherokee Chief (deep-red bracts), Cherokee Princess (white, very large bracts), Cloud 9 (white, profusely flowering when young), Plena (white, semidouble bracts), Rubra (the original pink dogwood), and Fragrant Cloud (white, lightly scented, and rare).

The show of Kousa dogwood (above) is a display of white bracts that enclose the small true flowers.

This dogwood (left) is a splendid size for its location.

Viewed from underneath, dogwood is a study of line and pattern.

The Kousa dogwood (*Cornus kousa*) is a smaller Oriental cousin of the native flowering dogwood. In early summer, Kousa's show is a display of white bracts that enclose the small true flowers. But the bracts unfold after the foliage emerges; also, the bracts taper to a point rather than being cupped at the outer ends like flowering dogwood. The bracts of Kousa dogwood are carried on a stem that often rises 6 inches above the background of glossy-green foliage.

In late September, fruit develops and hangs at the end of the long stem. The fruit has a remarkable size and looks like a Bing cherry.

Kousa's brilliant-scarlet fall color is another hallmark of the plant. The outer bark is a deep mahogany that peels back to reveal the light-brown inner covering.

In the landscape, Kousa is best displayed where it will be viewed up close or from above—as the feature tree in a courtyard or on the lower side of a retaining wall that supports a terrace. The ascending habit of Kousa dogwood also makes it a superb specimen plant for a patio or along a walkway, as the branches will not interfere with people walking beneath or beside it. Two outstanding selections are Chinensis and Summer Stars.

The two essentials for healthy dogwoods are shade and good drainage. Dogwoods will not do well in full sun. They are understory trees and need the shade of a canopy to protect

Small Trees

Late in summer, dogwood sets next year's flower buds.

Dogwood should be planted as an understory tree. Here is an excellent use, with pine as the canopy.

them. Dogwoods planted in full sun will flower profusely, but the wandering, reaching growth that gives the dogwood its grace will never be realized. Instead, the tree will be stunted and the foliage seared, withered, and oftentimes droopy.

Dogwoods must be planted high enough to drain well. Plant them similar to rhododendron, the root ball set 2 to 3 inches high in a shallow excavation with rich topsoil mounded up over the ball. In heavy clay, dig a hole at least twice as wide as the root ball; either replace the clay with topsoil, or work finely ground bark or peat moss into the soil until it is loose and friable.

Once a dogwood is properly planted and established, there is little that needs to be done to maintain a healthy tree. However, there are some common practices that must be avoided.

—Never till or plow underneath a dogwood. These trees are some of the most sensitive surface feeders, and tilling for a new planting bed or lawn will destroy the network of feeder roots. Also, do not pile dirt or pave beneath dogwood trees.

—Never allow a dogwood to dry out. The tree will signal water stress by dropping leaves and should be watered immediately. Maintaining a 3-inch layer of mulch around the tree will aid moisture retention.

—Avoid injuring the trunk of the tree. Open wounds in the trunk provide access for the dogwood borer, a serious pest, which can kill the tree. Repair any wounds immediately.

—Avoid removing any larger trees that provide shade for existing dogwoods; this will expose the trees to sunscald damage, as they have been accustomed to heavy shade.

Small Trees

178

Eastern Redbud
Limbs of magenta and heart-shaped leaves

AT A GLANCE
Light: full to partial sun
Water: moderate amount
Soil: any soil; prefers well-drained locations
Growth Rate: rapid
Size: to 25 feet

Contrasting with the stately and graceful white blossoms of dogwood is another native tree, the Eastern redbud *(Cercis canadensis)*, which electrifies the soft spring hues with its magenta display of flowers. Unlike the dogwood, which carries the flower at the end of its branches, the redbud's branches become covered with the tiny characteristic flowers of the pea family. The flowers are suspended by short pedicels that never extend farther from the branches than an inch. From a distance, the tree appears as a sculptural network of magenta lines and has a suprisingly delicate appearance. In fact, this fragile appearance at flowering is misleading, for redbud is one of the most dependable native trees; it is tolerant of extreme drought, temperature variation, and, most importantly, wide-ranging soil conditions.

When in foliage, redbud is a coarse-textured plant. The heart-shaped foliage is large; individual leaves may be as wide as 5 inches; and, as summer progresses, the foliage takes on a weathered, seared look. In fact, in early autumn, the foliage seems to sag under the burden of summer heat, and the leaves fold in the center as if trying to protect themselves. In fall, Eastern redbud turns a translucent yellow that sometimes fades to a tawny, parchment brown.

In winter, the tree becomes a study in dark, sharply angled branches. Close inspection of redbud during the dormant season reveals the striking branching pattern of the plant—a slightly zigzag directional growth. In sun, redbud becomes a symmetrical, rounded crown tree; in the shade, it becomes a wandering, loose-branched tree, reaching for available light. The young branches have a sandy brown color and slightly rough texture, while the older parts of the tree have a rougher and more scabrous bark.

Redbud is an excellent plant for naturalizing a woodland edge, but, since the color is difficult to use, caution must be exercised when planting it. For example, redbud is often used to provide an accent flower prior to the blooming of the dogwoods or other white flowering trees. Remember, one redbud tree can offset or balance 4 to 5 dogwoods, so keep that ratio in mind when planning a garden. If possible, avoid planting redbud against a red-colored background; in fact, a dark drapery of evergreen trees like pine is best since it allows both the flower color and form to show clearly.

Being a member of the pea family, redbud is important to soil reclamation. It reseeds rapidly; the pealike pods that are suspended from the tree in late summer add an ornamental look that contrasts with the delicacy of the redbud's springtime character. They drop to the ground during fall and late winter and generate countless seedlings capped with heart-shaped foliage. Because of its tenacity, this tree is frequently found in colonies along roadsides or at woodland edges where man has disturbed the earth.

Several selections are available from the nursery trade: Alba has the same characteristic form, but the flowers are white; Rosea has true pink flowers; and Forest Pansy is a red-leaved form, retaining a purplish cast to the leaves throughout the summer.

The characteristic pea-shaped flowers of Eastern redbud are aligned closely along the twigs.

Eastern redbud has a graceful, airy look when in bloom.

Flowering Cherry
Soft pastels of spring

AT A GLANCE
Light: full to partial sun
Water: moderate amount
Soil: any well-drained soil
Growth Rate: moderate to rapid
Size: varies up to 30 feet

All flowering cherries are noted for their interesting, heavily scarred trunks.

Flowering cherries reflect the energy of early spring, accelerating in bloom from a few blossoms to an abundant wash of pastel color seemingly overnight. Even when in full, profuse bloom, flowering cherries seem vulnerable, and they bloom as if each spring might be their last.

Cherries grow well in most of the South, particularly the middle and upper regions. They perform well in either full sun or under the lighter shade of a tall canopy planting, making them easy to use in the landscape—as mass plantings in full sun or to lighten and grace a semishady portion of the garden. They should be planted in well-drained but moist soil of medium fertility and mulched heavily.

Except for the weeping type, they have a strongly ascending form, branching upward and outward to form a vase-shaped canopy. In most cases, the plants will maintain an erratic upward branching structure, forming a wide, flat crown.

Cherries are best used in more formal gardens, such as a parterre, or in landscapes where the garden design is controlled. With some exception, they do not naturalize well and look out of place in naturalistic plantings.

Flowering cherries are excellent single specimens for a small entrance court; they provide a beautiful flowering show, a comfortable amount of shade, and their bark, heavily scarred with horizontal lenticels, is an interesting winter feature. In a similar use, a single specimen is a delightful feature tree in a sitting garden.

Cherries also work well as a mass planting. A group of three or four trees can be drifted to shape and form one corner of the landscape.

The weeping cherries offer a different landscape challenge. Because of their form, they are visually powerful throughout the year and should not be used indiscriminately. If they are located arbitrarily, they will tend to draw the eye from other important landscape features and dominate the entire design.

The two basic types of ornamental cherries are grafted and nongrafted. If possible, select a nongrafted tree; but if the desired type is grafted, be sure that the union between the root stock and the scion (the grafted upper portion) is free of scars or open wounds in the bark.

The presence of peachtree borers is indicated by small pencil-size holes and masses of gum exuding from the portion of the trunk between the ground to about 1 foot high. See page 245 for control.

The flowering cherries vary in type and color of bloom and in habit of growth. The ones best adapted to the South are Japanese flowering cherry (*Prunus serrulata*), Higan cherry (*Prunus subhirtella*), and Yoshino cherry (*Prunus yedoensis*).

Higan Cherry

Higan cherries (*Prunus subhirtella*) have small delicate blossoms and characteristically flower before the foliage appears. The single blossoms are soft pink to white and about 1 inch in diameter. The growth habit varies with the selection. The original species reaches about 25 feet and has an upright-spreading crown. Selections suitable for the South include the following.

Higan cherry (far left) is the focal point of this side garden.

Shirofugen Japanese flowering cherry is one of the most spectacular of the selections.

Yoshino cherry (below) is the famous flowering cherry of Washington, D.C.

Autumnalis is an unusual type with pink semidouble flowers that bloom both in the fall and in the spring. Because of its time of bloom, Autumnalis makes an unusual accent tree.

Pendula, as the name implies, is the weeping flowering cherry. The weeping cherries have soft-pink single flowers that appear before the leaves. The foliage is deep green and will reach to the ground. It is the most popular of all flowering cherries; because of its weeping form, it is the most difficult to use in the landscape. One caution about weeping cherries: most of them are grafted. So specify bottom or ground-level grafts; that way, all branches of the plant will weep from ground level in a fashion similar to weeping willow.

Japanese Flowering Cherry

The Japanese flowering cherries (*Prunus serrulata*) are some of the most spectacular of the genus. While the original species has white, single flowers 1½ inches across, the more popular types are double flowering. Following are some of the most widely available.

Kwanzan, also called Sekiyama, has profuse rose pink double flowers covering the entire tree. The young foliage is slightly copper red in color.

Shirofugen is probably the most spectacular of the species. The soft-pink buds open into 2½-inch pink double flowers that quickly fade to pure white.

Shirotae, widely known as Mount Fuji, is a small (20 to 25 feet) double-flowering tree. The blossoms are white and can be 2½ inches across.

Yoshino Cherry

Yoshino cherry (*Prunus yedoensis*) is the famous flowering cherry of Washington, D.C., and is the most widely available and horticulturally adaptable cherry in the South. Its habit of growth is identical to mimosa, with several low, upright-spreading branches that ascend to form a wide, flattened crown. Yoshino cherries flower profusely with single blossoms that open pink, then fade to white. Akebono is a white-flowering type of Yoshino that is a slightly more prolific bloomer.

Small Trees

Flowering Peach
A dark and weathered beauty

AT A GLANCE
Light: full to partial sun best
Water: moderate
Soil: well-drained, fertile soil
Growth Rate: moderate to slow
Size: to 25 feet

The Oriental look of flowering peach is strikingly portrayed here by the gnarled, seemingly contorted branches which terminate with clusters of soft, almost contradictory blossoms.

Flowering peach is deserving of careful display in the landscape; here it is used as a lawn specimen.

While the flowering cherry has become the celebrated tree of Oriental gardens, the flowering peach *(Prunus persica)* is perhaps almost a symbol of the delicacy and craftsmanship that graces this type of landscape. The flowering peach and its selections best express the essence of Oriental design. The deep-black ink strokes in Oriental artwork, depicting gnarled, seemingly contorted branches which terminate with clusters of soft, almost contradictory blossoms, must be paintings of the flowering peach, a native of China. For these highly variable trees seem to grow simply to express the severity of climate and then to gently temper it with a bountiful early-spring flower show.

This two-fold character, soft and pastel carmine in spring, followed by a rugged and withered fall and winter show, makes flowering peach especially expressive and deserving of careful display in the landscape. They are plants expressing form and line in winter, exploding into color that will last at least 10 days in spring, and then essentially blending into the summertime green canopy.

Although they are in the same family as the cherries, the flowering peaches have a more diverse landscape application than their close cousins. Where the cherries can become formal drifts of delicate light flowers and clean foliage—suitable for open-lawn specimens or to shelter a sitting area—flowering peaches need an almost rugged or weathered context. For unlike the flowering cherries, which have essentially uniform landscape character the entire year, the peaches change character substantially with leaf fall, and this phenomenon should be accommodated in the garden.

Accordingly, use flowering peaches to accent rock formations or to bring a feeling of strength and durability into the landscape. Remember to locate flowering peaches where the branch structure will be silhouetted in winter, since the bark is characteristically a deep, black brown; a tawny backdrop, or weathered fence, will enhance the visibility of the form.

Horticulturally, the flowering peach is highly variable; there may be as many as three colors of flowers on a single tree. If cuttings are taken of the branches, they may either be grafted to a root stake or rooted, and they will maintain their selected color.

Flowering peach will grow well throughout the Piedmont and the Upper South. In the deep South, the tree is more susceptible to pest damage and does not perform reliably over a long period of time. Generally, the tree will do well wherever peaches and ornamental cherries are grown commercially.

The flowering peach prefers full to partial sun and a moderately dry soil. It will tolerate either acid or alkaline soil but will grow best with slightly acid soil. This tree is susceptible to the same pests that infect commercial peaches, the peachtree borer and the lesser peachtree borer. See page 247 for controls. In addition, sapsuckers may damage the bark in their search for food.

Several selections of flowering peach are available in the nursery trade; some of the more widely available are: Alba (white flowers, single); Alboplena (white flowers, double); Atropurpurea (purple-leaved selection); and Pendula (grafted, weeping selection).

Flowering Plum
Flowers with foliage color

The flowering plums are another group of plants of the prolifically flowering genus that includes the cherries, almonds, and the peaches. When flowering, their landscape effect is more subtle than the other members of the family, but they put forth a showy display and fragrance. The plums also provide a bonus of deeply colored foliage that brings color into the summer garden as well.

While there are many plums which can achieve various landscape effects, the most noted members are the selections of Myrobalan plum *(Prunus cerasifera)*. And it is the foliage color, as well as the twiggy weathered appearance, that makes the selections valuable landscape accents.

Generally speaking, the plums may be used like the ornamental cherries—as accent plants, with certain considerations. The plums are smaller plants and more suited to smaller, hard-to-fill garden spots. Their foliage color throughout the summer season makes them especially valuable as accent plants. For example, a small grove of grouped plums could be used in conjunction with a weeping willow. The deep-maroon color of the plums would contrast handsomely with the soft-green flowering lines of the willow. The foliage color can also be a surprising accent to the color of a house—a cream- or beige-colored house is an excellent backdrop color for the plums.

In addition, the plum's deep, maroon-colored bark, usually almost smooth, and its twiggy character give it an aged look. It is a handsomely rugged plant, and so has a character that is stronger than the more delicate cherries yet not as powerful as the weathered look of the peaches.

The flowers appear in early spring, usually as the greenish red tips of the foliage are beginning to emerge. The flowers are borne in heavy profusion along the length of the stem and look soft and fuzzy because of the long stems. The fragrance is a characteristic cherry pollen odor. The individual flowers open from red buds and are white with dark-maroon centers. The fruit that follow are 1 inch in length and are small reddish purple plums.

Plums may be planted in any well-drained, rich soil and will reach 15 to 20 feet high with a rounded or even slightly flattened crown. They should be planted in at least full or partial sun to insure that the foliage will retain the characteristic coloration. If planted in deep shade, the color will fade substantially.

Two selections are commonly available and are tolerant of most disease problems.

Newport Plum

Newport has a more purple color to its foliage than does Pissard plum. In addition, the foliage is much larger, giving the tree a coarser texture; and it has an upright, rounded growth habit.

Pissard Plum

This old-time Southern plum favorite has small, deep-maroon leaves. It is not hardy in the cooler parts of the Upper South. The foliage is finely toothed and maintains its coloration if planted in full sun. Generally, the tree has a wandering growth habit and is more carefree and free form in its branching habit than is Newport plum.

AT A GLANCE
Light: full to partial sun best
Water: moderate
Soil: well-drained, fertile soil
Growth Rate: moderate to slow
Size: to 20 feet
Remarks: not adaptable to Florida

Flowering plum blossoms in early spring, and the flowers are borne in heavy profusion along the length of the stem.

Small Trees

Goldenrain Tree
Summertime refreshment in yellow

AT A GLANCE
Light: full to partial sun
Water: moderate to dry; drought tolerant when established
Soil: any well-drained soil
Growth Rate: moderate to slow
Size: to 20 feet

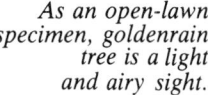

Goldenrain tree is a beautiful accent tree which can reach up to 20 feet in height.

As an open-lawn specimen, goldenrain tree is a light and airy sight.

In early summer, the goldenrain tree (*Koelreuteria paniculata*), with its panicles of airy yellow flowers, is a refreshing sight. This deciduous tree—native to the Far East—is a rugged and undemanding as it is attractive. Goldenrain tree is a small ornamental tree that is undeterred by the blinding heat of summer and early fall. Consequently, its ornamental flower display comes in mid-June, at a time of comparative quiet in the landscape.

The flowers are bright yellow and are borne on upright panicles up to 1 foot long that resemble the chaste tree. The compound light-green foliage gives the tree a light and airy appearance, which is reinforced by a very wide-spreading and upright branch structure.

Goldenrain tree is not only a beautiful accent tree but also a splendid planting for a small allée or border grove. It is a tree to bring a light-hearted look to either a formal or informal landscape. The tree is very clean and provides light shade, thus making it an excellent choice for planter spaces left in terrace locations. Not only will the goldenrain tree withstand the reflected heat of the terrace, but it will bring a comfortable shade and flower at a time of year when the terrace is likely to be in use. However, it does not naturalize (mix) very well, although goldenrain will spread rapidly from seed. It is best planted in a garden that has some structure or form to make the tree look its best.

One of the tree's most attractive delights is the fruit. These small, parchmentlike pouches begin to develop in late June and are vivid yellow (the same yellow as the flowers) until they mature (much slower than the flowers) into tiny, lanternlike pods that will remain on the tree long after the foliage has fallen. They are surely a landscape curiosity and an exceptionally attractive, unusual ornamentation in the garden. The flower and fruit show coincides with the blooming of yellow and gold daylilies, which makes a good planting combination.

Once established, goldenrain thrives in practically any soil, including alkaline soils, provided drainage is adequate. Hardy throughout the South, goldenrain tree can tolerate wind, drought, and extremes of heat and cold better than most woody ornamentals.

Goldenrain trees grow at a moderate rate to a height of about 20 feet. The bloom period coincides with that of the common mimosa or silk tree (*Albizia julibrissin*). The top of the tree is open and spreading, with compound leaves composed of elliptic leaflets that have serrate margins. The popular name, goldenrain tree, is derived from the plant's habit of dropping its spent tiny golden flowers on the ground around the base of the tree.

Grow goldenrain trees in full sun for optimum performance. It will get off to a better start if the planting hole is large and supplemented with compost, manure, or other organic matter.

Care of goldenrain tree is minimal. Fertilize established plants in early spring with 5-10-10 or other complete fertilizer at the rate of 1 cup per plant. Goldenrain tree has no particular insect or disease problems. Mature plants seldom require pruning. Young plants, however, may need some corrective pruning in late winter or early spring.

Goldenrain tree is best used in the landscape as an individual specimen. Be sure to plant it where it will receive the attention it deserves. In much of the Lower South and especially Florida, Flamegold (*Koelreuteria elegans*) is used instead of the common goldenrain tree.

Hawthorn
Tangles of flowers and fruit

The hawthorns (*Crataegus sp.*) have to be one of the most complex groups of plants. Botanically, the genus is as tangled as the growth habits of the plants; so variable and prone are they to cross-pollination that many times the types are indistinguishable. Fortunately, several species of these attractive, almost shrublike trees have been selected for landscape use. Among them are: Parsley Hawthorn (*Crataegus marshallii*), Washington Thorn Tree (*C. phaenopyrum*), Green Hawthorn (*C. viridis*), and their selections. These plants give homeowners an attractive choice for naturalizing in the garden border and are excellent plants to use to attract wildlife to the garden. In addition, they provide interest in all four seasons.

The word Haw is an old English word for hedge, and so it was that these trees were frequently planted for hedgerows in Europe. Generally speaking, the growth habit is thick and dense. Frequently, the trees are multitrunked and branch heavily from the ground up into a widespreading crown. Many times, they look like large shrubs instead of small trees. In addition, the plants are armed with long spines and twiggy spurs that make them slightly forbidding. The selections mentioned above share these characteristics but are also available in single trunk specimens, yet the crown will retain the dense and heavy thicket appearance. Accordingly, they may be used for specimen planting in an open lawn or as accents to frame a woodland edge.

All of the hawthorns have white to pinkish flowers that open into a cloudlike display in early spring. But the hallmark of the tree is not so much their flowers, as it is the abundance of fruit that follows in the fall. The berries are bright scarlet and cover the tree from late August through the winter, if they are not consumed by birds. In between flower and fruit is a steady foliage display that glows to a reddish orange during the fall color season. When the foliage and berries disappear, the ornamentation is carried by the beautifully exfoliating bark, similar to the habit of crepe myrtle.

The hawthorns are landscape plants that are tolerant of a wide range of conditions. They prefer a rich, well-drained soil in full sun, but these trees may be located in partial sun and in slightly wet locations without jeopardizing the health of the plant.

However, these are trees that perform best in the Upper to Middle South where they are native, doing quite well as far south as Atlanta. They are least susceptible to lacewing, bacterial canker, and fire blight, their major problems, in the colder regions than in the warmer areas of the South. In addition, the hawthorns are cohost to cedar-apple rust, a fungus infection that afflicts junipers as well as hawthorns. See page 248 for controls.

Some of the selections available are: Parsley Hawthorn—multitrunked with beautifully exfoliating bark, white flowers, prominent spines, featuring a full berry show in fall; Washington Thorn Tree—widely planted in the Upper South, one of the most dependable selections, pinkish to white flowers, followed by a profuse covering of berries in fall and winter; Green Hawthorn—several selections have come from this parent, among the best is Winter King Hawthorn, a light open-branched specimen that has a beautiful light-gray bark in addition to large, bright-red fruit.

AT A GLANCE
Light: full to partial sun
Water: moderate amount; drought damages fruiting show
Soil: any moist, well-drained soil
Growth Rate: moderate
Size: to 25 feet

The doubly-serrated leaves are one of the hawthorn's hallmarks.

Winter King hawthorn, shown here as an open-lawn specimen, is a light, open-branching plant with beautiful light-gray bark.

Small Trees

Holly
Dignity in an evergreen

AT A GLANCE
Light: sun to partial shade
Water: moderate
Soil: rich, fertile best; will tolerate poor soil
Growth Rate: moderate
Size: to 25 feet

Foster #2 holly is a hybrid holly with a strongly conical shape.

Hollies are more than the Christmas plant, although their bright-red berries and spiny foliage have become the veritable symbol of the Christmas season—they are stately and dignified throughout the year. In fact, a full mature native American holly, laden with fruit, may well be one of the most enduring and classic small trees that can be planted in the garden; the plants seem to have a presence and appearance that is at once reassuring and timeless. And although extremely old trees will reach 25 feet tall, the holly can be considered one of the premier small evergreen trees for the landscape—used either as understory evergreen plantings or as open-lawn specimens. The stately tree form of the large hollies make them ideal for accenting an entrance, walkway, terrace, or other landscape feature.

American holly makes a handsome specimen in a large, open garden or for framing a two-level home. In this situation, you can enjoy an uncluttered view of their pyramidal to rounded growth habit and horizontal branches that grow from the base of the trunk, with lower branches resting on the ground. In companion plantings, these hollies combine well with such native materials as mountain laurel, dogwood, and rhododendron.

Among the many kinds of hollies, there is great variation in size, texture, growth habit, leaf size, and color. Each tree has individual landscape attributes that make it more desirable than the parent types, although in some instances the landscape character of the plant when used at a distance in the garden is not noticeably different, even among some of the hybrids.

Most hollies are deciduous, which means they produce male and female blossoms on separate trees. In order for fruiting to occur, female flowers must be fertilized with pollen from a nearby male tree. So if you want berries, be sure to have both a female and male holly of the same species within 30 to 40 feet of each other.

The best time to plant or transplant hollies is in fall or early spring, but a container-grown holly may survive if set out at any time. Hollies prefer slightly acid, well-drained, fertile soil but will tolerate sandy or poorer soils. In heavy soils like clay, add sand, leaf mold, or other organic matter to help make the soil more friable. Most hollies are shallow rooted, so mulch the root area to prevent loss of moisture and winter injury. Avoid putting mulch up next to the tree trunk. Fertilize hollies in spring with 5-10-10 at the rate of ½ cup per inch of trunk diameter.

Occasionally, leaf drop and yellowing may be caused by drought or winter injury. Another problem that sometimes occurs is insect injury. See the chart on page 249. Do not prune hollies other than removing a wayward limb or one that is damaged or diseased.

American Holly

American holly (*Ilex opaca*) is a native evergreen that may still be unsurpassed in the landscape. The plant is slow growing, but mature specimens are elegant. Unfortunately, the American holly is not widely grown in the nursery trade and is replaced by several hybrids that do not have the same layered look that makes the tree so desirable. There is a noticeable difference between the male and female trees besides the obvious berries. The male tree has a loose, open form; the female is characteristically denser.

American holly may attain heights up to 25 feet; growth is pyramidal in form and generally slow. It can be recognized by green, spiny leaves and dull, scarlet berries. Selections of American holly include Croonenberg, noted for abundant fruit and dark-green foliage with a slight gloss; Howard, with denser foliage and a more compact form; and Xanthocarpa, unique because of its yellow berries.

Dahoon Holly

Dahoon holly (*Ilex cassine*) has a remarkable resemblance to sweetbay magnolia when viewed from a distance. In fact, although the Dahoon holly lacks the flowers of the magnolia, it makes a credible substitute in the understory.

Dahoon is a native evergreen and has pale-green, thin, lancelike foliage. It does well in moist locations and attains a mature height of about 25 feet. The color of the berries is a dull red; unlike some hollies, the leaves are pliable. Alabama dahoon (*I. cassine* Angusti-folia) has narrower, semirounded leaves and more abundant berries.

Luster-Leaf Holly

Luster-leaf holly (*Ilex latifolia*) is a massive, densely crowned tree (to 25 feet) with a coarse texture. It is a profusely berrying tree, with the berries clustered along the stems in massive aggregations. The clusters of large leaves sometimes hide the berries.

Luster-leaf holly performs best in partial shade. Because it is less hardy than the other large hollies, it does best in the Lower and Middle South. This pyramidal to rounded evergreen holly has very large, slightly glossy, leathery leaves with serrate margins and is sometimes called magnolia-leaf holly. Its berry color is a dull, reddish brown.

Hybrid Hollies

Hybrid hollies are the result of work by horticulturists and botanists who are in search of superior growth characteristics, such as heavier fruiting, improved shape, and more rapid growth. The following are among the most popular, large evergreen types.

East Palatka holly (*Ilex* x *attenuata* East Palatka) bears abundant red berries and has rounded, dull-green leaves and a loose, pyramidal shape. Mature height is 30 feet.

Foster #2 holly (*Ilex* x *attenuata* Foster #2) has long lance-shaped leaves with soft spines at the tips and red berries; females are profuse berriers. Its height is about the same as East Palatka, but its shape is more strongly conical.

Hume #2 holly (*Ilex* x *attenuata* Hume #2) has rounded, almost spineless dull-green leaves; the berries are red. Its growth is loosely pyramidal and vigorous, reaching a mature height of nearly 30 feet.

Savannah holly (*Ilex* x *attenuata* Savannah) has leaves with few spines; berries are scarlet red. Growth is rapid; shape and height are similar to Hume #2.

Nellie R. Stevens holly (*Ilex* x Nellie R. Stevens) has very glossy, dark-green leathery leaves with stiff spines; berries are scarlet red. Its dense, pyramidal growth while young becomes rounded with age. This holly may be used as a possible substitute for Southern magnolia on a small lot. The mature height of this holly is about 25 feet.

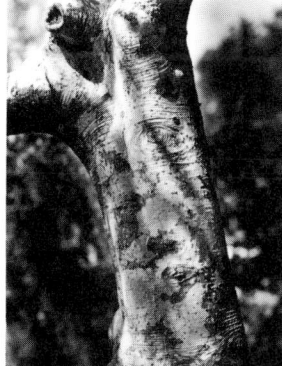

The trunks of typically large hollies have pale-gray bark.

Luster-leaf holly is a pyramidal to rounded evergreen holly with very large, slightly glossy, leathery leaves.

Small Trees

Japanese Maple
A special gift from Japan

AT A GLANCE
Light: partial shade best; some types will burn in full sun
Water: moderate amount
Soil: moist, well-drained soil; rich in organic matter
Growth Rate: slow
Size: standard to 20 feet; some types only to 4 feet

Tucked in the corner of this courtyard, this red-leaved Japanese maple (right) provides the garden with a small tree accent.

Many Japanese maples have an attractive, multistemmed branching habit of growth (below).

The airy, intricate foliage of Japanese maples appears as embroidery in the landscape, making these trees among the most prized ornamentals. In fact, there are numerous types of Japanese maples, each displaying a different color or leaf shape.

The Japanese maple (*Acer palmatum*) captures the essence of fall color with a brilliance that seems luminescent. As the chlorophyll matures, it gives way to a dark burgundy that changes to rich orange red. This coloration then yields to a soft butter-yellow hue. The entire transition from soft green to the final bleaching of the foliage to parchment may take almost three weeks.

But not all types of Japanese maple will have this vivid show. Extensive work by plant breeders has resulted in trees with varigated leaves, monochromatic leaves, and some with little fall color change at all. For instance, a red-leaved type of Japanese maple (*A. palmatum* Atropurpureum) maintains a steady burgundy color throughout the growing season, changing only slightly during fall.

Besides color variation, Japanese maples offer variety in leaf shape. Basically, the leaves of Japanese maple appear as an open hand that is dissected (divided into segments)

to form 5 to 11 lobes (the fingers of the hand). The depth of dissection and the length and width of the lobes depend on the type of Japanese maple. For example, threadleaf Japanese maple (*A. palmatum* Dissectum) has deeply dissected leaves with extremely thin, delicate lobes.

Some types of Japanese maple offer both intricate leaf shape and different coloration. Burgundy Lace (*A. palmatum* Burgundy Lace) has a deeply dissected leaf with a burgundy color in early spring that changes to a greenish burgundy for the summer. And one of the oldest and rarest Japanese maples (*A. palmatum* Dissectum Atropurpureum) is a threadleaf type with reddish foliage. Some specimens of this plant have reached only 4 feet in height even after 50 years of growth.

Their visually striking foliage makes Japanese maples splendid accent trees in the landscape. The large types (*A. palmatum* and *A. palmatum* Atropurpureum) reach a mature height of 15 to 20 feet and are excellent small shade trees for courtyards and terraces. While the upright, spreading growth habit is pleasing from a distance, the tree is best appreciated in close quarters where the foliage texture can be enjoyed.

The small, weeping Japanese maples are 4 to 6 feet tall at maturity and include the more elaborately leaved types, such as Threadleaf and Burgundy Lace. These are best used as accent plants in small gardens only, as they will be visually lost in large border plantings. Because of their particularly delicate form and slow growth rate, these types are excellent container plants for terraces or decks. In fact, they have been extensively cultivated as bonsai plants.

While Japanese maples can grow in direct summer sun, they will do best if they receive three to four hours of filtered shade daily. This is a particularly true of the smaller-leaved types. A moist, well-drained soil that is neutral or slightly acid is best.

Burgundy Lace Japanese maple offers both intricate leaf shape and different coloration.

Japanese maple is a popular tree for confined planting locations.

At maturity, the weeping Japanese maple selections are outstanding botanical specimens.

Small Trees

Jerusalem Thorn
A fountain of feathery foliage

AT A GLANCE
Light: full sun
Water: drought resistant
Soil: any well-drained soil
Growth Rate: rapid when young
Size: 25 to 30 feet

Looks can be deceiving, and the delicate, feathery foliage of Jerusalem thorn as seen from a distance looks almost fragile. In reality, Jerusalem thorn *(Parkinsonia aculeata)* is one of the most durable, tropical trees for the extreme Lower South. Native to the American tropics, Jerusalem thorn tolerates the extremes of desert and seacoast climates with equal immunity to distress.

Jerusalem thorn is a semievergreen tree, losing its leaves in the cooler regions of Florida and the Gulf South. It usually grows to a height of about 25 to 30 feet with an equal spread. Trees grow rapidly when young, gradually slowing as they approach maturity. The crown is loose and open, with branches drooping at the ends to create a willowlike effect.

Viewed close up, Jerusalem thorn takes on a different dimension. The branches and twigs are lined with 1-inch thorns, and the leaves are compound and nearly serpentine in appearance, with many tiny leaflets growing along 10- to 12-inch petioles. In late spring, small yellow flowers appear in clusters that peek through the sparse foliage. The bloom continues intermittently into summer. Most prominent through the remainder of the year are the green trunks and branches, a stem color that is distinctive to the south Florida plant.

Jerusalem thorn is not a shade tree. It is, however, a commendable specimen for its somewhat unusual texture and pleasant, irregular form. In areas where few other trees will tolerate the extremes of heat or drought, Jerusalem thorn is a good candidate for the garden or for use as a street tree. Lawn grass is not hampered by the filtered shade cast by the Jerusalem thorn. In fact, Jerusalem thorn could also be considered the Florida equivalent of the river birch (see Chinese Tallow on page 166), which also casts a similar leafy light shade. In large gardens, Jerusalem thorn is sometimes used as a clipped hedge, since the thorny branches provide an impenetrable barrier and the plants will tolerate repeated shearing. Some leaves may drop during prolonged drought, but the plant quickly recovers. Plant Jerusalem thorn in full sun and in almost any well-drained soil. This tree is considered generally pest free.

One of the plant's finest characteristics is that it is salt tolerant. In fact, it is one of the most tolerant plants and should be considered a superlative plant for beachside plantings where few trees can endure the weathering effect of salt spray.

Jerusalem thorn is a popular, small flowering tree in Florida landscapes.

Jerusalem thorn is an effective, small tree that can be used in a planter.

Loquat
One of the hardiest tropicals

Coarse, rugged, and somewhat unusual are characteristics that sum up the loquat (*Eriobotrya japonica*). Grown as a small tree or a large shrub, the loquat, or Japanese plum, as it is also called, forms a broad canopy of large, leathery leaves that inevitably makes the gardener who is unfamiliar with the plant ask, "What's this?"

Native to Japan, loquat bears heavy crops of clear yellow fruit in late winter and early spring when grown in the Lower South. In the Middle South, loquat is a popular landscape plant, although it seldom, if ever, produces fruit. The loquats mature at 15 to 20 feet tall, spreading to 10 to 15 feet. Do not plant this tree in the Upper South.

Among the most coarse-textured plants in the garden, the loquat is an eye-catching contrast to the other plants. The evergreen leaves, 4 to 12 inches long and up to 4 inches across, are elliptic, dark green on the upper surfaces, and gray green with rust-colored fuzziness beneath. White flowers, appearing in dense clusters in fall, are not very showy but they are fragrant.

Loquats, grown as trees, are most often used as specimens or accents, but the supple branches make the plants easy to train as espaliers. Do not plant loquat trees in the Gulf South where the unharvested fruit can be littersome.

In the Middle South, where plants seldom fruit, loquats can be used as lawn specimens or background plants in the shrubbery border. Unpruned, plants develop a dense, irregular crown, and it is best to locate loquats where you do not have to control their size. It is best used as a free-standing specimen, where its coarse texture and deep color will allow it to be visually powerful. For example, while both loquat and wax myrtle are approximately the same mature size, loquat planted in front of wax myrtle will be an outstanding accent planting. The broad, coarse leaves will provide an elegant silhouette against the finer texture of the wax myrtle. They can also be espaliered.

Loquat can also be considered a coarse-textured substitute for Southern magnolia in smaller gardens. Also, in areas not subject to ice damage, loquat may be successfully planted in planters against a wall and allowed to mature. The plant will arch gracefully from the wall and create a pleasant, shady sitting area beneath its cascading branches.

Plant loquats in full sun for best plant form. Although loquats are moderately drought resistant and will tolerate alkaline soil, plant growth is best in fertile, loamy soil that is well drained. Avoid planting loquats near other fire blight-susceptible plants, such as pear trees and pyracantha. Never overfertilize loquats, as rapid flushes of new growth tend to be susceptible to fire blight.

AT A GLANCE
Light: best in full sun
Water: moderately drought resistant
Soil: tolerates alkaline; best in rich, well-drained soil
Growth Rate: moderate
Size: 15 to 20 feet; equal spread

Loquat is popular as a street tree planting.

The flowers (far left) which appear in early fall are not very showy, but they are fragrant.

Loquat's edible fruit is orange and is found almost exclusively in the Lower South.

Small Trees

Magnolia
Spectacular flowers and interesting branching

There is no genus of ornamental small trees whose solitary flowers are as spectacular as those of the magnolias. So large and delicately sculptured are the flowers that these trees are known by a variety of common names. The middle-size trees have earned the collective name of tulip tree (so called for the shape of the blossoms) or saucer magnolia (perhaps because of the relative size of the blooms—to 6 inches across), and many people have also called the yulan magnolia species saucer magnolia. These middle-size magnolias are widely known throughout the entire South for their faithful, spectacular (though short-lived) show in early spring. And the smaller species are known by popular names as well; for example, the star magnolia and the lily magnolia. Each of these looks almost like a shrub, but when they are in flower, their grace is almost unsurpassed.

Surprisingly enough, the magnolias with the most prolific flowering show in the landscape are the deciduous species. The deciduous magnolias divide into three groups: the large trees (see "Large Trees," page 214); the middle-size trees, saucer magnolias (*Magnolia soulangiana*) and yulan magnolias (*M. heptapeta*); and the small trees or shrubs, (*M. stellata*) star magnolias and lily magnolias (*M. quinquepeta* Nigra).

While the color of the various species and selections will remain true throughout the entire region, magnolias exhibit markedly different characteristics depending on where they are planted—and, in some respects, can be considered more dependable flowers for the Upper rather than the Middle and Lower South. Generally speaking, they will withstand the heat in all but the most demanding areas.

In the regions of the Upper South—the Appalachian highlands of North Carolina and Tennessee, and parts of Virginia and Kentucky—the magnolia's growth is retarded by the cold. Rather than adapting the wide-ranging, ambitious growth habit of the Lower South locations, these plants grow more slowly and attain a more weathered and sculptural look. In the Lower South, the trees mature so rapidly that they almost appear ungainly; yet, at the same time, this rapid growth is advantageous where rapid landscape effect is desired in a relatively short time.

Also, in the Lower South, the flowers are far more prone to damage by freezing than in the more gradual warming that occurs in the Upper South. If a sudden freeze should occur while the magnolia is covered in delicately sculptured, tulip-shaped flowers, the tree will be draped in withered brown petals the following morning. Where the shift in temperature from spring to summer is more gradual, the trees are less likely to be affected by sudden freeze damage.

Generally speaking, the middle-size magnolias should be considered as specimen plants or spring accents for a border. Their winter interest (silver gray bark and great, hairy, terminal buds) is novel, and, in spring, if the weather permits, their flower show is spectacular. The trees are best used in conjunction with architecture or with other plantings for their greatest visual effect. It is as if the fragility of the blossoms is a character trait in the rest of the tree also—they do not seem quite strong enough to stand alone as specimens in the landscape.

However, an exception to tucking these plants aside can be to use several to create a

The fruit of sweetbay magnolia is part of the plant's winter interest.

The foliage of saucer magnolia is lush and attractive.

The flower of sweetbay magnolia is extremely sweet and appears in late spring.

grove. The wandering trunks and musculature of the branches are very effective in an accent planting—especially when underpinned with a planting of a medium height, an evergreen ground cover, or shrubbery.

While the foliage has a coarse look due to its texture, it is not overpowerful. When the pleasant light-green color is placed against a darker background, the tree can become visually attractive in any landscape planting.

Magnolias will grow best in a rich, well-drained soil either in full or partial sun. The flower show will improve if the trees are planted in full sun, although these plants will flower even with smaller amounts of light. In the Lower South, they should receive some protection from the direct rays of the noon and afternoon sun. Once planted, the trees are

Star magnolia (top) is a medium-textured small tree which, in many cases, may be used as a large shrub.

The large buds of star magnolia will unfold as the weather begins to warm.

essentially carefree and maintenance can be confined to an annual pruning to remove ungainly spots, water sprouts, or suckers that interrupt the form of the plant.

The hallmark of these trees is their flowers, however. Here is a look at the different species and their landscape assets.

Lily Magnolia

Lily magnolia (*Magnolia quinquepeta*) is more of a shrub than a small tree, reaching 12 to 15 feet in height. Its growth habit is very similar to the star magnolia. One selection that is widely distributed and makes an elegant landscape show in a shrubbery border is nigra (*M. quinquepeta* Nigra), which has a many-petaled flower that appears before the leaves. The petals are tightly grouped in a tulip shape and are a rich, deep-royal purple on the outside, with a lighter purple on the inside.

Saucer Magnolia

Saucer magnolia (*Magnolia* x *soulangiana*) is the most popular of the deciduous magnolias. The tree has a wide, ascending form with coarse-textured foliage. The flowers which appear before the foliage are variable; hence, there are a large number of selections in the nursery trade. Mature trees will reach 30 feet. Some selections are: Alexandrina—large flowers, purplish pink on outside, white inside; Lennei—large flowers, saucer shaped, deep purple outside, white inside; Rustrica Rubra—flowers rounded and lighter purple than Lennei.

Star Magnolia

Star magnolia (*Magnolia stellata*) is a profusely flowering tree (10 to 15 feet in height) that offers one of early spring's finest displays. The large buds begin to unfold as the weather begins to warm; the petals force the bud scales apart until the rays of the flowers open into a spectacular star-shaped fragrant bloom.

The flowers are broad (3 to 4 inches across), with 9 to 18 petals radiating from the slightly yellow center that contains the fertile parts of the bloom. Like most magnolias, the flowers of star magnolia do not last long, usually about 5 days; but not all the buds open at once, so the duration of the flowering can be as long as 10 days.

One of the features that make star magnolia such a versatile landscape plant is its small mature size and its form, which is similar to that of native azalea. Like native azaleas, star magnolias frequently have several trunks, a single plant often appearing as a cluster of several smaller shrubs. In addition, the branch structure is informal and slightly irregular, creating a delicate silhouette of lines.

While the most widely distributed selection is the straight species that bears white flowers, several selections that offer slightly different flower characteristics are available. Some of these are: Royal Star—double-white flowers, generally bloom earlier; Rubra—red-tipped buds; Rosea—pink, nonfragrant flowers.

Sweetbay Magnolia

Sweetbay magnolia (*Magnolia virginiana*) is the smallest evergreen magnolia widely distributed in the nursery trade. The plant in its native habitat, the wet or boggy bottomlands of the Piedmont and Coastal Plains, can reach 40 feet in height, developing a smooth, silver gray bark. More often, in its home landscape, the tree reaches around 25 feet with a spread of about 6 feet. Frequently, sweetbay is specified as a multitrunked tree, a form that is becoming as either an accent or a free-form screen.

Sweetbay is tolerant of both sunny and shady locations, but it must have well-drained soil for best growth. One of the plant's highlights is the silvery underside of the leaves, which give the tree a feeling of motion or movement in the landscape when a breeze moves the limbs. In addition, the tree has an extremely sweet blossom that appears in late spring and is followed in early summer by a bright-red, seed-bearing body.

The tree is native in the Coastal Plains up to Virginia and may be considered for landscape plantings throughout the South. If used in sheltered locations, it may be planted as far north as Lexington, Kentucky, but may become deciduous.

Yulan Magnolia

Yulan magnolia (*Magnolia heptapeta*) resembles saucer magnolia in its overall landscape appearance. The large flowers precede the leaves and are held upright; they are tulip shaped, pure white, and extremely fragrant. The tree will reach 30 feet with a wide-spreading crown. Although it is difficult to locate in the nursery trade, this tree is a good plant to use when large, white, fragrant flowers are desired.

The small magnolias make excellent accent trees for small gardens.

The flowers of star magnolia are broad, with 9 to 18 petals radiating from the center that contains the fertile parts of the bloom.

Small Trees

Palm
Exotic for the garden

AT A GLANCE

Light: full sun to partial shade
Water: moderate to drought tolerant
Soil: sandy to fertile soil
Growth Rate: slow to moderate
Size: 2 to 90 feet
Remarks: hardy in Lower South only

Pindo palm is easily recognized by its blue gray foliage and old leaf bases which are often retained all the way down the trunk. It is a fine, small palm well suited to the size of an average suburban lot.

Exotic is the word for palms. When looking through a garden framed by palms or sitting beneath a grove of these graceful trees, you are transported across oceans. Large palms are slender-trunked trees capped with great manelike crowns of foliage. They are trees in motion, and even when the air is perfectly still, the form of palms seems to create a breeze in the garden. Above all, palms are accent plants and immediately dominate the garden where they are planted.

Yet unlike most accent plants that work best as solitary specimens, palms can be successfully used as mass plantings. In fact, using palms to establish a grove or as the major planting in a landscape creates a garden effect that is both honest and direct in its approach, as well as unique in appearance.

The smaller types of palms are used in the landscape as punctuation points to contrast with other foliage or to call attention to a specific location or feature. The large palms, however, can be used as shade trees (although only casting a light shade) or as accent plantings in an open lawn. Differing from many evergreen trees in that most do not provide significant shade, tall palms can be used to frame a house, planted to form an allée, or clustered to create a grove. In addition, coarsely textured palms may be used in clumps or singly as accent plants.

Palms may be loosely divided into two groups according to their foliage: the feathered-leaved palm and the fan-leaved palm. Feathered-leaved, or pinnate, palms have foliage that is divided into leaflets which originate from a central midrib. Pinnate palms in this book include pindo palms and the date palms. The fan-leaved types are named for their resemblance to an open fan. Cabbage palmetto has an intermediate leaf shape, called costa palmate, which has characteristics of both the feather- and the fan-leaved types.

Because of limited hardiness, palms have only been planted in Florida and along the Southern coast from Texas to South Carolina. However, it has been found through the latest research and experimentation that the hardier palms may be grown in protected locations in cities such as Birmingham, Alabama; Columbia, South Carolina; Nashville, Tennessee; and Dallas, Texas. But, in general, if temperatures drop below 20 degrees, even the most cold-tolerant palms are susceptible to damage.

For the best growth palms should be planted in a fertile, slightly acid, well-drained soil. Palms which respond best to fertile soil are date palms, lady palms, windmill palms, and European fan palms. However, many palms, such as the pindo and cabbage palmetto, grow very well in sandy soils. Incorporate organic matter into sandy soil when you plant palms. Unlike other plants, the best time to plant palms is during the late spring or summer when the ground is wet and root growth is vigorous. Most palms have a small, shallow root system which is inevitably damaged in planting or transplanting. Warm soil temperatures encourage new roots that are necessary to establish the plant in its new location. After planting, be sure to keep the plant well watered. Remove some outer foliage on transplanted palms (not container grown) to reduce moisture loss through the leaves. Otherwise, the palm may lose more water than it can take up through its unestablished root system. Fertilize in the spring and fall (summer also in Florida). For the correct fertilization dosage, contact your county agent for recommendations according to soil type and tree size.

When planting single-trunked, nonsuckering palms, be especially cautious. These palms have a single growing tip at the top of the trunk from which all the leaves grow. If it dies, your palm will be a leafless trunk. Landscape contractors sometimes tie the leaves up around the treetop to protect the bud. Palms should be secured with guy wires or guide lines until the root system is established.

Large Palms

Cabbage palmetto, Canary Island date palm, and windmill palm are the tallest growing palms, reaching over 35 feet.

Cabbage palmetto (*Sabal palmetto*), native to the South, is a most dependable palm. Growing to 90 feet tall, this palm is extremely salt, drought, heat, and cold tolerant. It will also grow in wet soils. Cabbage palmetto is dependably hardy in Florida and along the coast from lower Texas to the southernmost coastal tip of North Carolina. This palm is very easy to transplant and is often moved when it is 20 feet tall or more. Plant cabbage palmetto in full sun or partial shade.

The Canary Island date palm (*Phoenix canariensis*) is a massive, very slow-growing palm. With its umbrella-shaped crown that may spread 15 to 20 feet and reach an ultimate height of 50 feet on a trunk 3 feet wide, this palm requires more space than most others. For best growth Canary Island date palm should be planted in full sun and in a fertile, moist soil; however, it will tolerate poorer soil. It is also salt tolerant and can be planted in beach landscapes. In areas where the temperature frequently drops below 20 degrees in winter, Canary Island date palm is not reliably hardy. The Senegal date palm (*Phoenix reclinata*) is a clump-forming palm with many slender, leaning trunks and suckers; it is less massive than the Canary Island date palm and is better suited for a small residential scale. It has the same cultural characteristics as the Canary Island date palm, but it is not as hardy and should be used only in southern to north central Florida and the warmer regions of Texas. Ultimately, a clump of Senegal date palms will reach a height of 35 feet and can easily spread to a width of 10 to 15 feet.

Windmill palm (*Trachycarpus fortunei*) is a single-trunked, slow-growing, slender palm that grows from 6 to 20 feet high (or higher in south Florida). The trunk is wrapped in a dark-brown fiber at the base of the leaf petioles, and the foliage is very dark green. One of the hardiest palms, this tree grows as far inland as Greenville, South Carolina, and Dallas, Texas, in a protected location. Moderately drought tolerant, windmill palm will also tolerate salt spray and sandy soil, making it a good palm for beach areas. However, for best growth, plant it in sun to partial shade in a fertile soil. It is also good for containers and indoor planting in bright locations.

Small Palms

Some of the smaller palms (less than 35 feet high) which are available at garden centers include the European fan palm, the lady palm, the needle palm, the pindo palm, and the saw palmetto.

The multitrunked character of Senegal date palm deserves an uncluttered, simple planting to set off its form. Most of the suckers that frequently come up from the base of the clump have been removed from this plant to give it a more sculptural look.

Never reaching much more than 20 feet in height (largest are in extreme Lower South), windmill palm is an excellent specimen for a restricted location. It is also salt tolerant, making it a good choice for landscapes along the coast.

Small Trees

European fan palm (*Chamaerops humilis*) is a clump-forming, slow-growing palm; it is hardy where temperatures drop to 20 degrees or slightly below. This palm has been observed to tolerate even lower temperatures but should be planted in a protected location or in a planter that can be moved indoors on severely cold nights. Growing to 20 feet high, European fan palm may form clumps that spread 6 to 8 feet or more. By removing suckers from the base of the main trunk the slightly salt-tolerant palm may also be trained as a single-trunked tree. European fan palm is difficult to transplant, so purchase container grown plants and plant them immediately in a permanent location in sun or partial shade.

Lady palm (*Rhapis excelsa*) and slender lady palm (*Rhapis humilis*) are tough and dependable but slow growing; consequently, they are expensive plants. Growing from 5 to 10 feet tall (tallest in tropical areas) and dark green in color, clump-forming lady palms tolerate low-light situations such as under a sheltered entry. They also grow well in containers and are excellent palms for indoor locations. The canelike branches are similar to heavenly bamboo.

One very hardy native palm, needle palm (*Rhapidophyllum hystix*), is native to wetlands and swamps in parts of the Southeast. This low-growing (2 to 3 feet high), fan-shaped, clump-forming palm has been used in areas where it survived temperatures of zero degrees and colder and could possibly be considered for areas as cold as Atlanta and Nashville. Unfortunately, availability of this palm is very limited. It may be available locally in areas where the plant is native or from very specialized plant sources. Needle palm grows best in moist, fertile soil and in a shady location; it will also grow in deep shade.

Pindo palm (*Butia capitata*), with its blue gray, salt-tolerant foliage is a good choice for beach landscapes. It is tough, withstanding drought and cold weather. The slow-growing pindo palm does well in the poor sandy soils of Florida and the Lower South coast. Plant single-trunked pindo palm in full sun and give it plenty of space to develop into its 20-foot-high and 10-foot-wide mature size. The orange fruit, which ripens in summer, is edible and can be used to make jelly.

Saw palmetto (*Serenoa repens*) is a low, spreading palm, native to the Lower South. If you build a house on an undeveloped lot where a few of the saw palmettos are already present, then you should try using a landscape design which will include these palms. Control their roots and rhizomes (grown on the ground surface) with regular pruning.

Trunk size and a limited, round crown make the hardy native palm, cabbage palmetto, excellent for grouping. Planted in clusters, the tall, single-trunked palms have more visual stability in the landscape.

Saw palmetto is a low, spreading palm, native to the South.

Sourwood
Pearl of the Southern summer

Sourwood (*Oxydendrum arboreum*) is native to every Southern state, but it is most abundant in the hardwood forests of the foothills and highlands of the Upper South. Sourwood adorns the August landscape with drooping clusters of tiny bell-shaped flowers. After the draping of the foliage with flowers in late summer, sourwood continues its display into autumn with the entire tree becoming a vivid rust red. Even in winter, the reddish twigs, erratic branch structure, and rugged multicolored bark make this native tree an outstanding landscape feature.

The flowers, which are the tree's hallmark, appear on long drooping clusters (panicles) at the end of the branches. Individual blossoms are suspended from tiny stems borne on a long raceme, with as many as 8 to 10 racemes forming the panicle.

Almost immediately after flowering, sourwood begins a slow change to its rust red fall color. When viewed from a distance, the tree seems a uniform color; up close, it is a study in intricate hues. The fall-color show is highlighted by the persistent flower racemes that now bear seeds. Where flowers were, there are attractive strings of tiny beadlike seeds that weather to a parchment color as the season wanes.

Sourwood grows unpredictably, and each tree is a unique tangle of deeply fissured bark and reddish winter twigs. Even when planted in uniform sunlight, sourwood branches in a random fashion, developing a singular character that is best described as generally upright.

Sourwood should be used as an accent plant in the landscape. The most successful uses are at the edge of an expanse of lawn or at the termination of a lawn vista. In either location, keep in mind its fall color. The vivid rust red of sourwood is at its best in the understory against a backdrop of yellow fall color, such as oaks, hickories, and tulip poplars.

Given proper attention, the sourwood will adjust to either deep shade or full sun. It will perform best, however, when planted in circumstances similar to its native habitat: deep, well-drained, acid soil, rich in humus, and limited exposure to direct sun (about four to five hours daily). Fortunately, it is adaptable enough to use in almost any landscape except the extreme climate of south Florida.

AT A GLANCE
Light: partial sun best
Water: moderate amount
Soil: moist, well-drained acid soil
Growth Rate: moderate
Size: to 30 feet
Remarks: a superb understory tree in all seasons—difficult to transplant when old

Sourwood adorns the August landscape with drooping clusters of tiny bell-shaped flowers.

At maturity, sourwood (right) enhances most Southern gardens with three seasons of interest.

The bark of sourwood is rugged (far right) and helps make this native tree an outstanding landscape plant even in winter.

Small Trees

Yellowwood
A native with grace and reserve

Yellowwood (*Cladrastis lutea*) drapes itself with drooping clusters of white flowers in June and then turns a splendid, glowing yellow in autumn. In contrast, the sourwood tree shows long panicles of white flowers in July and August; then, it turns brilliant scarlet in fall. Yet, while the sourwood tree is widely known, yellowwood, its native companion, is comparatively obscure. But this seldom-used native of the Southern Appalachians can be an attractive addition to any garden in the Piedmont and Upper South.

Yellowwood brings a different landscape character to the garden than sourwood. Unlike the flamboyance and flair of the sourwood, yellowwood is colorful and showy, yet slightly reserved. This small ornamental tree, which will reach 20 to 30 feet, is more regular in its growth habit than the erratic sourwood and adopts a spreading round–headed crown when mature. This uniform growth, even in varying light conditions, gives the tree a dignified appearance. Immature trees, however, are openly vase shaped in habit, and they spread out gradually as they approach mature form.

The tree is named for the bright-yellow color of the inner wood when it is cut and exposed. The bark of yellowwood is smooth and gray, although the younger branches may have a reddish tint. Yellowwood branches form a sharp upward angle with the trunk, a structural quality that adds to the strong, durable look of the tree.

The show of the plant is the flowering panicles that drape from the axils of the leaves in early summer. The panicles, which are as much as a foot in length, boast a shower of white flowers that are lightly fragrant. The flower show can be so prolific that the entire tree looks like it is covered with wisteria.

The foliage is clean and unusual; the leaves are compound and appear alternately along the branches. The individual leaflets are rounded in shape and taper to a small point. The color of the plant is a deep, fresh green that yields to a splendid yellow in fall.

Yellowwood is a slow-growing plant that needs rich, moist soil. Although this tree is normally grown in the Upper South, it may be planted in full sun in locations with adequate moisture. In the Piedmont or Middle South, the leaves will scorch if the tree is planted in an arid location. In fact, it is better to plant yellowwood where it will receive some shade from the noon or late afternoon sun. In addition, this member of the pea family can be recommended for alkaline locations.

The yellowwood will reach 20 to 30 feet and forms a spreading, round-headed crown when mature.

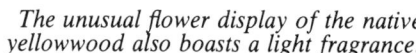
The unusual flower display of the native yellowwood also boasts a light fragrance.

Seasons in the garden can become painted in the memory by the effect that special plants bring: the shower of the golden flower bells of forsythia in early spring, the sweet fragrance of gardenia in summer, or the vivid and extreme color of winged euonymus in fall. But the majesty of the garden, the immediate and long-lasting impressions that make a garden individual and unique, belong to the large trees. They create the background and structure against which all other garden effects are staged and presented. Their contribution is not limited to a composite effect; single mature specimens can dominate a garden with incomparable beauty, subordinating all other plantings so that the memory of the garden becomes a picture of one special tree.

Trees are the largest and the most significant element of the garden; consequently, they become the most urgent consideration when the landscape is planned. Whether the raw landscape is wooded or open, the size and species of tree selected to bring shape and structure to the garden will impart an individuality that will orchestrate the character of the

Large Trees
Majesty in the garden

Southern magnolia, page 214.

Bald cypress, page 208.

201

Sugar maple, page 223.

American beech, page 205.

completed landscape. Therefore, tree selection should be based first on those qualities that trees in general bring to the garden, and secondly, on the individual expression that each species gives these qualities.

—Trees provide shade. It can be the deep, impenetrable shade of Southern magnolia or live oak, the high, clean shade of willow oak or tulip tree, the motion-filled shade of river birch or weeping willow, or the quiet, reflective penumbra of tall pines. The quality and amount of shade that a tree provides will determine the plantings that will eventually fill in and bring form to the remainder of the garden. While any tree offers shade, the type of shade will vary with the species. It is important to remember that in the South, shade is necessary; properly located shade trees can result in substantial energy savings.

—Trees provide greenery. While this may seem obvious, it is the most overlooked quality of large trees. Like shade, the green color of trees varies in hue and character. American plane tree is a coarse-textured, light green that contrasts with the deeper green and more lustrous foliage of white oak. Sweet gum has one of the deepest, steadiest green colors of the large shade trees; and, along with the sugar maple and American ash, it can form a stable, reliable backdrop for other plantings. Bald cypress has a feathery, soft color that is finely textured because of the needle foliage. In contrast, white pine and deodar cedar, which both have needle foliage, are strong, bold, bluish green in color, frequently with a slightly white cast at the edges. The other pines vary as well; Virginia pine is coarse and black green, while loblolly and long-needle pine have a softer appearance with a more yellow green cast. A discriminating look at the healthy foliage of mature trees will provide a good indication of how a younger tree will fit in with the existing specimens when it matures, or how the contrast in greens can contribute a subtle and pleasing harmony during the summer months.

—Trees provide different forms and growth habits in the garden. While older specimens of almost every species will give the feeling of a wide and spreading shape, particularly when viewed from underneath, large trees have a characteristic form. It is this maturing form that must be considered when designing with trees. For example, sweet gum, tulip tree, and common horse chestnut are strongly upright, almost pyramidal, in form but tend to relax and spread out as they mature. American beech, white oak, black gum, and scarlet oak have upright oval forms that tend to be rounded across the top and taller than they are wide. By contrast, laurel oak and live oak are more wide spreading than they are tall. The form of some trees is so striking that they are readily identifiable from a distance—river birch is linear and upright, maidenhair tree is erratic and angular,

American plane tree, page 206.

weeping willow is extremely pendulous, and Japanese zelkova has the upright vase shape that was peculiar to the American elm. The pines are upright with a flattened crown when mature. In any landscape, the particular form of a tree can be used to soften or accent a landform or the shape of a building.

—Trees provide the most colorful display in the landscape. Fall is the season of the deciduous hardwood trees, and the carnival of color that brightens the month of October may be the landscape's greatest show. It is also a challenge to decide which of the splendid displays will dominate the landscape. Perhaps the most rewarding approach for smaller landscapes is to select a dominant color range, like the reds or oranges, and use this as the backdrop color. Some of the most noticeable trees and their colors are: the sugar maple, brilliant orange red; red maple, ruby red; American beech, bronze gold; white ash, orange purple with a luminescent quality; maidenhair tree, soft butter yellow; sweet gum, yellow to wine to deep burgundy; black gum, the brightest lacquer red; white oak, bronze red; scarlet oak, brilliant scarlet; and Shumard's red oak, bright blood red.

If possible, pick trees that will complement the facade of your house in fall. If the tree is to be at the end of a vista, then select a spectacular color that will stand out against the surrounding or enframing foliage of other trees. An example might be to display a black gum (broad, oval, slightly weeping form with red color) against a backdrop of tulip trees (tall, upright, growth habit with mustard yellow color).

—Large trees provide flowers in the landscape. While flowers are more noted on the small, ornamental trees, some of the larger trees have pronounced flower shows. Combined with a species' other desirable qualities, this can come as an unexpected bonus. The most striking flowers belong to the magnolia family; the evergreen Southern magnolia produces the well-known, highly scented blossom in late summer. Cucumber tree, a deciduous species, has greenish yellow flowers that form in late spring. Bigleaf magnolia, another deciduous type, boasts 10- to 12-inch flowers that are pure white. Umbrella magnolia also has immense white flowers in late spring that are from 8 to 10 inches in diameter. Tulip tree, a magnolia relative, is another large tree that flowers—the upright, tulip-shaped flowers, light green with an orange center, are borne in early spring when the tree is completely foliated. Additional spectacular flowering trees are: red maple, whose bright-red flowers in late February give the tree its name; and common horse chestnut, which bears upright spikes of red flowers in early spring after the foliage has emerged.

—Trees can be selected to provide winter interest. A tree's contribution to the winter landscape can come from the bark, fruit, or in the case of evergreens, the foliage and the seed-bearing parts of the plant.

The bark is perhaps the most immediate show in the landscape. American plane tree, with exfoliating, brown upper bark and pure white underbark provides one of the most startling winter effects, as does the river birch with its paper thin curls of bark. White ash bark is corded and thick, while the bark of white oak is plated and imbricated (overlapped); in contrast, the bark of American beech is smooth and gray.

The fruiting bodies are also attractive. Sweet gum and sycamore suspend round ornaments from the tips of the branches through the winter season, while the fruiting bodies of the deciduous magnolias are like upright candlesticks.

The evergreen trees, of course, carry their foliage through the year and are more noticeable in the winter months; but subtle seasonal changes also enhance their appearance. The most conspicuous change is the presence of the cones in the pines—they vary from the short, stubby cones of Virginia pine to the full, long cones of longleaf pine. While the landscape effect of these cones is minimal, they do bring attention to the tree during a

White pine, page 232.

Tulip poplar, page 237.

Sweet gum, page 236.

Black gum, page 209.

much quieter season. Although selecting trees is never easy, it is made slightly less difficult by differentiating between deciduous and evergreen trees and by knowing exactly what you wish the trees to accomplish.

Usually, evergreen trees will be the strong focal point of the winter landscape. They will function as a visual mass to balance a building, to screen, or to enframe a vista. In addition, most needle-leaf evergreens are rapid growing and will provide quick cover or screening. The pines are particularly effective when used this way—both loblolly and long-needle pine are dense and full when young and will screen effectively to 15 feet. Virginia pine and white pine will retain their lower branches when planted in full sun and can provide an effective visual barrier from the ground to as high as 40 to 60 feet.

If an evergreen is needed for full shade, the logical choice is hemlock. It will retain its lower branches and foliage even in the deep shade, making it effective for gardens. Southern magnolia, in contrast, is a full-sun specimen or screening plant. Due to its massive mature size, Southern magnolia needs a lot of room to develop into a specimen plant. Eastern red cedar is also effective as a screening tree, especially if planted in lime soil. While full and symmetrical when young, the older trees develop a weathered character that has a handsome, enduring look.

Choosing a deciduous tree is a complex decision based on many of the factors that were listed earlier. Here is some additional information about specific trees.

—Sweet gum, American plane tree, and tulip tree are fast-growing trees that will provide quick shade. All of them prefer rich, moist, well-drained soil.

—American beech likes to be planted near a stream or water source, although in areas with good rainfall it can become a fine, open-grown specimen. It also enjoys rich, slightly acid soil.

—River birch is a surprisingly tolerant tree that will withstand severe heat. While it is usually found in wetlands, it can be established in poor soil.

—Red maple enjoys a lime soil; in fact, it can be planted in those areas of the country with limestone subgrade. It cannot tolerate drought, though; and if allowed to dry, red maple will die back.

—The deciduous oaks are hearty and enduring and will grow (albeit slowly) in almost any location. Willow oak, which is an excellent, rapid-growing tree, has invasive roots and should be kept from sewer and waterlines.

—White ash is a durable tree in cold locations but will grow anywhere from the Middle to Upper South. If allowed to dry out, it will go into fall color and the leaves will drop.

—Corkscrew and weeping willows are definitely accent plants. Both prefer wet locations and also have invasive root systems. They can be planted in full or partial sun.

—The deciduous magnolias are splendid screening plants in full and partial shade. While they will tolerate full sun, they will retain their foliage beneath the high canopy of oaks and beeches.

Homeowners will find that several common Southern species are unlisted in this section—for instance, the hickories, walnuts, black locust, and honey locust. Some of these species are not commercially available, others have severe disease problems that restrict their distribution, and still others are difficult to transplant. This is not to say that these trees are unacceptable as landscape plants; it is just difficult to establish them. The trees listed here are reliable performers from nursery stock and will bring a variety of landscape effects to the garden or contribute to the beauty of existing plantings with their individual qualities.

American Beech
Our stateliest native tree

The American beech (*Fagus grandifolia*) is one of the stateliest of all our native trees. A striking accent tree both for summer shade and brilliant autumn color, American beech has a handsome upright form, light-gray bark, and boldly spreading branches. However, its most distinctive feature is not revealed until winter.

Instead of the leaves dropping after the fall-color show, the foliage gradually changes from the yellow gold of autumn to an appealing parchment brown. The faded leaves may remain on the tree until spring.

American beech can be found in almost every Southern forest. Growing in association with maples, birch, and hemlock in the Upper South, the beech is mixed with sweet gum, oak, and sycamore in the lower portions of the South. Since these forests tend to become more open in the winter, the special effect of the beech—the light-brown, papery foliage and smooth gray bark—provides an unexpected richness in the winter woodland landscape.

When planted in a home landscape, the special characteristics of the American beech become even more pronounced. Set within a framework of shrubs, lawn, and ornamental trees, the bold, architectural quality of the beech creates a powerful effect.

To be enjoyed to its fullest, American beech should probably be planted as a specimen tree, especially on smaller lots. Even though it has a rather slow rate of growth, the beech eventually gets to be quite large (as much as 100 feet tall and 65 to 70 feet broad). So give it plenty of room to develop to its fullest form.

Size is not the only reason for using American beech as a single specimen. A heavy surface-feeding tree, it develops a dense network of hairlike roots just below the surface of the soil, making it extremely difficult for smaller, less aggressive plants to compete for nutrients. But by setting the beech apart, you can avoid this problem altogether; the extra separation also helps to emphasize the special qualities that make it unique.

AT A GLANCE
Light: full sun to partial shade
Water: moderate to wet
Soil: rich, well-drained soil
Growth Rate: moderate to slow
Size: to 100 feet; 35 feet in 20 years

The massive trunk structure of this American beech shows how large a mature tree can be.

The fall color of the American beech foliage (above) is yellow gold which gradually turns to parchment brown.

Young American beech trees (right) may hold their leaves all winter, even though the foliage is dead.

American Plane Tree
The correct name for sycamore

AT A GLANCE

Light: full sun
Water: moderate to wet
Soil: rich soil high in humus is best; will tolerate poorer soils
Growth Rate: rapid; a 10-foot tree will reach 25 feet in 8 years or less
Size: to 80 feet

Mature American plane trees are native to moist areas of the South, but they will tolerate most soil conditions.

This wide-leaved, light-green shade tree is well known throughout the South as sycamore *(Platanus occidentalis)*, the name given to it by the American Indians. The accepted common name is American plane tree; but, regardless of the common name used, the tree's wide-spreading, open-branched habit, rapid growth rate, and characteristic exfoliating bark have made it one of the common trees for the home landscape.

Native to the wet bottomlands and creek banks throughout the eastern United States, American plane tree is a primary shade tree that will adapt itself to a wide range of soil conditions. While it grows best in the rich, water-saturated, alluvial soils of its native location, American plane tree has been successfully used as a street tree in harsh urban locations. The vigorous root system, which enables it to withstand severe environmental pressures in the wild, sustains the tree in the nutrient-restricted soil beneath sidewalks and even in the poor soil that sometimes remains after the construction of a new home. This flexibility in planting makes it an ideal "first tree," where quick growth and shade are a necessity.

The tree's hallmark is its wide-spreading crown and large mature size. American plane tree can be expected to reach a height of 80 feet with a spread of almost 60 feet, and it is a dependable disease-free grower. The trunk will be huge and rugged, covered with a grayish brown bark that peels in vertical flakes to reveal the pure white underbark that distinguishes the tree's upper branches.

The wide, multilobed leaves (that can be up to 10 inches across) cast a light shade, since the crown of the tree, while covered with leaves, is actually sparsely foliated. American plane tree is not noted for its fall color; the leaves will turn slightly rust and then fall.

The leaves are followed by single sycamore balls, the seed capsules that give the tree still another name, buttonwood. These balls remain suspended from the branches throughout the winter and, along with the whitish bark, provide superb winter ornamentation. Eventually, they do fall and usually readily disintegrate, thus not becoming a nuisance for lawn maintenance.

The landscape strength of the plant is its beautiful winter interest plus its rapid growth. Because of its generally uniform shape, two or more trees will look good together. It is also a fine tree for wet locations, where excessive water may be a deterrent to other deciduous trees.

The wide, multilobed leaf of the American plane tree can grow to 10 inches in width.

Ash
An overlooked tree

One of our hardiest and most dependable native trees, white ash (*Fraxinus americana*), has been overlooked as a landscape plant. Rugged and adaptable to a wide variety of horticultural conditions, white ash makes a splendid shade or street tree. Its wide, ascending crown and open foliage is reminiscent of American elm, and white ash is widely used as a substitute street tree for the elm.

White ash is a rapid-growing plant eventually reaching over 70 feet tall. Mature plants have a deeply fissured bark and an upright-spreading crown. Because the leaves are compound (five to nine leaflets per leaf) and the branching habit is so open and upright, the ash does not cast a heavy, deep shade. In fact, it is one of the few shade trees that both shields from the sun but allows sufficient light to reach the ground for a healthy lawn growth. The foliage is a deep green that turns a luminescent purple in the fall. It is an unusual fall color, because the purple coloration is lightened by a yellowish pigment, making the leaves appear to glow as though illuminated from behind.

Ash trees have separate sexes, and the female tree produces inconspicuous flowers that develop into heavy clusters of one-winged samara (seeds similar to those of the maple). These seeds will germinate readily and can lead to a profusion of young seedlings. Although the heavy clusters of seeds are not unattractive, many gardeners find them objectionable. Therefore, the nursery profession predominately markets the male tree, which lacks the flowers and fruit.

White ash is extremely hardy and tolerant of soil conditions. It will do well in a well-drained neutral soil (pH 6.0 to 7.5) and in open sun. Since the root system is widespread and penetrates deeply, it prefers a deep soil.

Several selections that offer brilliant autumn color are available from commercial growers: Autumn Purple, seedless with brilliant purple color in fall; and Rosehill, seedless with unusual bronze red fall color and an upright, wide-spreading habit that withstands poor or alkaline soils.

AT A GLANCE
Light: full or partial sun
Water: moderate amount; Rosehill is more drought resistant
Soil: medium fertility; well-drained soil
Growth Rate: rapid—to 25 feet in 10 years
Size: large tree—60 to 70 feet tall
Remarks: will grow throughout the South except in subtropical climates

A mature white ash has an open yet dense canopy.

Here (right) is a young white ash.

Shown here (far right) is the rugged, interesting bark of white ash.

Bald Cypress
A surprising conifer

AT A GLANCE
Light: full or partial sun
Water: prefers moist locations
Soil: any rich, acid soil; will tolerate poor soil
Growth Rate: rapid under optimum conditions
Size: large tree—to 120 feet; 40 to 50 feet in 15 to 20 years

Note the striking form of bald cypress (right) in winter.

As a native tree, bald cypress (*Taxodium distichum*) towers above swampy and wet locations. Emerging from its watery habitat, this tree's wide-ribbed trunk tapers to a narrowly branched, flat-topped crown. The watery location forces this often giant tree to develop "knees" or rooty extensions that protrude above the surface of the water to collect oxygen for the tree's growth. Quite often, the feathery foliage remains obscured by the understory foliage; all that is visible of the tree are the black knobby knees and the rich red, shredding (exfoliating) bark.

However, bald cypress is more predictable in the home landscape. Young trees, grown in the open, have an almost perfect conical shape; and if allowed to grow without pruning, they will hold their branches low and maintain their symmetry to maturity. The foliage casts a light shade, making it possible to establish a lawn beneath the tree. The conical form has a soft outline, a characteristic that the delicate, featherlike foliage brings to the tree. Bald cypress is a conifer, but it is not evergreen—a surprising contrast to most coniferous trees. In fall, the soft, light-green needles turn a golden brown and fall, littering the ground beneath the tree so that it looks like a beautiful rust carpet.

Although it is native to wet locations, bald cypress shows remarkable tolerance for both poor soil and severe environmental conditions. It has done exceptionally well as a street tree in many cities. This hardiness makes the tree a useful landscape plant in virtually every region in the South. Once established, the plant grows very rapidly, particularly if planted near a source of water, such as a lake or a stream bed. Eventually bald cypress will become 120 feet tall, although it predictably will reach 40 to 50 feet in about 15 to 20 years if planted in ideal conditions.

Male and female cones are carried on each tree. Both are spherical in shape; the female cone is approximately 1 inch across and remains on the tree throughout the winter. The male cone is much smaller and is carried on long panicles (similar to those of sourwood) that are extremely conspicuous in winter.

A species of bald cypress, called pond cypress (*Taxodium ascendens*), is also available. It differs from bald cypress in two obvious ways: the tree is more irregular in form, with a conical shape when it is young which later develops into a wider, flatter crown, and the needles lie closely along the twigs, resembling more closely the foliage of the Japanese cedar (*Cryptomeria japonica*).

The conical shapes of these young pond cypresses (far left) will develop into wider, flatter crowns when they are mature.

The rich, shredding bark of the bald cypress (left) is one of the plant's hallmarks.

Black Gum
The most vivid red of fall

Black gum (*Nyssa sylvatica*) turns the original fire-engine red in fall. Often called pepperidge, this wide-spreading shade tree is one of the best native plants for the landscape—offering durability, handsome deep-green foliage, and unsurpassed fall color. While black gum blends handsomely with other trees throughout the year, it is in the fall that the tree becomes prominent, turning a bright lacquer red—a color so vivid that it almost seems painted. What gives the color that special quality is the glabrous (lacking of any fine hair or pubescence) foliage; it appears as though the fall color in the leaf has been covered with a clear shellac. Even in summer, the leaves may be bright and shiny, as if they were wet.

Black gum is a widely-distributed tree that is indigenous to the Piedmont and highlands of the South. A close relative, tupelo or sour gum (*Nyssa aquatica*), is native to the swampy and wet regions of the Coastal Plains from eastern Virginia to Texas. Sour gum and black gum are among a select group of trees that will give dependable fall-color shows to the warmer regions of the South; thus, they are particularly valuable landscape plants for the Gulf South.

Black gum has an upright and slightly spreading habit of growth. Older trees develop a slightly weeping habit that makes them especially attractive. In addition, the bark of the older trees is deeply furrowed and dark. Younger trees tend to be very symmetrical in growth habit, with a tapering crown of foliage that flattens out as the tree matures. The foliage is deep green, with the leaves tapering and slightly pointed at the ends. The tree is not heavily foliated and thus creates a light shade, making it possible to establish a lawn.

Male and female flowers are borne on separate trees. Pollination of the female tree results in extremely attractive cobalt blue fruit, called drupes, that occurs in pairs suspended from long peduncles or stalks from the twigs. The fruit matures in summer and remains on the trees throughout the fall show, contrasting handsomely with the intense red foliage.

Black gum tolerates a wide variety of soil conditions, but it prefers a moist location and will readily signal a lack of water by premature coloration and leaf drop. The tree cannot be easily transplanted from the wild and the chances of successfully establishing a plant are best if a small (under 6 feet tall) nursery-grown plant is selected. Even though it occurs naturally in the understory, black gum may be planted in full sun; and, if kept watered, the tree will establish itself and do quite well. Mature trees will reach 100 feet tall, and a young tree can reach 25 to 30 feet in 10 years; when planting, be sure to give them adequate room to grow.

AT A GLANCE
Light: full sun to partial shade
Water: prefers a moist location
Soil: tolerant of almost any soil (pH 6.0 to 7.0)
Growth Rate: moderate
Size: to 100 feet eventually—25 to 30 feet in 10 years (difficult to transplant)

Black gum is one of the South's most durable landscape trees.

Large Trees

AT A GLANCE

Light: full sun
Water: moderate amount; once established is drought hardy
Soil: any well-drained soil; prefers loam or sandy clay
Growth Rate: moderate to rapid
Size: to 40 feet ultimately; 20 to 25 feet in 20 years

Deodar
A cedar for the South

The most exciting plants to watch mature are those that undergo the most noticeable changes over the years. The deodar cedar (*Cedrus deodara*) rewards its watchers with a procession of sizes and forms, from the almost spindly nursery plant, to the pyramidal form of the tree in its active years, to the neatly mounded, matriarchal nature of the mature tree.

With its dense, weeping boughs, deodar cedar can be used for screening, as an accent with pines and other needle-leaved trees, or as a majestic specimen tree. In the Southeast, mature trees may reach 40 feet in height, with lower limbs spanning 20 to 25 feet. After 20 years, the green to blue green foliage of deodar cedar provides contrast with other trees.

The bark is another point of interest. On young trees, the bark is gray and smooth, becoming brown and furrowed (resembling pine bark) as the tree matures. Although the plant is classified as a conifer, cone production is rare on plants grown in this country.

Native to the Himalayas, deodar cedar is hardy in the Middle and Upper South. It can also be grown in northern Florida; and in Texas it can be grown as far south as Houston. Several selections of deodar cedar are available. Of particular interest is Aurea, which has almost yellow foliage in early spring, turning yellow green late in the season. Another notable selection is Pendula, which is distinguished by weeping branches whose ends are turned upward. Deodar may be confused with other cedars, particularly the popular atlas cedar. However, the leaves of deodar cedar may be 1½ to 2 inches long whereas those of the atlas cedar are about 1 inch long and denser.

Because of its size, deodar cedar should be located where it will have plenty of room to spread. Space plants at least 25 feet from buildings or other plants. Do not attempt to prune nursery plants to train a central leader; deodar cedar develops a main trunk naturally, and early pruning may damage its later form. Plant in loamy soil that is well-drained. Deodar cedar prefers full sun but also grows well in partial shade as long as it receives full sun for at least half of the day. Deodar cedar responds well to an annual fertilization program, but do not overfertilize; growth resulting from excess fertilization may be spindly and weak, detracting from the plant's natural form.

In its early stages, deodar cedar is very conical (left); but as it matures, it becomes more globose (right).

Hemlock
Gracefulness in the Southern shade

There are very few needle-leaf evergreen trees that will retain their foliage and full form naturally in shady locations. Fortunately, two species of the shade-loving hemlock may be adapted to gardens beyond their natural habitat, the Southern highlands. Canadian hemlock (*Tsuga canadensis*) and Carolina hemlock (*Tsuga caroliniana*) can be expected to reach 60 to 70 feet tall eventually; the taller Canadian hemlock easily reaches well over 100 feet in its native habitat—the Appalachian mountains.

Both of these trees will retain their lower branches and conical habit of growth in all but the deepest shade. And even those trees planted as an accent or screen beneath a hardwood canopy will maintain sufficient low foliage to create a dense visual barrier. Only when hemlocks become extremely old will they gradually begin to lose their lower limbs, revealing the deeply furrowed and ridged bark.

While it grows naturally in the understory or partial shade, the hemlock may readily adapt to full sun locations. This flexibility makes it an especially desirable landscape plant, since the hemlock is one of the few Southern conifers with a low-branching pyramidal form. This makes it a suitable accent plant or hedge plant. In fact, since hemlock has needle foliage and is relatively fast growing, in the Upper South it is often used in a formal way as a sheared hedge—an effective landscape use but one which destroys the tree's natural form.

While Carolina and Canadian hemlock are both adaptable to the same landscape uses, there are noticeable differences between the two trees. Canadian hemlock is more widely available and will grow in a wider geographic range than the Carolina species. Roughly speaking, Carolina hemlock is hardiest in the cool, upper elevations of the mountains, while Canadian hemlock will survive in moist, shaded conditions as far south as Jackson, Birmingham, and Atlanta. Neither plant will do very well in Coastal Plains locations.

In addition, the two trees differ significantly in appearance. Carolina hemlock is soft and more weeping in form, with a textured outline that more closely resembles deodar cedar. This is because the needles on Carolina hemlock are longer and are attached to the twigs in whorls, while the shorter needles of Canadian hemlock lie flatter on the stems. Also, Carolina hemlock is a slightly lighter green than its Canadian counterpart. When full grown, both of the trees are magnificent specimens that will dominate other plantings in the garden.

One other selection is available with a unique pendulous habit of growth. Sargent's weeping hemlock (*Tsuga canadensis* Pendula), a broad mounding plant with extremely graceful branches, is very slow growing. It is an unusual specimen and best used as an accent plant.

Hemlock prefers filtered shade in most of the South.

AT A GLANCE
Light: full to partial sun
Water: a moderate amount
Soil: any well-drained, rich, slightly acid soil
Growth Rate: moderate
Size: 40 to 60 feet; usually 30 to 35 feet in 15 to 20 years

The common horse chestnut makes a beautiful landscape plant.

Horse Chestnut
Brings flowers and shade

One of late spring's spectacular flower shows belongs to a magnificent shade tree, common horse chestnut (*Aesculus hippocastanum*). This towering native tree, with an upright (almost columnar) form, opens its leaf buds extremely early. After the foliage has emerged, the tree becomes covered in upright spikes of flowers that are 10 inches long from the tips of the branches.

The flowers may last as long as two weeks and, depending on the species and selection of the tree, will be either red or white or greenish yellow. There are actually several species of *Aesculus* that are misleadingly labeled horse chestnut. Each of the native selections makes an excellent landscape plant in its own right, and hybrids between the different types have generated some superb ornamental shade trees.

The species that are used as ornamentals are: common horse chestnut (*Aesculus hippocastanum*)—white flowers in 10- to 12-inch spikes; Ohio buckeye (*A. glabra*)—greenish yellow flowers with gold autumn color; and red buckeye (*A. pavia*)—shrub or small tree, to 12 feet with 8-inch spikes of red flowers.

The most striking flower show belongs to the hybrid ruby horse chestnut (*A.* x *carnea* Briotii), which is a cross between common horse chestnut and red buckeye. This handsome tree grows to 40 feet and has a symmetrical oval crown. The flower spikes are 8 to 10 inches long and bright scarlet. Another selection, Rosea (*A.* x *carnea* Rosea), has pink flowers.

All of these species have deep-green, distinctively palmate compound leaves. The actual number of leaflets varies from five to nine, and the size of the individual leaflets on each leaf will vary. Characteristically, the foliage layers and spreads over itself, creating a very deep, dark shade. And, except for the Ohio buckeye, which turns a gold autumn color, all species exhibit minimal fall coloration. The fruit of these species is the hard buckeye that falls from the tree in late autumn.

In winter, the horse chestnuts and buckeyes offer deep-black bark and a stiff thick-limbed branching structure that is characterized by very large terminal buds. Their winter character is rugged and durable, and the species are extremely hardy, tolerating both urban pollution and the salt spray of ocean breezes.

Because of the deep shade beneath them and the large seed husks, which can create a nuisance for lawnmowers, these trees are more successfully used in a woodland setting or in a mulched planting bed. Here, the seeds will fall inconspicuously, and the heavy shade will not interfere with lawn growth.

The flowers of the common horse chestnut (far left) may last as long as two weeks.

After the foliage has emerged, red buckeye (left) becomes covered with upright spikes of flowers that are 8 inches long.

Japanese Zelkova
Zelkova arches like an elm

The passing of the American elm due to Dutch elm disease has left a gap in the landscape designer's repertoire of tree forms. The vase-shaped branching of the elm made it an unsurpassable street and shade tree—but fortunately, there is a hardy Oriental native that can rapidly fill this important design role. Japanese zelkova (*Zelkova serrata*) offers the same wine-glass shape as the American elm. In addition, it is a rapid-growing tree that will ascend 40 to 60 feet in its mature state.

Although the shape and branching structure of the tree make it a useful elm substitute, the leaf shape and bark resemble still other familiar landscape plants. The leaf is serrated and ribbed and looks remarkably like the leaf of ironwood. The bark is smooth and silvery and resembles the bark of American beech (but much darker).

As a rule, Japanese zelkova has a single trunk, although multitrunked trees are not at all unusual. The tree is a vigorous grower and has been known to sucker (send up separate leaders from the base), which can be a nuisance if a single-trunked specimen is desired.

Both male and female flowers occur on the same tree but at different levels. The upper branches of the tree bear the fertile flowers and generally have shorter leaves than the lower branches, where the male flowers occur. The flowers do not have an outstanding ornamental quality. In fall, Japanese zelkova turns deep maroon red (occasionally yellow) and retains the color display for a long period.

Village Green is one selection that is exceptionally cold hardy and has extended the range of the tree considerably. In addition, it is uniform in growth habit; thus, several specimens may be easily matched for a street planting.

Several factors restrict the use of Japanese zelkova in the Lower South. It is subject not only to heat damage but also to sunscald of the exposed trunk. It will be necessary to be sure that the trunk is properly wrapped when planted. One other caution with Japanese zelkova: the bark that is so attractive can be severely damaged by lawnmowers or other equipment; care must be taken when mowing around these trees. These wounds will provide access for borers and other damaging insects.

AT A GLANCE
Light: full sun
Water: moderate amount
Soil: any soil except wet
Growth Rate: rapid
Size: 40 to 60 feet; a 1- to 2-foot tree will reach 20 feet in 5 years

The vase-shaped form of the Village Green Japanese zelkova is distinctive in this Southern landscape.

Planted in mass, the young Japanese zelkova trunks resemble groves of young American elms.

Magnolia
Large flowers and larger leaves

AT A GLANCE

Light: full sun or partial shade
Water: most species not drought resistant
Soil: best in deep, moist, well-drained soil
Growth Rate: moderate to rapid
Size: 50- to 90-foot trees at maturity—20 to 40 feet in 15 to 20 years

Although cucumber tree magnolia is pyramidal in its youth, mature trees tend to become more rounded.

To most people, the word magnolia conjures up that magnificent evergreen tree with the big, white, fragrant flowers. Southern magnolia is one of the best ornamental large trees for the South, but the group includes several other noteworthy large trees, too, particularly cucumber magnolia, large-leaved magnolia, and umbrella magnolia. These three species are deciduous and much hardier than the evergreen Southern magnolia.

The magnolias, as a group, are large-leaved trees, rapid growers, and abundant bloomers. Most magnolias also have bright-red fruit (seeds) that are showy, starting in late summer. The group is relatively free from insect pests and fungus diseases.

Because of their size and coarse texture, the larger magnolias must be situated in the garden with great care. The once-popular practice of espaliering Southern magnolia was impractical for most gardeners since the tree can become a maintenance problem when grown in this manner. All large magnolias are best planted where they can grow as rampantly as they may be inclined to, away from buildings and thereby eliminating the need to prune the plant to control its size.

This is not to say that magnolias cannot be used in combination with other plants, particularly the larger ones. A combined canopy of magnolias and pines can provide a simple, low-maintenance evergreen area that can be used for screening or for reducing street noise.

Southern Magnolia

Few plants are sufficiently distinctive to compose an entire garden in themselves, but Southern magnolia (*Magnolia grandiflora*) is such a plant. Thought of by many as a prime symbol of plantation days, the Southern magnolia grows to a monumental pyramid of year-round foliage. The late springtime fragrance of the blossoms can perfume an entire neighborhood, and, at Christmas, magnolia branches are often used for indoor greenery. Native to the region, this magnolia can be grown throughout the South, except in western Texas, Oklahoma, south Florida, and mountain areas.

Maturing when around 60 to 90 feet tall, Southern magnolia will have a 30- to 40-foot spread. Leaves are oblong to ovate and between 5 and 8 inches long. They are glossy, bright green, and leathery to the touch. The flowers, which appear most abundantly in April and May, are 6 to 10 inches across, waxy white, and extremely fragrant. They may occur sparsely through September, followed by seedpods that are red enough to create landscape interest.

Everything about the Southern magnolia is big—the leaves, the flowers, and most of all, the plant itself. It is, therefore, not a tree for the small garden unless you intend to have very little else. In a good-sized lawn, however, Southern magnolia is the specimen par excellence. A triad of magnolias can also make a long-lived, but fast-growing, screen or noise barrier. And a single magnolia at the edge of a wooded or naturalized area can provide a perfectly natural contrast for accenting either conifer or hardwood trees.

In closer quarters, enough lower limbs may be removed to allow movement under the tree. A word of warning, however—Southern magnolia constantly drops a few old leaves, seedpods, or blooms in season. Plants whose lower limbs have been removed can be messy, and the area under them will require daily raking. Grown away from buildings and outdoor living areas, the lower limbs can be left on the tree, creating a solid mass of foliage. This is also a practical measure; with the lower limbs growing all the way to the ground, Southern magnolia conceals its own debris.

Locate Southern magnolia in either full sun or partial shade, depending on soil conditions. In moist, peaty soil, magnolias can tolerate the hot summer sun. In areas where rainfall is irregular or the soil is too light to retain moisture naturally, plant magnolias in partial shade, protecting the tree from the afternoon sun, if possible.

There are many superb selections of Southern magnolia, including Glenn St. Mary, with bronze leaf undersurfaces, and Majestic Beauty, with deep-green foliage and a profusely flowering habit. Also, here is a tip with regard to cold hardiness: the "brown-backed" leaves tend to be more cold hardy than those that are green on the undersides.

Bigleaf Magnolia

It is hard to believe that a plant with such tropical-looking leaves as the bigleaf magnolia (*M. macrophylla*) could be hardy as far north as New England, but it is. This unusual native tree matures at about 50 feet tall with a spreading crown. The large, paddlelike deciduous leaves may be from 12 to 36 inches long and 12 inches wide near the tips, but they narrow toward the petiole. The flowers, appearing in early summer, are cup shaped, about 12 inches across, waxy white, and fragrant. Bigleaf magnolia grows well in the Upper and Middle South but adapts poorly to summer heat in warmer areas.

Exotic and unusual plants, such as the bigleaf magnolia, are often difficult to use in the landscape. The enormous leaves do create a tropical atmosphere, but this fact does not necessitate the use of tropical plants as companions. Bigleaf magnolia seems as much at home in the Southern garden as the other native magnolias. Used alone as a specimen, the large leaves and flowers of this tree are overpowering in the landscape. An underplanting of late spring bulbs or summer cannas can help de-emphasize this tree within the garden. Situated at the edge of a woodland planting or within a grove of pines or other magnolias, bigleaf magnolia accents the other trees effectively and receives protection against winds. It is important to plant bigleaf magnolia in a protected place since the leaves flop around in the wind and tear easily, leaving the plant in an unsightly condition until fall when the leaves drop.

Bigleaf magnolia prefers deep, moist, peaty soil although the plant should grow satisfactorily in less than ideal soil. Plant in full sun or partial shade.

Cucumber Tree

Another popular magnolia is the cucumber tree (*M. acuminata*). This deciduous tree grows rapidly to about 90 feet with a 30- to 40-foot spread. Although cucumber tree is pyramidal in its youth, mature trees tend to become more rounded. Native to the east-central United States, cucumber tree can be grown throughout the South except in western Texas and Oklahoma. In Florida, cucumber tree is limited to the panhandle.

Like the other magnolias, cucumber tree tends to have large leaves, 6 to 9 inches long, with light-green undersides. Leaf shape is irregular but is somewhat ovate with wavy

Shown here are the foliage and fruit of Southern magnolia.

The bigleaf magnolia is named for its extremely large leaves, which may be 3 feet long and up to 1 foot wide.

Large Trees

Southern magnolia is best used as a specimen tree in a landscape which has large, open spaces.

Here is a young Southern magnolia that has been recently planted.

margins. Flowers are yellowish green, 2 to 3 inches across, and not very conspicuous, since the tree blooms in early summer after the leaves have come out. In the fall, the leaves turn yellow to brown before falling.

Because of its coarse texture and deciduous habit, cucumber tree makes a good accent tree when planted with other trees for screening purposes. Cucumber tree also makes a good lawn specimen. Locate cucumber tree in either full sun or partial shade. Soil requirements for this magnolia are more stringent than for most trees. The plant needs deep, fertile soil that is moist and yet well drained.

A smaller form of this tree, called yellow cucumber tree (*M. acuminata* Cordata), is sometimes used as a substitute, particularly in a smaller garden. The plant reaches a height of about 30 feet and may be grown as either a tree or a large shrub. The flowers are a brighter yellow and more conspicuous than those of the regular cucumber tree.

Umbrella Magnolia

With leaves nearly rivaling those of the bigleaf magnolia, umbrella magnolia (*M. tripetala*) forms a less pyramidal tree than most other magnolias, often growing as an open-crowned tree or, in the wild, as a large shrub. The branch structure is distinctive; the branches themselves are often rugged and contorted, adding to the winter appeal of the tree.

Native to the eastern United States, umbrella magnolia grows to around 40 feet tall with a 20- to 25-foot spread. Found most frequently in boglands and wooded areas of the Upper and Middle South, umbrella magnolia can be expected to grow well across most of the South, including southeastern Oklahoma and northeastern Texas. It does not grow well in Florida or in the rest of the Lower South.

Leaves of umbrella magnolia are generally obovate to oblanceolate. They are about 10 inches wide. They grow alternately along the branches, becoming crowded toward the ends of the branches. The white flowers are multipetaled, often 8 to 10 inches across, and mildly odiferous.

Umbrella magnolia, because it is smaller than bigleaf magnolia, can be used as a substitute for the latter in gardens where the bigleaf magnolia would be disproportionately large. Umbrella magnolia makes a good specimen or accent tree in addition to blending well with other large deciduous trees and conifers in a naturalized area or at the edge of a woodland planting. Situate umbrella magnolia where its winter form can be enjoyed. Some find the scent to be less than pleasant; to be on the safe side, plant umbrella magnolia away from the house and outdoor living areas.

Like the cucumber tree, umbrella magnolia is more particular about soil and moisture than other members of the genus. Plant umbrella magnolia in moist, fertile, well-drained soil and in either full sun or partial shade.

Maidenhair Tree
A plant that is eons old

If there is any question about the hardiness and durability of the maidenhair tree (*Ginkgo biloba*), then consult fossil records. Imprints made millions of years ago indicate that this erratically branched shade tree was one of the first plants to evolve a seed-bearing means of reproduction. It is still hardy and viable today and is one of the more durable shade trees.

The common name comes from the peculiar fan-shaped leaves that closely resemble the leaflets of maidenhair fern. The foliage characteristically lines the branches and, instead of forming a wide broad crown, emphasizes the branching structure of the tree. The branching habit is perhaps the tree's most distinctive characteristic and, besides the fall color, the feature that likely caught the Western gardener's eye when the tree was discovered in the Orient during the seventeenth century. The maidenhair tree's branches seem to grow in every direction—in a thoroughly arbitrary fashion. The crown shape, which varies greatly with individual trees, seems full of erratically projecting branches and gives the tree an eccentric scarecrow appearance (like modern sculpture). This unusual display makes the tree an excellent specimen plant, particularly where there is sufficient space to appreciate its character from all directions.

The maidenhair develops leaves comparatively early in the spring and carries an even, green foliage into early fall. Fall is perhaps the tree's finest season. Beginning at the edges of the leaves, the chlorophyll seems to drain down the veins and into the stems of the branches, leaving behind a beautiful butter-yellow coloration. Thus, the leaves during the fall change will be a soft butter yellow with the veinage still prominently etched in its characteristic summer green. The change is gradual and prolonged, with the full display lasting almost two weeks—leaving the tree in a crown of perhaps the purest yellow of the season. But once the leaves start falling, the tree will become completely bare in 3 to 4 days. In winter, the wild branching structure and knobby protrusions along the branches, where the leaves are attached, give the maidenhair tree a distinctive shape.

If there is a drawback to this singularly fine specimen, it is that maidenhair tree may be one of the slowest growing large shade trees. It will spend many years in an awkward adolescent stage until it finally begins to develop a full mature crown.

Maidenhair tree seems to adjust to any environmental condition. It is so hardy that substantial trees may be seen in just about every old estate planting in almost every region of the South. Maidenhair tree prefers a rich soil, but it is so adaptable it will thrive as a street tree or in poor soil.

It is important to remember to plant only male trees. The female tree, which flowers, bears an obnoxious-smelling fruit in the fall. The crushed or bruised fruit smells of rotten eggs and may take away from the attractiveness of the tree. Interestingly though, the seed inside the pulpy covering is considered a delicacy in the Orient.

Several selections are available that offer an appearance that is slightly different from the erratic growth that is the species' hallmark. They are: Aurea, with bright-yellow leaves; Fastigiata, a tree with a pyramidal habit; Laciniata, with leaves deeply divided; and Pyramidalis, a tree with a strongly pyramidal habit and a name that is patented.

AT A GLANCE
Light: full or partial sun
Water: moderate amount; generally drought hardy
Soil: any well-drained soil
Growth Rate: slow to moderate
Size: to 80 feet

While slow growing, maidenhair tree can become an effective landscape tree at an early age.

Tulip poplar, page 237.

Bald cypress, page 208.

Sweet gum, page 236.

Red maple, page 221.

Large Trees

Sugar maple, page 223.

Maidenhair tree, page 217.

Large Trees

Maple
Shade tree for the South

AT A GLANCE

Light: full sun
Water: moderate amount; red maples tolerate wet locations
Soil: any well-drained soil; red maples tolerate high alkaline soil
Growth Rate: slow to moderate; silver maple and Norway maple, rapid
Size: some to 100 feet with 50- to 60-foot crown spreads

The maples are among the most widely planted shade trees for several reasons. All members of the species are free of debilitating diseases or insect pests; they thrive in a wide variety of horticultural conditions; and they produce dependable deep shade and a wide range of fall color.

Yet in spite of being one of the important shade trees for this region of the United States, the maples are usually considered a northern species. This is especially ironic since maples are native to every Southern state. While the climatic conditions that permit the making of maple syrup do not exist in the South, horticulturally, this genus will grow with every bit of the dependability and flair that is so proudly proclaimed elsewhere. In fact, because of the warmer climate, the maples can be expected to mature faster and become more effective in the landscape in a shorter period of time.

The hallmark of the maples is their fall color. The colors range from rich lemon yellow, characteristic of silver maple (*Acer saccharinum*), to the ruby red of red maple (*A. rubrum*), to the boisterous flaming orange of sugar maple (*A. saccharum*). Invariably, maples can be counted on for a brilliant fall show, but that is only for one season of the year; the appeal of the maples extends throughout the growing season and into the dormancy of winter.

Characteristically, maples are among the first flowering trees of spring (especially the red maple) and one of the few large deciduous trees that produces a noticeable flowering

Note the distinctive shapes of the two maples, Crimson King Norway maple (left) and sugar maple (right).

show. Following the flowers, the seed bodies or samara develop. These are the familiar maple wings that flutter to the ground just prior to the leaf emergence. The foliage, which emerges shortly after the fruit develops, is a deep steady green among all the trees except silver maple, which has a lighter underside reminiscent of the true poplars. In winter, the bark and branching habit of each tree is distinctive enough to be a valuable key in winter identification.

Maples should be planted for shade and for show. Mature trees are large, and most residential landscapes can be shaded completely by three of four of any of the species. When planted in good conditions, all of the species will easily develop a crown width of 30 feet in about 15 to 20 years. Keep in mind the fall color when selecting a maple. Since it is so vivid, the trees should be selected so that the color complements the color of the house facade. For example, if your house is red brick, then the yellow fall color of silver maple will be visually more complementary that either the ruby of red maple or the flame orange of sugar maple. Except for specific soil and climate compatibility where certain species are better adapted, color is one of the most important considerations in choosing a maple.

Shown here is the fruit of Crimson King Norway maple.

Norway Maple and Crimson King Norway Maple

Norway maple (*Acer platanoides*) is a large-leaved tree that develops an upright, rounded crown. The tree is a durable, rapid grower and performs best in the Mid- to Upper South. Fall color on the standard type is bright yellow. Characteristically, the tree is very hardy and tolerates both city conditions and the severe demands of a seashore environment. It is a vigorous feeder with a root system that is close to the surface, as are those of all maples, sometimes making it difficult to establish a ground cover planting underneath the tree. The leaves are slightly broader but similar to sugar maple. Since the sap of Norway maple is a milky white and bleeds readily from the base of the leaf petiole if the leaf is removed, the trees may be easily distinguished.

Crimson King Norway maple is a species that has deep maroon leaves year-round. The crown is lightly flattened and more globose than Norway maple. Since the leaves have such deep color throughout the year, the fall color change is minimal. Crimson King needs sunlight to retain its foliage color. The leaves that are shaded will revert to the characteristic green coloration. Thus, if you look at the foliage from underneath a mature Crimson King, it will appear to be basically a green tree with a very deep shade. However, when viewed across an open space or in a planting, the tree will be deep maroon. Because of this foliage color, Crimson King is best used as a single accent plant in the landscape.

Sugar maple is an excellent tree for scale in the home landscape.

Red Maple

Ironically, the red maple (*Acer rubrum*)—the shade tree heralded for its vivid fall color—is actually named for the flowers that it brings to the waning winter landscape. In a season of browns, ochres, and muted greens, and bronzed grasses still pressed by frost, red maple hovers above and is washed with ruby red flowers. And against the clear, still cold, blue sky, the flowers are suspended like tiny jewels.

The tree is easily picked out from a woodland edge—the gray tangle of still-dormant twigs and branches beyond is a perfect backdrop for the seasonally unexpected color. The

Here is an attractive row of young silver maples used as street trees.

The upright, branching structure of sugar maple makes it an excellent street tree.

color of forest edge trees seems muted by the gray winter woods, but the individual flowers are bright ruby, delicately suspended from the twigs on long, red pedicels in clusters of as many as twenty individual flowers.

Another fine feature of red maple is the smooth, silver gray bark that becomes slightly rugged and striated with age. Older red maples have rugged trunks that bring character to the tree during early winter.

Red maple is not bothered by either heavy clay soils or wet lowland conditions. The root system is vigorous and can sustain the tree during adverse conditions. Regardless of the soil structure, whether clay or sandy, red maple prefers a rich soil.

The red maple is widely available from the nursery trade. There are several named types that will do well in the South: Autumn Flame, a round-shaped crown with a

prolonged fall display; October Glory, brilliant crimson color, with longer display than Autumn Flame; Columnare, a dense, upright form; and Drummondii, leaves deeply cut with five lobes—leathery above and pubescent below.

Silver Maple

Silver maple (*Acer saccharinum*) is the fastest-growing popular maple, and it is considered a "weed tree" by many horticulturists. Eventually, the tree can be expected to reach a height of 60 feet with a 60-foot crown spread. Because of its rapid growth, silver maple is a good selection for fast shade cover in a barren landscape. But the rapid growth that enables the tree to provide quick shade has a drawback—the wood of silver maple is brittle and weak. The tree is likely to be damaged by high winds.

Silver maple has bark and leaf characteristics that make it markedly different from the other maples. The bark is shaggy and flaky; it is silver gray with light-brown highlights. The leaf is deeply cut, and every breeze shows off the light green on top and light silver underneath. In fall, the tree turns lemon yellow.

Silver maple will adapt to any soil condition from sandy loam to heavy clay. Since it grows very rapidly and is easily propagated, it is widely available in nurseries.

Southern sugar maple has smaller leaves than the common sugar maple.

Most maples blend easily into the native landscape, as does this silver maple.

Southern Sugar Maple

Southern sugar maple (*Acer barbatum*) can bring the rich fall color of the common sugar maple into the landscape of the Lower South. Southern sugar maple has smaller leaves and a more irregular open habit of growth than sugar maple. In addition, the edges of the leaves curl under slightly—an appearance that makes it noticeably different. The tree has admirable fall color; when it is mature, it can reach 50 feet in height and is more adapted to the alkaline soils of the coastal areas.

Sugar Maple

The durable sugar maple (*Acer saccharum*) is native to the extreme Upper South. It is probably the most widely planted shade tree and can be relied on to grow magnificently in almost any landscape. Without question, sugar maple provides the finest fall-color show of the large maples. It produces a deep-green shade underneath its uniform upright rounded crown. The tree frequently branches low from the trunk and makes a fine climbing tree with age.

One of the most delightful characteristics is the way it loses its brilliant-colored leaves in the fall. The leaves at the top of the crown fall first, and the bare leaves of the upper portion of the tree will emerge from a girdle of still-brilliant leaves on the lower branches. In addition, as the leaves fall, they retain their color and lighten the ground beneath the tree, reflecting the same hue that the still-attached foliage displays. Generally speaking, the tree is almost unsurpassable as a shade tree when given adequate room to mature. Old trees can be 80 feet tall with a 40- to 50-foot crown spread.

Sugar maple is tolerant of a wide range of soil conditions but prefers a rich soil. The bark of old trees is coarse, rugged, and slightly shaggy, somewhat similar to white oak. Specific selections are: Green Mountain, with a rounded crown and deep-green foliage; and Monumentale, a columnar selection.

Large Trees

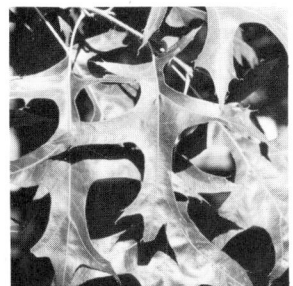

Oak
Symbol of strength and age

AT A GLANCE

Light: full sun
Water: best with regular irrigation; most species reasonably drought resistant
Soil: wide range
Growth Rate: slow to moderate
Size: large to very large trees

The laurel oak is one of the most adaptable large shade trees in the southeastern United States.

In the South, the word oak is nearly synonymous with the word tree. Few gardens are without oaks and, for this reason, oak trees are a part of the experience of everyone, gardener or not. From the subtropical live oak to the white oak of Virginia and Kentucky, nearly everyone has at some time sat under an oak, swung from an oak, or built a tree house in an oak.

Because of their size and slow rate of growth, oaks have come to be symbols of strength and age and wisdom. To plant an oak is to bequeath something ageless and enduring to future generations.

The oaks are familiar to the point of being taken for granted; and yet, the commonness of the oaks is the surest testimony to their ability to endure. Oaks occur naturally, in the wild and in the garden, from seed that is distributed by squirrels, the wind, and other natural forces. In some gardens, it is difficult not to have oaks.

Like the pines, the oaks are a widely distributed group from which you can select trees that will adapt to any locality in the South. Although most oaks are large, deciduous trees, the evergreen live oak is the exception. Oak is the most popular shade tree and, in many communities, the most widely used street tree. Parks and playgrounds are full of oak trees, campuses abound in oak trees, and the more appearance-conscious shopping malls have included trees—oftentimes oaks.

Because most oaks are deciduous, they bring seasonal change and drama to the garden. The leaves of summer provide shade that can help reduce wasteful overuse of air conditioning. Each fall, oak trees supply gardeners with leaves that can be used as compost, mulch, or soil conditioners to make unusable soil suitable for gardening. In winter, the bare branches allow sunlight into places where the summer sun never reaches—porches and windows where potted plants can thrive, and garden plots that are too shady in summer but receive plenty of light after the leaves fall to grow cabbages, turnips, and other winter vegetables.

Oaks provide the perfect shade for azaleas, dogwoods, rhododendrons, gardenias, and other popular ornamentals that require protection from summer sun. Mulching these plants with oak leaves helps maintain the soil at the acidity level required by azaleas and their relatives.

Oak wood is considered one of the best hardwoods for the fireplace. Occasional trimming of large branches can contribute to the season's supply of firewood.

Oaks are used as framing trees in the landscape. Planted near the house as shade trees, oaks can strongly influence the character of the garden, both for their own sculptural value and for the horticultural conditions created by the shade they cast. Planted away from the house, oaks can be used to determine property boundaries.

Laurel Oak

The laurel oak (*Quercus laurifolia*), because it is native to the southeastern United States, is one of the most adaptable large shade trees in our region. A popular street tree throughout the Upper, Middle, and Lower South, laurel oak is noted for its dense, rounded form. In the Middle and Lower South, laurel oak is evergreen. In the Upper South, the tree may retain most of its leaves during mild winters. Laurel oak has no fall color. The glossy green leaves of laurel oak are oblong to obovate and resemble those of the willow oak, except that they are larger, sometimes lobed, and 2 to 6 inches long. The acorns are ovoid and about ½ inch long.

Locate laurel oak in full sun. In the warmer, wetter areas of the South, laurel oak grows rapidly and may develop weak wood. In drier soil, however, the rate of growth is slowed, and the trees are generally sturdier. Although laurel oak is seldom bothered by pests, scale insects may pose an occasional problem.

An avenue of laurel oaks along a street or long driveway is an impressive sight, but the tree is not limited to this use. Laurel oak makes a handsome specimen tree for the lawn and is a useful shade tree. One selection that has received attention from commercial growers is Darlington. This type grows more densely and retains a more compact form than the species.

Live Oak

The matriarch of the Southern garden is the grand live oak (*Quercus virginiana*). This massive, sprawling evergreen tree is hardy everywhere in the South except in West Virginia, northern Kentucky, and the westernmost areas of Texas and Oklahoma. The branches of an aged live oak are often as stout as the trunks of many other trees, and their irregular, sometimes horizontal branching habit can cause the branches to arch to the ground and then turn up again. The evergreen leaves of the live oak are 2 to 4 inches long, ½ to 2 inches wide, smooth margined, and elliptic in shape. The ovoid acorns, about 1 inch long, appear either singly or in clusters. Male flowers are borne in slender, yellow clusters in early spring.

Live oaks are powerful trees due to their size and dramatic form. A common host of Spanish moss, the moss-draped live oaks of the Gulf Coast have come to be an almost magic symbol of the Deep South. A single tree can dominate any garden, large or small, and the conditions created by such a monumental tree should be considered. One of these conditions is dense shade, making it difficult, if not completely impossible, to grow a lawn underneath. With so many good ground cover plants available, however, the lack of a lawn should not necessarily be considered a disaster. Live oaks make spectacular street trees, particularly when they are planted on both sides of the street, forming a canopy. For sheer drama in the garden, no tree can match the live oak, particularly an old one.

Grow live oaks in full sun. Few plants are less demanding about soil conditions than live oak. This remarkably durable native thrives in clay, sandy, or depleted soil. It is tolerant of wet soil and dry soil. For the most vigorous growth, however, plant live oaks in rich, well-drained soil. Few, if any, pests are truly damaging to live oaks. In some areas, galls may develop in older trees, but these are not destructive. In the wetter areas of Louisiana

The branch shown here emphasizes the sculptural effect of live oak.

When mature, live oak has a spread equal to its height. This live oak is over 100 years old.

Large Trees

Scarlet oak makes a valuable street tree because it provides strong seasonal interest in the fall.

Shumard's red oak is a moderate to rapid grower, reaching 80 to 100 feet or more at maturity.

and the Gulf Coast, mushroom root rot may become a problem. See page 252 for pest controls on all oaks. To encourage a pleasing branching pattern, it may be necessary to prune young live oaks during their first years in the garden.

Pin Oak

Pin oak (*Quercus palustris*) is one of the most unique oaks in the South. This large, pyramidal tree combines several desirable traits—unusual form, good fall color, dependable cold hardiness, and pest resistance.

Pin oak grows to a mature height of 75 to 100 feet with a 40- to 50-foot spread. The limbs of unpruned trees reach nearly to the ground. Grown as a lawn specimen, the lower limbs should be left on the tree, but they should be removed if the plant is used as a street tree. The glossy green leaves turn to orange red in the fall, often remaining on the tree throughout the winter. Leaves are 4 to 6 inches long and deeply lobed; the lobes taper to points. Leaves may have from 5 to 9 lobes on mature trees. Acorns are about ½ inch long and subglobose in shape.

Hardy in the Upper and Middle South, pin oak prefers the cooler climates and may not perform well along the Gulf Coast, in Florida, or west of east Texas. Locate pin oak in full sun or partial shade. Tolerant of a wide range of soil conditions, pin oak grows satisfactorily in all but extremely poor or alkaline soils. Two selections are available in the nursery trade: Sovereign, noted for its upright branches, and Crownright, which is even narrower and more columnar in form than Sovereign.

Scarlet Oak

The showiest oak is scarlet oak (*Quercus coccinea*). As the common name suggests, this tree lights up like a blaze in fall when the leaves turn a dazzling red. In form, the scarlet oak is a rounded, open-crowned tree with narrow, deeply lobed leaves that are glossy on the upper surfaces and glabrous on the undersides. Leaves are 4 to 8 inches long. Scarlet oak may reach 75 feet or more at maturity with a 35- to 40-foot spread. Locate scarlet oak in full sun and in well-drained, acid soil. This oak is at its best in soil that is slightly dry, but this does not indicate extreme drought resistance, only that the plant performs poorly in soggy soils.

Native to the eastern United States, scarlet oak is hardy in the Upper and Middle South and in much of the Lower South, although not in central and southern Florida. Farther west, in Arkansas, Oklahoma, and Texas, the scarlet oak may become increasingly less reliable.

Scarlet oak makes a valuable street tree since it provides strong seasonal interest in the fall. In a large lawn, scarlet oak is a fine specimen, but, in the small garden, such a large tree soon grows out of scale with its surroundings. The most commonly available selection of scarlet oak is Splendens. This type is noted for its brilliant, long-lasting autumn color.

Shumard's Red Oak

The Southern answer to the famed northern red oak is Shumard's red oak (*Quercus shumardii*). Relatively new to the nursery trade, Shumard's red oak is a moderate to rapid grower, reaching 80 to 100 feet or more at maturity. This spreading to rounded tree takes on an almost oval form with a 50- to 60-foot spread. Native to the central and southeastern United States, Shumard's oak has adapted throughout the South, including north Florida and east Texas.

The leaves of Shumard's oak are 5 to 8 inches long, 3 to 6 inches wide, and deeply lobed with thistles at the tips of some lobes. The leaves are dark green during the growing season, turning to orange red in the fall. The 1-inch subglobose acorns require two years to mature.

Like the other large oaks, Shumard's red oak is a majestic lawn tree in a large garden. The orange fall color blends well with the red of scarlet oak or the purple red coloration of white oak. In areas where the other large oaks are not reliably hardy, Shumard's red oak may be the answer, due to its remarkable tolerance of urban conditions.

Plant Shumard's red oak in full sun. Although this oak will grow in a range of soils, including heavy and depleted soils, it is best in deep, fertile, well-drained soil where it grows rapidly. To ensure desirable branching, young trees may require some shaping during their first few years in the ground.

White Oak

Thought of by many as the most desirable of the deciduous oaks, white oak (*Quercus alba*) is a large, spreading tree with a rounded to pyramidal crown. Mature trees may exceed 100 feet in height with a 50- to 60-foot spread. The branches are stout and contorted enough to give the tree a dynamic character during winter when they are exposed. White oak is also one of the most vividly colored trees in fall.

Native to the eastern United States from Maine to northern Florida, white oak does well in the Upper and Middle South but may be disappointing in the Lower South. It is adaptable as far west as east Texas and Oklahoma.

The leaves of white oak are 5 to 9 inches long and about 4 inches wide; they are lobed but not sharply and turn orange red to purplish red in fall. Leaves tend to remain on the young trees into winter and may fall continually for several months, necessitating a weekly raking.

White oak is a prized shade tree when it reaches maturity. Because of its slow rate of growth, it is not recommended where shade is needed immediately. Scale is an important consideration when planting white oak. Because of its mammoth size, white oak is often out of scale with one-story homes. But if your house is large and you have the patience to wait twenty years or more for the tree to grow to its potential size, then few choices of shade trees can exceed the white oak. As a street tree, white oak is a good choice—even where electrical and telephone wires may be present. The open growth habit of white oak allows wires to pass through the crown with a minimum of interference from branches.

Plant white oak in full sun and in fair to good soil. This species is not particularly drought resistant, so consider the irrigation demands before planting if precipitation is notoriously sparse in your locale.

White oak is a prized shade tree (above) when it reaches maturity.

The winter branches of white oak (left) take on a striking sculptural quality.

Large Trees

The branching structure of oaks emphasizes the strength of the tree.

Willow Oak

Not all oaks look alike, and nowhere is the difference more apparent than in the case of willow oak (*Quercus phellos*). The common name reflects the similarity of the leaves of this tree to those of the weeping willow, which are long, slender, and smooth margined. As a result, this tree is much finer in texture than most of the other oaks, and the smaller leaves give the plant a more open, airy appearance. Leaves of willow oak are 3 to 5 inches long, ¼ to ½ inch wide, and lance shaped. The fall color is yellow to light brown.

Willow oak is an upright, nearly rounded tree, with a horizontal branching habit, unlike the true willow, with its sweep of arching branches. Willow oaks are moderate to rapid growers, reaching 50 to 80 feet at maturity with a 30- to 40-foot spread. Willow oak is hardy throughout the South, including north Florida and east Texas, but beyond these areas, the performance of willow oak may not be optimum.

Where it adapts, however, willow oak is a valuable landscape tree. The fine-textured foliage draws the eye, making willow oak a commendable specimen tree. The filtered shade cast by willow oak is ideal for bedding plants and shrubs that need protection from the summer sun. Since it is easier to transplant than the other oaks and can be installed when it is several years old, willow oak is also a valuable street tree.

Locate willow oak in full sun. Because of its shallow root system, willow oak prefers loamy, moisture-retentive soil that is well drained. The soil pH must not be highly alkaline. In alkaline soil, iron is not available to the plant, resulting in yellowed leaves and a weakened plant.

The branches of an aged live oak are often as stout as the trunks of many other trees.

Willow oak is an upright, nearly rounded tree, with a horizontal branching habit, unlike the true willow.

Large Trees

Pine
South's most popular evergreen tree

So popular are the pines in the South that three states, Alabama, Arkansas, and North Carolina, claim one or more species of pine as their state tree. The pines are not a tremendously varied group, but few trees are as dependable or as versatile. Because of the wide distribution of pine species across the South, it is usually possible to find a pine that will grow in any area, from the drought-loving Japanese black pine to the native longleaf pine, which is most at home in rich, bogland soils. Many species, in fact, tolerate a wide range of growing conditions, further contributing to their attractiveness as trees for the home landscape.

Many pines become large, stately trees in a comparatively short time. Even young pines, five to ten years old, are appealing landscape plants. Although some exotic species may be hard to find, most species are widely available and inexpensive.

Pines have a multiseasonal appeal, beginning in winter when the lustrous green needles stand out against the dormant and sometimes barren landscape. Pine branches and cones are popular decorations for the winter holidays. Pines have a pleasing fragrance all year, but it is most pronounced in the spring as new growth begins. During the hot Southern summer, pine trees provide filtered shade reminiscent of a forest. And in the fall, many pines drop their oldest leaves, providing a plentiful source of pine straw to use as mulch in the garden.

As landscape features, pines are as versatile as they are durable. A well-placed pine can act as a specimen, but a group can make pleasing companions for other ornamental plants, particularly those requiring light shade cast by a small grove of trees. Pines are plants whose appeal can be enhanced and regionalized by the proper selection of companion plants. Nature may be the best teacher of companion selection. In the Lower South, the native yellow pines and palmettos spring up together in forests from Florida to the Carolina coast. Inland, and farther north, white pines and rhododendrons are likely combinations that you may find in the wild. The tranquil effect of white dogwood flowers in a grove of green pines is another naturally occurring combination that is easy to emulate in the home landscape. Pines and azaleas, both native and imported, are yet another combination.

A stand of pines can provide a fast-growing screen. As the plants grow, use evergreen shrubs as an underplanting to maintain a screened effect at eye level. To complete the woodland effect and embellish multiseasonal interest, plant woodland perennial wild-flowers in a pine grove. When planting a stand of pines, spacing is important. Space plants at least 15 feet on center. Avoid planting in straight lines; instead, stagger the plants or drift them informally. When planting near a building, plant pine trees 20 to 25 feet away from the building so that you will not have to remove lower limbs as the plant grows. Pines are also widely used for windbreak plantings and for erosion control on steep banks.

Most pine species are grown from seed. Germination may require two years for some pines, and it is advisable to purchase nursery-grown plants in 1- to 2-gallon containers rather than to try to grow them from seed. To ensure rapid establishment, dig planting holes twice as deep and wide as the root ball. Work plenty of organic matter, such as peat

AT A GLANCE
Light: full sun or partial shade
Water: moderately drought resistant but prefers good drainage
Soil: wide range; best in improved soil
Growth Rate: moderate to rapid
Size: medium to large trees

At maturity, loblolly pine may easily reach 100 feet.

Mature white pines are used here in a street tree planting.

moss, leaf mold, or compost into each planting hole. In windy areas, such as the Texas and Oklahoma plains, it is wise to stake young plants. Plant pines anytime from October through the following spring.

Although they are capable of growing well in the wild with no human supervision, pine trees grown in the home garden will fare better with regular fertilizing and watering during dry weather. Apply 5-10-10 fertilizer at the rate recommended on the label. Make the first application in early spring when new growth begins and make a second application in midsummer.

Pines also have several insect problems. These insects generally do not hinder the plant, if controlled; see page 253 for a tip on controlling these problems. Nonetheless, many species of pines are desirable home landscape plants.

Japanese Black Pine

A pine for the entire South, Japanese black pine (*Pinus thunbergiana*), can be expected to do well from Virginia to southern Florida and as far west as east Texas and southeastern Oklahoma. Native to Japan, this pine does well in coastal areas as well as inland gardens. It is also the only pine that adapts readily to container culture.

Grown in the garden, Japanese black pine can be expected to reach about 50 feet with a spread of 20 to 30 feet. The rate of growth is moderate to rapid.

Needles of this pine are stiff to the touch, usually 3 inches long, and grow in bundles of two. The leaves remain a uniform dark green throughout the year. Plants tend to lose their pyramidal form as they age, growing bushier and more open. The woody cones are about 2 inches long with a tiny prickle on each side.

Japanese black pine adapts to most soils but results are most satisfactory when grown in fertile, well-drained soil. This pine is easy to transplant when young. Locate it in full sun as a specimen. It is an ideal conifer for the Japanese garden or where a comparable effect is desired.

Loblolly Pine

More familiar to Southern gardeners and naturalists is the native loblolly pine (*P. taeda*). This moderate to rapidly growing tree may reach 100 feet at maturity when grown under ideal conditions and without competition from other plants. Loblolly pines grow throughout the South and may even be grown successfully in southern Florida.

Like many other pines, loblolly pines are pyramidal when young, developing a more

The needles of the white pine (right) grow in clusters of five.

The needles of the Scotch pine (far right) are 1 to 3 inches long, growing in twisted bundles of two.

rounded crown as they age. The long, soft needles are often 8 inches long and grow in bundles of three. Trees have a light-green cast throughout most of the year. Cones are ovoid to conical, 3 to 4 inches long, and grow in clusters of two to five. These cones remain on the tree for several years.

Although not the most attractive pine, loblolly is one of the most tolerant of both wet and dry soil. Grown in full sun, this species makes a good background or overstory for shade-loving trees and shrubs.

Loblolly pine may be attacked by the pine-tip moth and also by fusiform rust, a fungus disease.

Longleaf Pine

The best known pine in the South is the native longleaf or Southern pine (*P. palustris*). Noted for its unusually long needles, which may be from 8 to 18 inches long, longleaf pine grows to a tall, slender tree, 100 feet or taller. Its branches have been used for generations as Christmas decorations. Longleaf pine is hardy throughout the Southern region. Although considered primarily a timber tree, it can be used effectively as an ornamental in the home garden. The soft needles of a longleaf pine remain dark green throughout the year, growing in bundles of three. The upper branches are ascending, giving the tree an open, irregular crown. Cones are cylindrical, 6 to 10 inches long, and remain on the tree for 15 years or more.

Here is a grove of young and old longleaf pines, one of the best-known pines in the South.

White pine can reach 130 feet under favorable conditions.

Longleaf pine is grown throughout the South, except in west Texas, Oklahoma, and Arkansas. Capable of reaching 100 feet and more in height, longleaf pine grows best in deep, sandy loam. The Latin name, *palustris*, implies this pine's preference for the Southern marshlands to which the plant is native. Locate trees in full sun or partial shade.

Use longleaf pine as a specimen or background planting. This species is a highly desirable timber tree and would make a good crop for anyone with a few acres of land and an interest in putting the land to a profitable use.

Scotch Pine

Another hardy pine that is adapted to most of the South is Scotch or Scots pine (*P. sylvestris*). Familiar to many as a Christmas tree, Scotch pine is noted for its bushy form when young. As plants grow to maturity, they may reach 75 feet with a 30- to 40-foot spread. Mature plants tend to lose their pyramidal form, developing a more oval crown. The main stem may develop irregularly, adding character to the plant. Needles are 1 to 3 inches long, growing in twisted bundles of two. Bark on younger limbs often has an orange cast. The rounded cones are about 2 inches long.

Scotch pine makes an excellent background or windbreak planting. Selections include Argentea, with silvery leaves, and Fastigiata, a columnar tree with branches sweeping slightly upright.

Spruce Pine

Another fine native is spruce pine (*P. glabra*). Although not as well known as longleaf pine, spruce pine can sometimes be found in the same bottomlands of Louisiana and Mississippi as its more familiar cousins. Spruce pine, also known as cedar pine, is a large

Because of their rapid rate of growth, pines are popular landscape plants in the South.

The deeply fissured bark of pines is one of their most readily identifiable characteristics.

tree, reaching 100 to 120 feet at maturity. Because the needles are loosely tufted, the tree has a more open appearance, somewhat resembling a cedar. The drooping habit, often seen, further enhances the resemblance. Less hardy than longleaf and loblolly pines, spruce pine is adapted to the Middle and Lower South but may sustain damage from the cold in the Upper South.

The bark of the spruce pine is reddish brown and smooth on the young tree, becoming fissured with age. The 4- to 6-inch needles are borne in clusters of three and remain bright green throughout the year. The oblong cones, which may grow either singly or in clusters, are 1 to 4 inches long and about 2 inches wide and thickly scaled. This moderately rapid-growing tree grows in either full sun or partial shade. Use it as a specimen or in a grove with other pines where spruce pine, with its bright color and short, airy branches, becomes an accent plant. Spruce pine prefers deep, fertile, sandy-loamy soil.

Virginia Pine

The native Virginia or scrub pine (*P. virginiana*) is not a popular ornamental, but this tree is noted for its ability to grow in very poor soil where more desirable plants will not fare well. Depending on the conditions under which it is grown, Virginia pine may be a scrubby 10-foot tree or an open-growing, sparsely branched 30- to 40-foot pyramidal tree. Under rare conditions, this pine may reach 70 to 100 feet. Needles are stiff and twisted, growing in bundles of two, and 1¼ to 4 inches long. Cones are conical in shape, growing to about 2 inches long and 1 inch wide. They are borne singly or in pairs.

Grow Virginia pine in full sun or partial shade. This native pine is best used as a background or bank planting. Grown in full sun this pine, along with Japanese black pine and Scotch pine, will retain branches to the ground indefinitely. The other pines mentioned here will lose their lower branches.

White pine

White pine (*P. strobus*) is one of the hardiest native pine species found in the South. Native to the northeastern United States, white pine is a fine choice for gardens in the Upper and Middle South. It is not, however, adapted to the Lower South. White pine may reach 130 feet in our region and maintains a splendid pyramidal form during its youth, becoming somewhat more oval at maturity.

New needles of white pine often have a bluish cast. They grow in clusters of five and become greener during the remainder of the growing season. Cones are smooth, about 7 inches long and 2½ inches in diameter.

A rapid grower, white pine tolerates a wide range of soils and grows well in either full sun or partial shade. It does not grow well in heavy clay.

Several selections are available. Glauca has a bluer cast than the species. Three shrublike selections, Radiata, Prostrate, and Umbraculifera, are also available at some nurseries.

Red Cedar
A classic with age

AT A GLANCE
Light: full sun
Water: moderate to dry
Soil: almost any
well-drained soil will do;
cedar prefers a pH of 6 to
7—a soil approaching
alkaline conditions
Growth Rate: under good
conditions, slow to
moderate
Size: 20 to 30 feet

Obvious plants are often overlooked, and this is true of red cedar. The familiar green spire that pops up along fence rows across the South is considered a garden throwaway. But placed carefully in the landscape and allowed to mature, red cedar (*Juniperus virginiana*) becomes a classic in anybody's garden.

Cedar bark is a light, rich reddish brown that peels in handsome strips. As the tree matures, the trunk becomes twisted and misshapen, and it has a strongly corded character. The stiff, prickly foliage is a deep green that turns a purplish red in winter. There are some unnamed selections which have a bluish cast to their foliage.

Without question, cedar is a full-sun plant that loves alkaline soil. In fact, the presence of cedar in the landscape is often an indication of limestone or alkaline soil conditions. It is drought hardy and, once installed, maintenance free.

Red cedar brings a stately, formal look to a garden. In fact, parks and formal gardens of the late Victorian era and early twentieth century often feature this plant as a specimen, using it as a framing or enclosing plant for parklike vistas.

In addition to bringing a dignified, conical shape of green into the landscape, red cedar is durable, disease free, and readily available. A good feature of red cedar is its tolerance of severe weather. It will withstand both the searing heat of Texas and the salt spray of seaside locations. In fact, when planted by the sea, red cedar takes on a sculptured character that makes the plant almost look like a different species.

Red cedar needs space and a location that commands a view, such as in an entrance planting for a long drive. A group of three or four plants at a driveway entrance signals a handsome approach, but a better use still is a red cedar allée that lines a drive or roadway. In such a location the trees will mature and touch across the drive, creating a beautiful canopy.

Red cedar is also effective in a screen planting. If planted in a row, cedar provides a hedge that can be used as an evergreen backdrop for deciduous plantings.

In addition, cedar is a superb wildlife habitat. Birds can nest safely in its dense protective foliage. Many bird species are attracted by the bluish black berries that appear on female trees.

One drawback to cedar as a landscape plant is its slow rate of growth. The tree maintains its tight, sheared look for years; then it will suddenly become shaggy and weathered looking. A tree 20 years old will be 20 to 30 feet tall.

The compact, tight character of a young cedar is shown on the left, while the loosened, wispy shape of mature trees is evident in the cedar on the right.

AT A GLANCE
Light: full to partial sun
Water: will tolerate wet soil but very adaptable
Soil: any soil; grows best in rich, moist soil
Growth Rate: rapid
Size: to 25 or 30 feet in 10 years

River Birch
It is the bark that counts

The river birch (*Betula nigra*) is an outstanding native to use as a mid-scale ornamental tree. Its light, delicate canopy and upright, irregular habit of growth along with its exfoliating bark, make river birch a perfect choice for a courtyard, entrance walk, or other location where these special qualities can be viewed at close hand.

River birch is hardy throughout the eastern portion of the United States. It likes a lot of moisture, so avoid planting it where it would be exposed to hot, drying winds and excessive periods of drought. Although river birch may be difficult to transplant from its native environment, it can be moved in early spring with a fair prospect for success. But since the tree is generally available in nurseries and garden centers, there is no need to risk transplanting it from the wild.

At the nursery, inspect balled-and-burlapped specimens for signs of dehydration and winterkill. The young shoots should be extremely flexible: you should be able to bend a pencil-size stem almost double without breaking it. If available, plants grown in papier-mâché or other biodegradable containers may be your best choice, but check the tree for brittleness and weakened stems.

River birches are relatively fast growing and get to be quite large at maturity. A full-grown plant may be 60 feet tall, but 25 to 30 feet is a more common height for those grown in a residential situation.

River birch should require nothing more than an occasional maintenance pruning to remove dead or damaged branches. Never prune a birch in spring, as the plant is a persistent "bleeder." Any cuts made at this time of year will continue to ooze sap for several weeks, subjecting the plant to unnecessary infestations of insects and diseases.

The visual softness of the river birch is one of its most desirable attributes as a landscape material. The canopy has an airy, almost fragile appearance that responds to every breeze with a shimmering of delicately serrated leaves. But even the golden yellow autumn color cannot compare with the year-round beauty of the rough, exfoliating bark. Paper-thin strips of the creamy white bark peel away from the trunk, exposing a rich terra-cotta underside. As the strips curl back along the stems, the mottling of light and dark creates an effect that is the river birch's most distinctive and most desirable landscape characteristic.

Because of its rapid growth, attractive bark, and multistemmed habit of growth, this river birch gives quick shade plus an accent to this garden.

Spruce
Pyramidal grace in a conifer

The spruces (*Picea sp.*) are splendid trees for the colder parts of the Upper South. Characterized by stiff angled needles, pendulous cones, and strongly conical and symmetrical forms, this group of needle leaf evergreens brings dignity and grace into the landscape as specimen or group plantings.

If planted in full sun, they will retain the foliage on the lower branches, thus making them useful for screening. Even when used in mass, though, these spruces are eye-catching. Although sometimes grouped and used as a backdrop planting, it is difficult not to separate the individual trees from the group, since their conical shape silhouettes the top of each tree against the horizon or skyline. This tendency for the plant to attract the eye makes the spruce an excellent accent plant.

The plants are long-lived; and as the trees mature, they assume a graceful weeping stature, except for Colorado spruce (*P. pungens*), that is in marked contrast to their upright and stiff adolescent form. It seems fitting that spruces grow best only in the cooler Upper South and Piedmont, because one of the finest landscape shows associated with these trees is to view them when they are covered with snow. It is then easy to see why certain species are cultivated and sold commercially as Christmas trees each year. Spruces are highly variable plants, and there are many selections available.

Colorado Spruce

The Colorado spruce (*P. pungens*) is more widely known for its blue-colored selection than for the straight species. Colorado Blue spruce (*P. pungens* Glauca) does well only in the colder Upper South. The foliage is a silvery powder blue—a foliage color that is unmatched in the landscape. Generally Colorado Blue spruce is a stiff, conical tree with branches spreading stiffly horizontally from the trunk. Because of this rigid form, the plant is difficult to use in the landscape, although it can be successfully isolated as a specimen.

Norway Spruce

The Norway spruce (*P. abies*) is one of the most accommodating and widely planted spruces. It will do well in the Piedmont South, growing north of a line from Raleigh to Atlanta to Birmingham. Norway spruce is characterized by sweeping branches that dip down and are upturned at the tips. The lateral branches hang from the main branches and give the tree a relaxed, almost weeping, character. Norway spruce is fairly slow growing but eventually will become a large tree of 75 feet or more in height, with a breadth of 25 feet. It tends to retain its lower branches and creates a beautiful conical form in the landscape. The cones of older trees are pendulous and may reach 7 inches in length. The foliage is deep green. The plant is variable and many selections are available including dwarf and prostrate selections. One of the more striking specimens is Weeping Norway spruce (*P. abies* Pendula), which has a marked drooping habit of growth.

Oriental Spruce

Oriental spruce (*P. orientalis*) is a tree to be planted for its silhouette. The foliage is short and deep green; and because of this, the plant appears as lines in the landscape. The form is tall and narrow with a striking outline of branches. It is hardiest in the Upper South and makes a splendid accent plant in the landscape.

AT A GLANCE
Light: full to partial sun; sun will force the tree to retain the lower branches
Water: moderate amount; will tolerate slightly wet locations
Soil: any well-drained, moderately rich soil
Growth Rate: moderate to slow
Size: 50 to 75 feet in height and 20- to 25-foot spread after 40 to 50 years

Although not popular in areas below the Piedmont South, Norway spruce grows well there after its initial establishment.

Sweet Gum
A steady, stately shade tree

AT A GLANCE

Light: full sun to partial shade
Water: prefers wet locations; drought resistant
Soil: any soil; prefers rich, loamy soil
Growth Rate: rapid
Size: to 80 feet; 20 feet in 5 to 8 years under ideal conditions

As sweet gum ages, the rigid pyramidal form of the young trees will loosen slightly.

Pyramidal young sweet gum trees (*Liquidambar styraciflua*), often with corky growths (called wings) that edge the branches, begin the reforestation of the hardwood forests that cover almost the entire South. One species that has been recently introduced is Oriental sweet gum (*Liquidambar orientalis*), which is hardy in the Middle and Lower South. Its role in the reclamation of land is a valuable key to the versatility of sweet gum, because this plant, which favors moist locations and fertile soil, can tolerate poor soil and dry conditions. This makes it an excellent choice as a first tree in the landscape for homeowners with treeless gardens. In addition, it will respond well to fertilization and watering and is a rapid grower, quickly achieving a size that will offer shade and comfort and give shape and full color to the garden.

As mature trees, sweet gums maintain the pyramidal form they displayed as younger trees. Because of its constant form, sweet gum makes an exceptional street tree or formal allée. Given good growing conditions, any grouping of sweet gums will steadily and rapidly mature, forming almost identical crown shapes—a landscape characteristic that can be very desirable. Old trees can easily reach 80 feet with a spread of about 35 feet. Younger trees will ascend to 20 feet in as little as 5 to 8 years if 6 to 8 plants are installed in the landscape.

The foliage of sweet gum is a medium green—a perfect backdrop color for the contrasting foliage of flowering trees. The tree is heavily covered in palmately-lobed (star-shaped) leaves, sometimes mistaken for maple leaves. The leaves generally have five to seven lobes and cast a very narrow but dense shade pattern. The dependable, seemingly unvarying, green foliage yields to one of fall's most spectacular seasonal shows. The green fades to yellow, then to a red orange with some purple, eventually reaching a deep-burgundy color—one of the most vivid lasting colors of the season.

The ornamental effect continues after the leaves fall—prickly gum balls remain on the tree like ornaments, eventually falling in late winter. The bark, too, has winter interest, being a bright silver brown. Cut branches with their corky growth on the sides are useful in indoor arrangements.

Some gardeners find the prickly gum balls objectionable, although they can be readily raked up. Consequently, consider planting sweet gum in a mulched border, where the leaf drop and sweet gum balls will not be objectionable.

Sweet gum derives its name from the fragrant gummy material present in its sap, called styrax. It is widely used for perfume and was once commonly chewed prior to the development of chewing gum.

Tulip Tree
Summer flowers and fall color, too

One of the tallest hardwood trees native to the forests of eastern America is also one of the finest selections for use as a shade tree in the home landscape. The tulip tree (*Liriodendron tulipifera*), which can reach well over 100 feet in height, grows rapidly, is relatively long-lived, and produces a filtered shade. An added bonus is the late spring flowers.

A member of the magnolia family, tulip tree, also called yellow poplar, develops leaves extremely early in the season. The lime green new foliage, which resembles a tulip, is followed quickly by upright tuliplike flowers that are carried at the end of the twigs. The yellow green flowers, with an orange tint, are slightly fragrant, and can last as long as two weeks. They are hidden from view since they usually develop only on trees that are at least ten years old, whose branches are already above eye level. The distinctive foliage covers the tree in a light open canopy. Individual leaves are up to 8 inches wide with four distinct lobes. The end of the leaf is blunt, looking almost as though the true tip were cut off. The color is a clean, fresh, even green, similar to that of sugar maple.

In fall, tulip tree turns a brilliant mustard yellow; its conical crown is plainly visible, rising above the crowns of other fall colors. While it is one of the first trees to change, the color is persistent; the leaves slowly drop, gradually thinning at the crown until just a few adhere. Tulip trees are open and thinly branched; the winter form is extremely upright, conical, and clean. The bark of older trees is gray, deeply furrowed, and ridged with fissures sometimes as deep as ½ inch. Also, in winter, the tips of the branches support upright seed capsules that look like parchment-colored flowers.

The attractiveness of tulip tree as a landscape plant is increased because the plant is hardy and basically disease free. Suffering only from some brittleness and branch loss in old age, tulip tree is exceedingly durable and has often been used as a long-lived estate tree. The tulip tree prefers moist, well-drained soil. It is preferable to plant it in a soil rich in organic matter and nutrients—tulip tree can tolerate poor soil but will not perform well. If it is planted in fertile soil with adequate moisture, the tulip tree can be a rapid grower. If planted in full sun, tulip tree will develop an upright full crown. While foliage and crown development are best in full sun, tulip tree must have moisture for best growth. Fortunately, the plant will readily signal a lack of moisture by a premature yellowing and dropping of leaves. Should this occur, water immediately and thoroughly.

AT A GLANCE
Light: full sun is best
Water: likes to be moist
Soil: any well-drained, rich soil
Growth Rate: rapid when young
Size: to 150 feet; 25 to 30 feet in 6 to 8 years

Even a young tulip tree will take on its mature upright, conical shape.

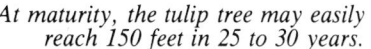

At maturity, the tulip tree may easily reach 150 feet in 25 to 30 years.

Large Trees

Weeping Willow
Accent for the landscape

AT A GLANCE

Light: full sun
Water: excellent for moist locations
Soil: any soil but prefers moist locations
Growth Rate: rapid
Size: 50 to 60 feet

Because of its preference for moist soil conditions, weeping willow is most often used in locations as shown here, near a lake.

Weeping willow (*Salix babylonica*) is one of the most elegant of all the weeping trees. Its graceful, fountainlike form and delicate texture make it a distinctive accent tree for sculptural effects; when it is planted in a grove, the weeping willow gives the landscape a romantic look.

While the term "weeping" generally refers to the willow's cascading form, the Victorians assigned the name a rather maudlin connotation; many people still identify the weeping willow with periods of mourning. An objective look at the plant, however, will dispel these negative impressions.

The weeping willow is unsurpassed for graceful motion in the landscape. The delicate branches seem to respond to every breeze; when it is planted in a lawn, the gently swaying willow creates the impression of flowing water.

Planted as a single specimen along a drive or at the edge of a lawn, weeping willow gives the garden a dramatic sculptural accent; when it is planted at the entrance of a drive or garden path, the arching form of weeping willow creates the impression of a gateway.

If several willow trees are planted in a grove, their slender trunks and branches create a mysterious, almost curtainlike effect. Viewed from a distance, the mounded, rolling form of such a planting also gives the landscape a dramatic sense of motion.

When weeping willows are planted against a background of darker evergreens, such as magnolia or pines, their pale-green color is enhanced and made to seem more dominant. An evergreen background also helps to emphasize the delicate linework of the willow tree in winter.

While they are most often seen along the banks of lakes and streams, weeping willows will adapt to less aquatic situations if they are given ample water. Although they may require irrigation during prolonged periods of drought, weeping willows can be grown throughout the South, including the drier areas of Florida and Texas.

Weeping willow is a fast-growing tree that may attain a height of 25 feet in only four or five years. At maturity (about 20 years), a willow tree may be as much as 50 to 60 feet high and 25 to 30 feet across, so give it plenty of room to reach its fullest form.

Size, however, is not the only reason to set the weeping willow apart from other plants and structures. Willow trees have an aggressive root system that can rob nourishment and moisture from surrounding plants. The roots also tend to seek out water sources such as septic fields and sewers. Since they can penetrate the smallest fissure in a clay or cast iron pipe, avoid planting willow trees within 50 feet of a water line or sewer to avoid the problem of intrusion.

This section is a guide to help you identify and control insects, diseases, and special problems in your landscape. A chart, which begins on page 243, lists the plants in this book and many of their problems. For information to supplement the chart and for suggestions on when to apply pesticides, contact the county agricultural extension agent in your area.

To decide whether you must use a pesticide, become familiar with recurring pests and monitor infestations and damage carefully. Never let pest populations build up; they become more difficult to control.

To control a recurring pest, begin applying pesticides before the pest develops. An inexpensive, labor-saving insect control is a dormant oil (petroleum oil) spray, which can be applied in winter or very early spring. Dormant oil kills overwintering insects and insect eggs by smothering them before they become active in spring. Lime sulphur (for deciduous plants) kills insects and also kills fungal spores that overwinter on plants and cause anthracnose and other diseases. It is most important to control diseases before they get started.

If you have a problem for which there is no pesticide recommended in this section, check with your county agricultural extension agent. The pesticides recommended here are only those registered with the Environmental Protection Agency, but some states may have pesticide registrations in addition to those at the federal level.

General pests that occur widely are described on the following pages. Their controls are also listed. The controls that are least toxic to humans are listed first and separated from other pesticides by a semicolon. The pesticides listed are for use only on the plants listed on the specific pesticide label. From the list, you must select a pesticide approved for use on your plant.

Insects, Diseases, and Problems

Insects

Aphids—Aphids are pear-shaped insects, ⅛ to ¼ inch long, pink, green, brown, or black in color, and are distinguished by two cornicles, or elongated protrusions, at the end of their body. Aphids suck sap from young leaves and stems which causes deformation and leaf curl and debilitates the plant. Unless aphid populations are limited by natural controls, such as parasites, predators, heavy rain, or hot weather (upper 90s), you should control them early. Tremendous populations can build up rapidly. Controls: dormant oil; acephate, diazinon, dimethoate, Isotox®, lime sulphur, malathion, rotenone, carbaryl.

Bagworms—Bagworms are caterpillars which live in oblong bags constructed of silk, leaves, and twigs; the bags hang from twigs of the plant. In spring and summer, caterpillars move about, carrying the bags and eating the plant foliage. Controls: hand-pick the bags; acephate, diazinon, dimethoate, Isotox®, malathion, rotenone, carbaryl.

Borers—Borers weaken or kill trees and shrubs by boring underneath the bark or into the wood of trunk and limbs. Sometimes they are easily detected by sawdust that may be present outside the hole where the borer has entered the wood. Because there are so many different borers, you should contact your county agricultural extension agent for positive identification of borers attacking your plants. He can also suggest the best time to spray a particular borer. Controls: weakened plants are most subject to attack, so keep plants healthy by planting them in a suitable location; by fertilizing and watering them well; and by protecting them from debilitation by other insects or diseases. If plants are not too badly infested, lindane is effective to kill some borers. On noninfested trees, it is used as a preventative. Badly infested plants may have to be cut down.

Cankerworms—Cankerworms are inch-long, green- to black-colored, inchworm-type

Aphids

Bagworm

caterpillars that damage trees in spring (spring cankerworms) and fall (fall cankerworms) by eating the foliage. (Spring cankerworms are more serious because they eat the young developing foliage.) After feeding for a few weeks, cankerworms drop from the trees and burrow in the ground; adult cankerworm moths emerge from the ground the next spring or fall. Controls: to prevent reinfestation, encircle the base of the tree trunk with a foot-wide band of tacky material (sold along with pesticides at garden centers). This prevents female moths, which are wingless and must crawl up the tree trunk to lay eggs, from ascending the tree. For spring cankerworms, apply the material in very early spring; for fall cankerworms, apply the material in the fall. For cankerworms already in trees: *Bacillus thuringiensis*; acephate, methoxychlor, toxaphene.

Japanese Beetles—Japanese beetles are heavy-bodied, oval-shaped, about ⅜ inch long, with a reddish green head and midsection and brown wing covers; they can seriously defoliate plants in a short time. Total control is difficult since the beetles are active fliers, constantly moving in from other plants after you have applied pesticides. Controls: carbaryl, Isotox®, malathion, methoxychlor, rotenone.

Lacebugs—Lacebugs are square-shaped, light-colored, lacy-winged insects about ⅛ inch long; they suck sap from the underside of the plant foliage. Dark-colored spots (secretions) are present on the undersides of leaves; the uppersides of leaves exhibit a yellow stippling damage. Controls: rotenone; acephate, carbaryl, dimethoate, Di-Syston, Isotox®, malathion.

Leafminers—Leafminer is a general name for the larvae of several different insects that feed on the inner tissue of a leaf, making a mine (which may be serpentine or blotchy) as they progress. Leaves turn brown in areas where they have fed and are ruined in appearance. Controls: acephate, carbaryl, diazinon, dimethoate, Di-Syston, Isotox®, lindane.

Mealybugs—Mealybugs are white, soft-bodied insects about ⅛ to ¼ inch long that are covered with a white cottonlike wax. Frequently seen on leaves and stems, they also like unexposed areas, such as inside an unfurling leaf or on other tight places on the plant. Mealybugs cause damage by sucking sap from the plant. Controls: dormant oil; acephate, carbaryl, diazinon, Isotox®, malathion.

Mites—Unless webs are present, minute red-, brown-, or black-colored debilitating mites are difficult for the inexperienced eye to find without a magnifying glass. They are generally found on the undersides of leaves, on buds, and on tender stems. Due to their pinpoint size, mites may be overlooked until damage has occurred; the damage involves a yellow stippling of the foliage and deformation of leaves and young stems. Controls: dormant oil, sulphur; acephate, diazinon, dimethoate, Di-Syston, Isotox®, karathane, kelthane, lime sulphur, malathion, rotenone.

Psyllids—Psyllids are 1/16 to ⅛-inch-long, insects which suck sap from plants, causing leaves to be deformed. Some are surrounded with cottonlike white waxy threads. They jump or move away quickly if you disturb them with your fingers. Controls: dormant oil; acephate, carbaryl, Isotox®.

Scales—Many scales attack plant leaves, stems, and occasionally the main trunk. Generally, scales are ⅛ to ⅜ inch long, sessile (crawl only when young), black, brown, red, purple, white, gray, gold, or yellow. Hard scales are flat or hemispherical with a hard outer covering; they are elongate, round, or pyramidally shaped. Some hard scales are so flat that they look flush with the leaf surface. Soft scales lack a hard outer covering and may be covered with wax as is Japanese wax scale. Scales suck sap from plants; leaves usually turn yellow where the scales are attached. Most scales feed on the leaf's underside; only a few feed on the upperside. Controls: dormant oil; acephate, carbaryl, diazinon, dimethoate, Di-Syston, Isotox®, lime sulphur, malathion.

Tent Caterpillars—Tent caterpillars defoliate branches of some plants in the spring. The Eastern tent caterpillar makes weblike tents in the branches of large shrubs and trees. It is brown, hairy, about 2 inches long, with white and reddish brown stripes down its back and blue and white spots on both sides. The forest tent caterpillar does not make a tent; it is light blue with light-colored, diamond-shaped spots on its back. Controls: dormant oil, *Bacillus thuringiensis*; acephate, carbaryl, diazinon, Isotox®, malathion, methoxychlor, toxaphene.

Thrips—Thrips are tiny, torpedo-shaped insects that feed inside the flowers of many ornamentals. The slender, 1/16-inch-long insects deface flowers, such as gardenias; the area where they feed turns brown. Buds attacked by thrips may not open properly. Although damage to flowers while they are outside may not seem significant, the cut flowers that you bring indoors will have brown spots on them. Controls: diazinon, Di-Syston, Isotox®, malathion. Spray the flowers thoroughly. Some flowers may fade or burn from the pesticide application.

Webworms—The fall webworm and other webworms are always protected by webs, which are spun across twigs and branches. Unlike some tent caterpillars, webworms stay inside the web while they feed on plant foliage; try to spray before large protective webs are formed. Controls: *Bacillus thuringiensis*; acephate, diazinon, methoxychlor, toxaphene.

Whiteflies—White, mothlike whiteflies about ⅛ inch long suck sap from the underside of plant leaves, which debilitates a plant and may deform the foliage. In the wingless (early) stages of their lives, whiteflies are almost transparent, difficult-to-see, flat, oval nymphs attached to the leaf underside. Controls: dormant oil; acephate, diazinon, dimethoate, Di-Syston, Isotox®, and malathion.

Diseases

Fire Blight—Fire blight is a bacterial disease that attacks flowering fruit trees, crabapples, cotoneaster, and other members of the rose family. Blooms and leaves of affected plants wilt, turn brown, and die, but remain attached to the stems. Cankers (sunken, dead areas) form on the limbs. In moist weather during spring, bacteria oozes from the cankers and is spread by rain or insects to infect other parts of the plant and other plants. Controls: streptomycin. Cut off diseased limbs 3 to 4 inches into healthy wood. To avoid reinfecting, clean the cutting tool with alcohol between cuts.

Powdery Mildew—Powdery mildew covers foliage (topside) with a white, powderlike growth. Worse during cool, humid weather (spring or fall), it does not usually cause serious damage but is unsightly. Control: sulphur; benomyl, cycloheximide, karathane, lime sulphur, triforine.

Leaf Spots—Leaf spot diseases (usually worse in wet weather) form small, dead areas on a leaf but may not be damaging enough to warrant control. If they defoliate or disfigure specimen plants, you may want to control them. Controls: copper sprays control many leaf spots, but for definite control, have a county agricultural extension agent identify the leaf spot and make a corresponding chemical recommendation.

Rust—Cedar-apple rust, hawthorn rust, and quince rust cause galls on Southern red cedar and other junipers that release spores which infect the foliage of crabapples, apples, hawthorn, and quince. The rust causes yellow, rusty-looking areas on leaves that later blacken; infections may result in defoliation, dwarfing, and poor fruiting. Controls: one

Leaf Gall (azalea)

Tent Caterpillar

Insects, Diseases & Problems

Whiteflies

control method is to avoid the production of infected spores by removing Southern red cedar and other host junipers from the area. However, on suburban size lots, this must be a collective effort because junipers on neighboring lots are close enough to affect your plants. Or, you may hand pick all galls from the junipers in winter before spores are released from long outgrowths of the gall. There are no federally registered pesticides to control cedar-apple rust on junipers, but apple hosts may be sprayed with zineb or ferbam for control. Zineb also controls rust on hawthorn and quince.

Root Rot—Root rot is a widespread problem which affects plants by rotting away the root system. Typical symptoms include sudden or gradual wilting which is not corrected by watering, stunting or very slow growth, mushrooms growing from surface roots, yellow foliage, and a general decline of the plant. In most cases, plants eventually die because the root system is no longer present to support them. Root rot often affects plants in a wet location or in poorly drained soil. When this is a problem, select plants adapted to wet locations. However, even when grown in well-drained soils, plants are sometimes affected by root rot. Controls: there is no control for root rot on infected plants; the plants must be removed. Before you replant in the same location, sterilize the soil with a soil fumigant. Liquid fumigants are applied to the soil several weeks before replanting.

Sooty Mold—Sooty mold is a black, sootlike fungus that often covers the foliage and stems of plants attacked by aphids, whiteflies, soft scale, psyllids, and other insects that secrete honeydew (a sugary substance on which the sooty mold grows). Sooty mold may indirectly harm the plant by blocking sunlight from the leaf surface. Controls: to avoid sooty mold, control the insects—aphids, mealybugs, soft scales, whiteflies (see Insects)—that secrete honeydew. It will also wipe off or eventually weather off the foliage.

Problems

Some plants are particularly susceptible to mineral deficiency, sunscald, leaf scorch, and other problems. These problems are listed in the chart in addition to the insects and disease pests that occur on the respective plant.

Lacebug Damage

PLANT	PROBLEM	CONTROL	COMMENT
American Beech (*Fagus grandifolia*)	aphids, borers, scales, tent caterpillars	See *Insects* on page 237.	
American Plane Tree (*Platanus occidentalis*)	anthracnose	copper fungicide or lime sulphur—Gather fallen leaves and twigs. Prune infected tree parts.	Humid, rainy weather and cool temperatures favor the disease. Young leaves look frostbitten; full-grown leaves die in spots between veins which may enlarge to kill the entire leaf. Twigs may dieback 8-10 inches and limbs may die.
	aphids, scales	See *Insects* on page 237.	
	sycamore lace bugs	See *Insects* on page 237.	Severe injury causes leaves to drop prematurely. Leaves curl; may be deformed.
	dogs		Consistent exposure to dog urine may damage lower part of trunk. Young trees with a diameter of 6″ or less may be killed.
Asian Star Jasmine (*Trachelospermum asiaticum*)	Generally pest free.		
Azalea and Rhododendron Alabama Azalea (*Azalea alabamense*) Delaware Valley White Azalea (*A. mucronatum*) Flame Azalea (*A. calendulaceum*) Florida Flame Azalea (*A. austrinum*) Glenn Dale Hybrid Azalea (*A. x glenn dale*) Gumpo Azalea (*A. x satsuki* Gumpo) Kurume Hybrid Azalea (*A. obtusum*) Oconee Azalea (*A. flammeum*) Pericat Hybrid Azalea (*A. x pericat*) Piedmont Azalea (*A. canescens*) Pinxterbloom Azalea (*A. periclymenoides*) Plumleaf Azalea (*A. prunifolium*) Rosebay (*Rhododendron maximum*) Rutherford Hybrid Azalea (*A. x rutherfordianum*) Satsuki Hybrid Azalea (*A. x satsuki*) Southern Indian Hybrid Azalea (*A. x indicum*) Swamp Azalea (*A. viscosum*)	azalea petal blight	Terraclor®, zineb, Fore®, captan. Remove blighted flowers from plant and ground.	Small brown spots on flowers enlarge to blotches; disease is worse during humid weather.
	leaf gall	Remove galled leaves by hand.	Leaves are grossly thickened; worse in wet or humid weather. Damage is not usually serious and disease disappears in hot weather.
	powdery mildew	See *Diseases* on page 239.	
	black walnut injury	Do not plant azaleas in the root zone of black walnut.	In the Upper South, azaleas and other plants planted in the root zone of black walnut may wilt and die, possibly due to toxins from the tree.
	lacebugs	See *Insects* on page 237.	
	Other than lacebugs, azaleas are generally insect pest free but may have problems with: aphids, leafminers, caterpillars, mites, borers, mealybugs, scales, thrips, whiteflies.	See *Insects* on page 237.	
Banana Shrub (*Michelia figo*)	Generally pest free but may have problems with:		
	mineral deficiency	Spray foliage several times a year with minor-element spray and add chelated iron to the soil around the plant.	In poor or alkaline soil, leaves may yellow between veins.
	wet feet	Plant in well drained soil	Will not tolerate poorly drained soil.
Barberry Chenault Barberry (*Berberis* x *chenaultii*) Japanese Barberry (*B. thunbergii*) Mentor Barberry (*B. x mentorensis*) Sargent Barberry (*B. sargentiana*) Three-spine Barberry (*B. wisleyensis*) Warty Barberry (*B. verruculosa*) Wintergreen Barberry (*B. julianae*)	Generally pest free but may have problems with aphids, scales, or webworms.	See *Insects* on page 237.	

PLANT	PROBLEM	CONTROL	COMMENT
Beautyberry (*Callicarpa americana*)	Generally pest free.		
Beautybush (*Kolkwitzia amabilis*)	Generally pest free.		
Big Blue Liriope (*Liriope muscari*)	tipburn	Mow over in spring to encourage new growth and get rid of burned foliage.	Cold weather may burn (brown) the foliage, especially the leaf tips.
	Generally pest free but may have problems with: scales.	See *Insects* on page 237.	Dormant oil after mowing and before new growth starts. Use catcher attachment on mower or rake the clippings before spraying.
Black Gum (*Nyssa sylvatica*)	Generally pest free but may have problems with: leafminers, aphids, scales.	See *Insects* on page 237.	
Border Forsythia (*Forsythia* x *intermedia*)	Generally pest free but may have problems with: crown gall	Remove diseased branches.	Galls develop on stems; stems may die back.
Boston Ivy (*Parthenocissus tricuspidata*) **Virginia Creeper** (*P. quinquefolia*)	Generally pest free but may have problems with:		
	leaf spot, powdery mildew	See *Diseases* on page 239.	
	Japanese beetles, scales	See *Insects* on page 237.	
Boxwood Common Boxwood (*Buxus sempervirens*) Harlands Boxwood (*B. harlandii*) Japanese Littleleaf Boxwood (*B. microphylla* Japonica) Truedwarf Boxwood (*B. sempervirens* Suffruticosa)	psyllids, scales, leafminers, mites, and webworms	See *Insects* on page 237.	
Bradford Pear (*Pyrus calleryana* Bradford)	Generally pest free.		
Camellia Common Camellia (*Camellia japonica*) Sasanqua Camellia (*C. sasanqua*) Tea Plant Camellia (*C. sinensis*)	dieback	Prevention is best control; buy disease-free or resistant plants. Avoid prolonged moisture from overhead watering (use drip irrigation if possible); space plants to allow good air circulation, especially in shady location. On infected plant, remove diseased wood; wash pruning cuts with solution of 1 part chlorine bleach to 9 parts water and paint wound with pruning paint or orange shellac on day of pruning so fungus will not reinfect plant. Avoid wounding plant; fungus enters through wounds, grafts, leaf scars.	Cankers form on branches and stems; infected branches eventually die. Sasanqua camellia is generally more susceptible than the common camellia. The *C. japonica* selections, Professor Sargent, Rose Emery, Governor Mouton, and Woodville Red, are resistant. Tea plant camellia is also resistant. Fungicides are not effective for killing disease already present.
	scales	See *Insects* on page 237. Dormant oil in spring; dimethoate. Most plants are eventually infested so it is best to spray once or twice a year as a preventive.	Persistent, serious pest of camellias, if allowed to become established.
	flower blight	Terraclor®, ferbam, zineb, Fore®. Remove blighted flowers from plant and ground.	Brown spots on petals in spring enlarge until bloom is blighted; Sasanqua camellia may not be affected.
	leaf gall	See recommendations for *Azaleas*.	
	root rot	See *Diseases* on page 239.	
	mealybugs, aphids, mites	See *Insects* on page 237.	
Cape Plumbago (*Plumbago auriculata*)	manganese deficiency	Apply manganese sulfate to ground or minor-element spray to foliage.	Leaves yellow; smallest veins remain green; possibly spots of dead tissue

PLANT	PROBLEM	CONTROL	COMMENT
	mites, mealybugs	See *Insects* on page 237.	on the leaves.
Carpet Bugleweed (*Ajuga reptans*)	southern blight	Remove plants and 6″ soil surrounding plants; replace with sterile soil or treat soil with a fumigant before replanting. Do not scatter infected soil.	Hot humid weather favors disease; spreads rapidly, turning entire plants black.
Cast-Iron Plant (*Aspidistra elatior*)	Generally pest free but may have problems with: mites, scales.	See *Insects* on page 237.	
Chaste Tree (*Vitex agnus-castus*)	Generally pest free.		
Cherry Tree Higan Cherry (*Prunus subhirtella*) Japanese Flowering Cherry (*P. serrulata*) Yoshino Cherry (*P. yedoensis*)	scales, aphids, tent caterpillars	See *Insects* on page 237.	
	leaf spot	See *Diseases* on page 239.	
	lesser peachtree borer, peachtree borer	See recommendations for *Flowering Peach*.	
Chinese Tallow Tree (*Sapium sebiferum*)	Generally pest free.		
Chinese Wisteria (*Wisteria sinensis*)	Generally pest free but may have problems with: scales, mites, aphids.	See *Insects* on page 237.	
Common Horse Chestnut (*Aesculus hippocastanum*) **Red Buckeye** (*A. pavia*)	anthracnose	lime sulphur	Shoots are blighted several inches below the buds.
	leaf blotch	Inspect nursery plants before purchasing.	Usually a problem in nurseries; foliage appears scorched. Disease is worse during cold, wet springs.
	scales	See *Insects* on page 237.	Flat, circular reddish gray or brown walnut scale is usually found on the main trunk several layers thick.
	leaf spot	See *Diseases* on page 239.	
	mealybugs, Japanese beetles	See *Insects* on page 237.	
Common Oleander (*Nerium oleander*)	oleander caterpillars	carbaryl, acephate	1½″-long orange larvae with black dots and tufts of black hair eat the foliage.
	aphids, scales, mealybugs	See *Insects* on page 237.	
Confederate Jasmine (*Trachelospermum jasminoides*)	Generally pest free but may have problems with: scales.	See *Insects* on page 237.	Problems with scale are most abundant in the Lower South.
Coral Vine (*Antigonon leptopus*)	Generally pest free.		
Cotoneaster Bearberry Cotoneaster (*Cotoneaster dammeri*) Brightbead Cotoneaster (*C. lacteus* Parneyi) Cranberry Cotoneaster (*C. apiculatus*) Franchet Cotoneaster (*C. franchetii*) Rockspray Cotoneaster (*C. horizontalis*) Willowleaf Cotoneaster (*C. salicifolius*)	lacebugs, webworms, mites, scales	See *Insects* on page 237.	
	fire blight	See *Diseases* on page 239.	Some selections are resistant or less susceptible to fire blight. Check with a nurseryman or county agricultural extension agent for the selections in your area.
Crabapple Callaway Crabapple (*Malus prunifolia* Callaway), r, fb Carmine Crabapple (*M. x atrosanguinea* Carmine) Chinese Flowering Crabapple (*M. spectabilis*) Dolgo Crabapple	scab	Fore®	Spots about ¼″ in diameter appear on leaves and fruit; leaves fall off early and fruit is disfigured.
	cedar-apple rust	Fore®. See *Diseases* on page 239.	
	fire blight, powdery mildew	See *Diseases* on page 239.	
	mites, scales, aphids	See *Insects* on page 237.	

PLANT	PROBLEM	CONTROL	COMMENT

Crabapple *continued*

(*M. baccata* Dolgo), s, fb
Eleyi Crabapple
  (*M. x purpurea* Eleyi)
Japanese Flowering Crabapple
  (*M. floribunda*)
Sargent Flowering Crabapple
  (*M. sargentii*), s, fb
Scheidecker Crabapple
  (*M. x scheideckeri*)
Siberian Crabapple (*M. baccata*)
Southern Crabapple (*M. angustifolia*)
Note: Symbols following the selections above indicate a tolerance to the diseases listed here: r—rust; fb—fire blight; s—scab. Southern Crabapple and Eleyi Crabapple may be more susceptible to disease than other selections listed and should be planted with that fact in mind.

PLANT	PROBLEM	CONTROL	COMMENT
Creeping Fig (*Ficus pumila*)	Generally pest free but may have problems with: whiteflies, mealybugs, thrips, scales.	See *Insects* on page 237.	
Crepe Myrtle (*Lagerstroemia indica*)	powdery mildew	See *Diseases* on page 239.	
	aphids, scales	See *Insects* on page 237.	
Cross Vine (*Anisostichus capreolatus*)	Generally pest free but may have problems with: mealybugs, scales, whiteflies.	See *Insects* on page 237.	
	leaf spot	See *Diseases* on page 239.	
Cycad Queen Sago (*Cycas circinalis*) Sago Palm (*C. revoluta*)	blight	Removing diseased plants is the only control.	An unknown blight may kill plants. Leaves turn yellow; plant declines in health and dies.
	scales, mealybugs, thrips	See *Insects* on page 237.	
Cypress Bald Cypress (*Taxodium distichum*) Pond Cypress (*T. ascendens*)	Generally pest free.		
Deodar Cedar (*Cedrus deodara*)	Generally pest free but may have problems with: aphids, bagworms, scales.	See *Insects* on page 237.	
Dogwood Flowering Dogwood (*Cornus florida*) Kousa Dogwood (*C. kousa*)	dogwood spot anthracnose	maneb, Fore®—Spray regularly—from early spring until late summer.	Infected flower buds do not open, flowers malformed; flowers and foliage covered with brown spots.
	water stress, sunscald	Plant in partial shade in moist, fertile soil; water during periods of drought.	In its native environment, dogwood is an understory tree with a shallow root system that makes it subject to heat, water stress, and sunburn when planted in full sun or hot, dry soil.
	twig blight	Prune dead twigs back 2″ or 3″ into healthy wood; keep trees in good health by watering and fertilizing regularly.	Fungus may cause dieback of twigs.
	flower and leaf blight	Use benomyl every 10-14 days during the flowering period. If possible, remove blighted leaves and flowers from the tree and the ground.	Worse during wet weather; white flowers are covered with a gray mold. Blight also affects leaves.
	dogwood borer	Wet trunk and branches thoroughly	½″-long white caterpillar bores into

PLANT	PROBLEM	CONTROL	COMMENT
Dogwood *continued*		with lindane; repeat according to label directions.	wood; may girdle small trees or branches to kill portions of tree or entire tree.
	clubgall	Remove galls during spring and summer before adult midges emerge from the gall.	Midge fly larvae produce ½" club-shaped galls on young stems—may stunt growth.
	crown canker	No treatment for infected trees. Avoid wounds when mowing, transplanting, or planting trees.	Leaves smaller, lighter green than usual, turn red prematurely in late summer; canker present at the base of the tree.
	powdery mildew	See *Diseases* on page 239.	
	scales	See *Insects* on page 237.	
Eastern Redbud (*Cercis canadensis*)	dieback	Prune infected branches; paint pruning wounds with orange shellac. Avoid injuries to tree when mowing or using other tools.	Cankers girdle stem, causing stem part above canker to die.
	scales	See *Insects* on page 237.	
Elaeagnus (*Elaeagnus pungens*)	Generally pest free but may have problems with: aphids, scales.	See *Insects* on page 237.	
	leaf spot	See *Diseases* on page 239.	
English Ivy (*Hedera helix*)	Generally pest free but may have problems with: aphids, scales, mealybugs, Japanese beetles.	See *Insects* on page 237.	
	leaf spot	See *Diseases* on page 239.	
Euonymus Dwarf Euonymus (*Euonymus alata* Compacta) Winged Euonymus (*E. alata*)	scales	malathion, dimethoate—Spray stems and undersides of leaves thoroughly.	Euonymus scale (white and brown flat scales on stems and foliage) is most serious. May build up several layers thick and become very difficult to kill. First sign of infestation is yellow spots on leaves.
	crown gall	Remove diseased plant; fumigate soil before replanting. If only a few galls present, remove galled stems.	Large galls develop at base of the plant.
	aphids	See *Insects* on page 237.	
	powdery mildew, leaf spot	See *Diseases* on page 239.	
Fescue Blue Fescue (*Festuca ovina* Glauca) Red Fescue (*F. rubra*)	Generally pest free.		
Firethorn Formosa Firethorn (*Pyracantha koidzumii*) Scarlet Firethorn (*P. coccinea*)	scab	No pesticide federally registered.	Leaves become covered with a moldy growth, turn yellow, and fall off.
	scale, mites, lacebugs, webworms	See *Insects* on page 237.	
	fire blight	See *Diseases* on page 239.	
Flowering Peach (*Prunus persica*)	peachtree borer	*To remove borers, uncover the surface roots and use a curved blade knife to dig out borer from roots and crown of tree by following the burrow along until you find the larvae. Spray with lindane as a preventive.	White, ½"- to 1"-long, brown-headed larvae bore into the bottom 10" of the trunk and surface roots of the tree; gum and excrement are present outside the holes; leaves yellow and the tree declines.
	lesser peachtree borer	*Eggs laid on trunk of tree hatch and young larvae enter (in summer) through wounds or openings in bark. Spray with lindane as a preventive.	Damage is like the peachtree borer but usually present in the limbs and along the trunk instead of low at the soil level.

Insects, Diseases & Problems

PLANT	PROBLEM	CONTROL	COMMENT
Flowering Peach *continued*	aphids, scales	See *Insects* on page 237. **Note:* Timing of spray for control of peachtree and lesser peachtree borer is very important—for the most specific recommendations on timing in your area, contact your county agricultural extension agent.	
Fringe Tree (*Chionanthus virginicus*)	borers	See *Insects* on page 237.	
Gardenia Dwarf Gardenia (*Gardenia jasminoides* Radicans) Gardenia (*G. jasminoides*)	mineral deficiency	Apply a minor-element spray to the foliage several times a year and chelated iron to the ground.	In deficient or alkaline soils (sometimes next to house foundation) foliage may yellow between veins.
	canker	Fungus enters plant through bark and stem injury. Avoid mechanical injury to plant. Make clean cuts when cutting flowers or taking cuttings.	Oblong cankers develop on stems and branches. At the soil level, large cankers develop on trunk.
	powdery mildew	See *Diseases* on page 239.	
	aphids, scales, mealybugs, whiteflies, thrips, mites	See *Insects* on page 237.	
Glossy Abelia (*Abelia* x *grandiflora*)	Generally pest free but may have problems with: iron chlorosis.	Use fertilizers that contain iron or apply chelated iron to the soil. Keep soil pH slightly acid.	Leaves turn yellow between veins while veins remain green.
Goldenrain Tree (*Koelreuteria paniculata*)	Generally pest free but may have problems with: scales.	See *Insects* on page 237.	
Hawthorn Green Hawthorn (*Crataegus viridis*) Parsley Hawthorn (*C. marshallii*) Washington Thorn Tree (*C. phaenopyrum*)	scab	No pesticide federally registered.	Spots on leaves and premature leaf drop; also affects fruit.
	fire blight, leaf spot, powdery mildew	See *Diseases* on page 239.	
	aphids, scales, borers, mites, tent caterpillars	See *Insects* on page 237.	
Heavenly Bamboo (*Nandina domestica*)	Generally pest free but may have problems with: mites, scales.	See *Insects* on page 237.	
	root rot	See *Diseases* on page 239.	
Hemlock Canadian Hemlock (*Tsuga canadensis*) Carolina Hemlock (*T. caroliniana*)	sunscald	Plant in shade in southernmost areas of its hardiness zone.	Ends of branches may die back several inches in temperatures 95° or above.
	drought injury	Water during dry periods.	More susceptible if planted with southern exposure or in shallow soils.
	aphids	See *Insects* on page 237.	Hemlock wooly aphid is covered with white woollike material; found on bark and needles, it is capable of killing a young tree.
	hemlock looper	carbaryl and kelthane (to discourage mites) when loopers are small.	Yellow inchworm-type caterpillar, 1″ long with double row of small black dots down body; feeds on foliage.
	hemlock scale	See *Insects* on page 237.	Circular, black scale on the lower surface of the leaves.
	elongate hemlock scale	See *Insects* on page 237.	Pest in Upper South; yellow to brown elongated scale on leaves; may be covered with old skins.
	other scales	See *Insects* on page 237.	
	mites	See *Insects* on page 237.	Space between needles protects mites from pesticides.
	pesticide damage	Apply pesticides according to label	Hemlock is particularly sensitive to

PLANT	PROBLEM	CONTROL	COMMENT
Hemlock *continued*		directions very early in the morning on cool days.	pesticides; foliage burn may occur if pesticides are applied when temperature is too warm.
	rust	No pesticide federally registered.	Young needles turn yellow; orange rust spores form at the base of needles, needles drop, and twigs curl. Most serious in the Upper South.

Holly
American Holly (*Ilex opaca*)
Chinese Holly (*I. cornuta*)
Dahoon Holly (*I. cassine*)
East Palatka Holly
  (*I.* x *attenuata* East Palatka)
Foster #2 Holly
  (*I.* x *attenuata* Foster #2)
Hume #2 Holly
  (*I.* x *attenuata* Hume #2)
Inkberry Holly (*I. glabra*)
Japanese Holly (*I. crenata*)
Luster-leaf Holly (*I. latifolia*)
Possum Haw Holly (*I. decidua*)
Savannah Holly
  (*I.* x *attenuata* Savannah)
Winterberry Holly (*I. verticillata*)
Yaupon Holly (*I. vomitoria*)
	powdery mildew, leaf spot	See *Diseases* on page 239.	

	leaf scorch	Plant in proper hardiness zone and avoid planting in wind tunnels.	In winter or early spring, leaves may be parched (with large, dry, brown areas) by cold.
	black root rot	Do not replant Japanese holly in the same location.	Affects only Japanese holly; top of plant dies back, plant is stunted and declines.
	dieback	Keep plants watered during dry periods.	Japanese holly plants often die back in summer after periods of drought; black root rot may follow.
	leafminers, scales, mites	See *Insects* on page 237.	
Holly Fern (*Cyrtomium falcatum*)	Generally pest free but may have problems with: mites.	See *Insects* on page 237.	

Honeysuckle
Everblooming Honeysuckle
  (*Lonicera* x *heckrottii*)
Trumpet Honeysuckle
  (*L.* x *sempervirens*)
Winter Honeysuckle
  (*L. fragrantissima*)
	powdery mildew	See *Diseases* on page 239.	

	aphids, mites, scales, mealybugs, whiteflies	See *Insects* on page 237.	
Horse Chestnut See *Common Horse Chestnut*			
Hybrid Clematis (*Clematis sp.*)	clematis leaf and stem spot	benomyl, sulphur—Remove diseased leaves and stems.	
	aphids, whiteflies, scales, mites	See *Insects* on page 237.	
Hybrid Trumpet Creeper (*Campsis* x *tagliabuana*)	powdery mildew	See *Diseases* on page 239.	

Hydrangea
French Hydrangea
  (*Hydrangea macrophylla*)
Oakleaf Hydrangea
  (*H. quercifolia* Snowflake)
Peegee Hydrangea
  (*H. paniculata* Grandiflora)
Snowhill Hydrangea
  (*H. arborescens* Grandiflora)
	aphids, mites	See *Insects* on page 237.	

	flower blight	benomyl; sulphur—Keep foliage dry by careful watering practices.	During wet weather flower buds and sometimes foliage become blackened with gray moldlike growth.
	powdery mildew, leaf spot	See *Diseases* on page 239.	
Indian Hawthorn (*Raphiolepis indica*)	leaf spot	See *Diseases* on page 239.	Causes leaves to drop; most serious in shady location where foliage remains wet from rain or dew.
	scales	See *Insects* on page 237.	
	fire blight	See *Diseases* on page 239. No pesticide federally registered.	

Insects, Diseases & Problems

PLANT	PROBLEM	CONTROL	COMMENT
Japan Cleyera (*Ternstroemia gymnanthera*)	Generally pest free but may have problems with: scales.	See *Insects* on page 237.	
	leaf spot	See *Diseases* on page 239.	
Japanese Andromeda (*Pieris japonica*)	Generally pest free but may have problems with: lacebugs.	See *Insects* on page 237.	
Japanese Anise Tree (*Illicium anisatum*)	mites, scales	See *Insects* on page 237.	
Japanese Ardisia (*Ardisia japonica*)	leaf spot	See *Diseases* on page 239.	
Japanese Aucuba (*Aucuba japonica*)	leaf spot	No pesticide federally registered.	May occur after scale infestation; brown spots form along leaf margins. Serious infection causes leaf drop.
	anthracnose	No pesticide federally registered.	Spots form on leaves and flowers; cankers form on stems. Tips of branches wilt.
	winter injury	Plant in a protected location in the northernmost area of its hardiness zone.	In freezing weather leaves may wilt; later, irregular black areas may appear on leaves.
	scales, mites	See *Insects* on page 237.	
Japanese Fatsia (*Fatsia japonica*)	Generally pest free but may have problems with scales and mites, especially in the more tropical areas.	See *Insects* on page 237.	
Japanese Pachysandra (*Pachysandra terminalis*)	Generally pest free but may have problems with: scales, mites.	See *Insects* on page 237.	Mites most serious when plants are crowded.
Japanese Zelkova (*Zelkova serrata*)	Generally pest free.		
Jasmine Primrose Jasmine (*Jasminum mesnyi*) Showy Jasmine (*J. floridum*) Winter Jasmine (*J. nudiflorum*)	scales, whiteflies	See *Insects* on page 237.	
	crown gall	Avoid injury to plant; remove diseased plant and sterilize soil with a soil fumigant before planting.	Round galls with irregular surfaces form at plant base near the soil level.
Juniper Creeping Juniper (*Juniperus horizontalis*) Parsons Juniper (*J. davurica* Expansa) Red Cedar (*J. virginiana*) Sargent Chinese Juniper (*J. chinensis* Sargentii) Shore Juniper (*J. conferta*)	juniper blight	benomyl. Remove infected branches. Check nursery plants carefully for blight before you buy.	Causes dieback of twigs and branches of plants less than 5 years old. On older trees, twigs are blighted.
	cedar-apple rust	See *Diseases* on page 239.	Many selections of creeping juniper may be resistant.
	juniper webworm	diazinon	Serious webbing and chewing damage in the Middle and Upper South. Larvae are ½″ long, light brown with reddish brown stripes. Early infestations are hard to discover because they feed inside the plant first; are difficult to kill if not controlled early.
	mites	See *Insects* on page 237.	Mites are difficult to kill because the tight spaces between the juniper needles protect them from sprays.
	wet feet	Plant in well-drained soil.	Junipers often die in wet or poorly drained soils.
	aphids, bagworms, scales	See *Insects* on page 237.	
	dogs	Dog repellents may be effective against some dogs.	Dog urine may kill foilage and stems.
Laurel English Cherry Laurel (*Prunus laurocerasus*) Schipka Cherry Laurel (*P. laurocerasus* Schipkaensis)	scales	See *Insects* on page 237.	
	root rot	See *Diseases* on page 239.	

PLANT	PROBLEM	CONTROL	COMMENT

Laurel *continued*
Southern Cherry Laurel
  (*P. caroliniana*)
Zabel Cherry Laurel
  (*P. laurocerasus* Zabeliana)
	wet feet
	Generally pest free.
		Plant in well-drained soil.	

Leucothöe Drooping Leucothöe (*Leucothöe fontanesiana*) Florida Leucothöe (*L. populifolia*)	Generally pest free.		
Loquat (*Eriobotrya japonica*)	fire blight scales	See *Diseases* on page 239. See *Insects* on page 237.	
Magnolia Bigleaf Magnolia (*Magnolia macrophylla*) Cucumber Tree (*M. acuminata*) Southern Magnolia (*M. grandiflora*) Umbrella Magnolia (*M. tripetala*)	scales, mealybugs spring defoliation leaf spot	See *Insects* on page 237. Terraclor®	Magnolias drop many leaves in spring as part of their natural cycle, which may be misinterpreted as a problem.
Mahonia Chinese Mahonia (*Mahonia fortunei*) Cluster Mahonia (*M. pinnata*) Leatherleaf Mahonia (*M. bealei*) Oregon Grape Mahonia (*M. aquifolium*)	Generally pest free.		
Maidenhair Tree (*Ginkgo biloba*)	Generally pest free.		
Maple Japanese Maple (*Acer palmatum*) Norway Maple (*A. platanoides*) Red Maple (*A. rubrum*) Silver Maple (*A. saccharinum*) Southern Sugar Maple (*A. barbatum*) Sugar Maple (*A. saccharum*)	anthracnose	copper fungicide, lime sulphur	May be serious on sugar and silver maple; anthracnose may kill the entire leaf, leaving a scorched appearance. Can cause severe defoliation in rainy weather.
	verticilium wilt	No control for severely infected trees. Trees wilting on only a few branches may be treated by a heavy application of fertilizer to slow disease by increasing tree vigor.	Leaves may suddenly wilt or die on certain limbs. Trees die suddenly or slowly, depending on extent of infection.
	tent caterpillars, scales, borers, Japanese beetles	See *Insects* on page 237.	
	scorch	If possible, water important landscape specimens.	Leaves look burned along the margins due to water stress during periods of drought.
	sapstreak	No control.	Symptoms are gradual thinning of tree, undersized yellowing foliage—then death of tree.
	aphids	See *Insects* on page 237.	Norway maple particularly susceptible.
	cankers	Cankers on trunk can rarely be successfully removed if they are large; remove cankers on stem by cutting off stem or branch several inches below canker.	Cankers develop on stems, branches, and occasionally on trunks. Severe infestations may kill tree.
Mondo Grass (*Ophiopogon japonicus*)	Generally pest free.		
Mountain Laurel (*Kalmia latifolia*)	leaf spot flower blight	See *Diseases* on page 239. See recommendations for *Azaleas*.	More often a problem on plants growing in shade or within the drip line of a tree.

PLANT	PROBLEM	CONTROL	COMMENT
Mountain laurel *continued*			
	borers, lacebugs, scales, whiteflies	See *Insects* on page 237.	
Myrobalan Plum (*Prunus cerasifera*)	lesser peachtree borer, peachtree borer	See recommendations for *Flowering Peach.*	
	Japanese beetles	See *Insects* on page 237.	
Oak Laurel Oak (*Quercus laurifolia*) Live Oak (*Q. virginiana*) Pin Oak (*Q. palustris*) Scarlet Oak (*Q. coccinea*) Shumard's Red Oak (*Q. shumardii*) White Oak (*Q. alba*) Willow Oak (*Q. phellos*)	anthracnose	lime sulphur	Rainy weather favors the disease. May cause defoliation; already weakened trees may be killed by complete defoliation.
	oak wilt	Infected trees cannot be saved. Trees are most susceptible to oak wilt in the spring; prevent infection by limiting all pruning to winter so insects and other vectors do not spread the fungus. Paint pruning wounds with orange shellac or a tree paint. Avoid wounds from lawn mower and pruning because fungus enters through wounds. Cut down infected trees to prevent disease spread. Oak wilt may spread from natural grafts of roots where oaks are planted close together. Avoid close plantings.	Red oaks such as pin and scarlet are most susceptible but others may also be affected. Leaves turn a dull green and later brown, then drop off; symptoms usually begin in mid-late spring at the top of the tree and spread downward. Red oaks usually die the first year, whereas white oaks may only lose a few branches per year; some recover.
	root rot	See *Diseases* on page 239.	
	scales	See *Insects* on page 237.	Golden oak scale is a 1/16" round, gold scale that grows in pits in the tree bark. Severe infestation year after year may kill large branches and small trees if not controlled.
Osmanthus Devilwood (*Osmanthus americanus*) Fortunes Osmanthus (*O.* x *fortunei*) Holly Olive (*O. heterophyllus*) Sweet Olive (*O. fragrans*)	Generally pest free.		

Palm
Cabbage Palmetto (*Sabal palmetto*)
Canary Island Date Palm
  (*Phoenix canariensis*)
European Fan Palm
  (*Chamaerops humilis*)
Pindo Palm (*Butia capitata*)
Senegal Date Palm
  (*Phoenix reclinata*)
Slender Lady Palm (*Rhapis humilis*)
Windmill Palm
  (*Trachycarpus fortunei*)
	scales, mites, mealybugs, aphids	See *Insects* on page 237.	

	palm leafskeletonizer	No pesticide federally registered.	5/8"-long yellow-white caterpillar chews leaves; silklike webbing and excrement are present.
	butt rot	Avoid wounds from cold damage, mowing, or planting. Do not plant in wet soil or overwater. Remove affected palms and sterilize soil with soil fumigant before planting.	Lower leaves die and young leaves become progressively smaller until the palm slowly dies.
	minor-element deficiency	Corrective procedures depend on your soil type, soil pH, and the size of the palm; check with your local county agricultural extension agent for recommendations.	Palms grown in poor or alkaline soils may be deficient in iron, manganese, magnesium, or other minor elements. Manganese- and iron-deficient leaves yellow between the veins (veins remain green); magnesium deficiency shows up on older leaves as yellowing of the entire leaf, except the base.
	lethal yellowing	In south Florida, resistant palms are being planted to replace those that die; check with your county agricultural extension agent for the latest list of resistant palms; some palms first	First, the older and then the younger leaves turn yellow and die; the palm is killed. Canary Island date palm, Senegal date palm, and windmill palm are susceptible.

PLANT	PROBLEM	CONTROL	COMMENT
Palm *continued*		believed to be resistant have been found with the disease.	
Periwinkle Bigleaf Periwinkle (*Vinca major*) Common Periwinkle (*V. minor*)	Generally pest free.		
Photinia Chinese Photinia (*Photinia serrulata*) Fraser Photinia (*P. x fraseri*) Japanese Photinia (*P. glabra*)	fire blight	No pesticide federally registered. See *Diseases* on page 239.	
	leaf spot	See *Diseases* on page 239.	May be most serious on Japanese photinia.
	powdery mildew	See *Diseases* on page 239.	More serious on Japanese and Fraser photinias than Chinese photinia.
	root rot	See *Diseases* on page 239.	
Pine Loblolly Pine (*Pinus taeda*) Longleaf Pine (*P. palustris*) Scotch Pine (*P. sylvestris*) Virginia Pine (*P. virginiana*) White Pine (*P. strobus*)	rusts	No pesticide federally registered.	Several rusts affect pines, especially Virginia and Scotch, causing galls, defoliation or deformation of branches and trunks. However, they are usually not serious enough to limit planting.
	Nantucket pine tip moth	acephate, dimethoate. Use in spring and early summer.	Larvae kill twigs by boring into them; affects Scotch, loblolly, and Virginia pines.
	aphids	See *Insects* on page 237.	Feeding of white pine aphid may cause winter injury on white pines due to drying out. Pine bark aphid may be present on limbs and trunk.
	pine sawflies	acephate, ISOTOX®, methoxychlor	Sawfly larvae look like caterpillars, about 1″ long, usually have greenish yellow bodies marked with spots or stripes and red or black heads.
	pine webworm	Use diazinon or methoxychlor spray before webs are formed or they are partly protected from pesticides by the web.	Masses of brown webbed excrement are present on yellowed, defoliated twig ends. Larvae is yellow brown, 4/5″ long with black stripes.
	white pine mortality	A fungus transmitted in the ground may be involved; remove dead trees and all roots; do not replant white pine in the same location.	An increasing number of white pines are dying rapidly in the landscape due to an unknown reason.
	white pine weevil	lindane. Spray to the terminal leader and the upper portion of the tree in early spring before adults lay eggs.	⅓″ pale-yellow grubs feed in the wood and kill tops of trees. Attacks white and Scotch pines.
	bark beetles	lindane. Keep trees in good condition by watering and fertilizing regularly.	Usually attack weak trees; mine bark and wood.
	scales	See *Insects* on page 237.	
	pales weevil	Wait about a year before planting young pines on a pine-covered lot that has been cleared for construction.	White grubs ½″ long with brown heads strip bark from young trees. Weevils are attracted to freshly cut pine stumps and will move to young newly planted trees in the area. May also feed on twigs of older trees.
	borers	Prevention is the only control; remove all infested trees from property and spray with lindane regularly according to label directions as a preventive. Spray the trunk and limbs thoroughly; if trees are too large, hire	Borers enter the trunk; small holes where pine pitch has run out is first sign of infestation. Later, pine needles brown and portion of tree or the entire tree dies.

Insects, Diseases & Problems

PLANT	PROBLEM	CONTROL	COMMENT
Pine *continued*		a professional to spray, spraying only the lower part that you can reach will not protect the tree successfully.	
Pineapple Guava (*Feijoa sellowiana*)	scales	See *Insects* on page 237.	
Pittosporum	scales, aphids, mealybugs	See *Insects* on page 237.	
Dwarf Pittosporum (*Pittosporum tobira* Wheeler's Dwarf)	leaf spot	See *Diseases* on page 239.	Worse in shade, during rainy season, or where there is poor air circulation.
Japanese Pittosporum (*P. tobira*)	root rot	See *Diseases* on page 239.	
Whitespot Japanese Pittosporum (*P. tobira* Variegata)	cold damage	Plant in a protected location in the northernmost part of its hardiness zone.	Leaves appear burned.
Podocarpus	root rot	See *Diseases* on page 239.	
African Fern Pine (*Podocarpus gracilior*)	aphids	See *Insects* on page 237.	
Broadleaf Podocarpus (*P. nagi*) Japanese Yew (*P. macrophyllus*)	scales	See *Insects* on page 237.	Scale problem is worse in warmer regions, such as Florida.
Privet Roundleaf Japanese Privet (*Ligustrum japonicum* Rotundifolium)	Generally pest free but may have problems with:		
	anthracnose, twig blight	Remove diseased branches. No pesticide federally registered.	Leaves die and remain attached to stems. Cankers form on stems.
Waxleaf Privet (*L. japonicum*) Yellow-edge California Privet (*L. ovalifolium* Aureo-marginatum)	root rot	See *Diseases* on page 239.	
	mealybugs, aphids, leafminers, scales, mites, whiteflies	See *Insects* on page 237.	
Quince	scales	See *Insects* on page 237.	
Japanese Quince (*Chaenomeles speciosa*)	fire blight	See *Diseases* on page 239.	
Lesser Flowering Quince (*C. japonica*)	leaf spot	No pesticide federally registered.	Worse in rainy or humid weather.
	rust	See *Diseases* on page 239.	
Red Buckeye See *Common Horse Chestnut*			
Rhododendron —See *Azalea* (*Rhododendron sp.*)			
River Birch (*Betula nigra*)	dieback	Water to prevent drought stress— prune infected branches back 2″ or 3″ into healthy wood; water and fertilize to revitalize tree.	Drought-stressed plants may be attacked by dieback fungus which causes the upper branches to die.
	aphids, borers	See *Insects* on page 237.	
Rosemary (*Rosmarinus officinalis*)	Generally pest free but is susceptible to root rot in poorly drained soils.	See *Diseases* on page 239.	
Santolina Green Lavender Cotton (*Santolina virens*) Lavender Cotton (*S. chamaecyparisus*)	Generally pest free but will not tolerate wet feet.	Plant in well-drained soil.	
Silver Lace Vine (*Polygonum aubertii*)	Japanese beetle	See *Insects* on page 237.	
Sourwood (*Oxydendron arboreum*)	Generally pest free.		
Spirea Bridal Wreath (*Spiraea prunifolia*) Bumalda Spirea (*S.* x *bumalda*) Garland Spirea (*S.* x *arguta*) Reeves Spirea (*S. cantoniensis*)	Generally pest free but may have problems with: aphids, mites.	See *Insects* on page 237.	

PLANT	PROBLEM	CONTROL	COMMENT
Spirea *continued* Thunberg Spirea (*S. thunbergii*) Vanhoutte Spirea (*S.* x *vanhouttei*)			
Sprenger Asparagus (*Asparagus sprengeri*)	Generally pest free but may have problems with: scales, mites.	See *Insects* on page 237.	
Sweet Gum (*Liquidambar styraciflua*)	scales, webworms	See *Insects* on page 237.	
Tulip Tree (*Liriodendron tulipifera*)	alphids	See *Insects* on page 237.	Leaf yellowing during hot dry periods in summer; many leaves yellow and drop off prematurely.
	scales	See *Insects* on page 237.	Trees may be seriously damaged by heavy infestations of brown, turtle-shaped tulip tree scale.
Viburnum Burkwood Viburnum (*Viburnum* x *burkwoodii*) Chinese Snowball (*V. macrocephalum*) Cranberry Bush (*V. opulus*) David Viburnum (*V. davidii*) Fragrant Snowball (*V.* x *carlcephalum*) Japanese Viburnum (*V. japonicum*) Judd Viburnum (*V.* x *juddii*) Korean Spice Viburnum (*V. carlesii*) Laurustinus (*V. tinus*) Leatherleaf Viburnum (*V. rhytidophyllum*) Maple-leaf Viburnum (*V. acerifolium*) Sandankwa (*V. suspensum*) Southern Black Haw (*V. rufidulum*) Sweet Viburnum (*V. odoatissimum*) Tea Viburnum (*V. setigerum*) Wright Viburnum (*V. wrightii*)	Generally pest free but may have problems with: borers. wet feet Occurence of problems with pests listed increases in the Lower South: aphids, mites, whiteflies, thrips.	See *Insects* on page 237. Plant in well-drained soil.	Most viburnums require well-drained soil for good growth. May decline in poorly drained soil.
Virginia Creeper—See *Boston Ivy*			
Wax Myrtle (*Myrica cerifera*)	Generally pest free.		
Wedelia (*Wedelia trilobata*)	mites	See *Insects* on page 237.	
White Ash (*Fraxinus americana*)	lilac borer	lindane	Sawdust and scarred outgrowths are present where borer entered trunk.
	fall webworms, cankerworms, scales	See *Insects* on page 237.	
Willow Corkscrew Willow (*Salix matsudana* Tortuosa) Weeping Willow (*S. babylonica*)	aphids, lacebugs, scales powdery mildew	See *Insects* on page 237. See *Diseases* on page 239.	
Winter Daphne (*Daphne odora*)	mealybugs root rot	See *Insects* on page 237. See *Diseases* on page 239.	
Yellow Jessamine (*Gelsemium sempervirens*)	Generally pest free.		
Yellowwood (*Cladrastis lutea*)	crotch rot		Water collects in deep crotches formed by branching pattern and rot sets in.

Insects, Diseases & Problems

Index